$2

Miller's Court

Miller's Court

ARTHUR R. MILLER

HOUGHTON MIFFLIN COMPANY
BOSTON 1982

Library of Congress Cataloging in Publication Data

Miller, Arthur Raphael, date
    Miller's court.

    Includes index.
    1. Law—United States.   I. Title.
KF385.M525   349.73   81–7246
ISBN 0–395–31323–6   347.3   AACR2

Printed in the United States of America

ACKNOWLEDGMENTS

THIS BOOK COULD NOT have been written without John J. Berry III. He is one of those students who every once and a while come into an academic's life and make it all worth while. John appeared in mine in 1967 when he was an entering student at the University of Michigan Law School. At the end of the academic year he became a research assistant, spending a great deal of time putting an earlier book, *The Assault on Privacy: Computers, Data Banks, and Dossiers* (1971), in final shape. After a few years with a big New York City law firm, John turned to writing as a full-time career. When the idea for this book came to mind early in 1980, it seemed obvious that John was the perfect man to make the project go. And that is what he did, as a writer, researcher, and devil's advocate. I am extremely grateful for his devotion to this effort.

Additional significant research and writing assistance was provided by Perry E. Bendicksen III, Nancy R. London, Maureen P. Manning, and Janet L. Sanders, all current students at the Harvard Law School. Valuable support and encouragement also has come from Lynn Thompson Long and Austin Olney of Houghton Mifflin. I am also indebted to Sarah Flynn, whose copy-editing enhanced the accuracy and precision of the manuscript, as did the efforts of my secretary, Peggy Geromini.

CONTENTS

Miller's Court

PROLOGUE:

Does the Law Work? You Be the Judge!

LET'S FACE IT, today many of us are dissatisfied with the "law" in all its works and manifestations. We question the integrity of lawyers and suspect that all too often they don't do an especially good job. The Watergate scandal presented the legal profession in an unflattering light, with lawyers constituting a large percentage of the cast of conspirators. It revealed plots being hatched in the Justice Department, in the presence of the attorney general — the nation's chief law officer — himself. Moreover, in recent years there have been increasing numbers of reports of lawyers stooping to unethical practices in representing clients or, worse yet, stealing from them. The mass media *often* portray lawyers as hired guns, shysters, or Mafia mouthpieces. Even poets have been known to be critical: Carl Sandburg once wrote, "Why does a hearse horse snicker/Hauling a lawyer away?"

Dissatisfaction runs much deeper than the feeling that lawyers aren't as honest and upright as they should be. Many people are convinced that the legal system itself just isn't working, that it has "broken down" or come to a "grinding halt." Some are concerned about the maddeningly slow pace at which the law moves, whether to resolve a dispute or to adjust to new social realities; some think that the law favors the rich over the poor, either through the way laws are written and cases decided or because of the staggering expense of litigation; many believe that the high cost of legal services results from excessive fees charged by venal lawyers; others think that the law, especially the decisions of the Supreme Court in such fields as school prayer and abortion, undermines our traditional values; still others charge that the system is not designed to arrive at a fair resolution of disputes, but rather subjects hapless litigants to a senseless, time-consuming, and costly game from which only confusion and injustice emerge. Even judges aren't beyond the critics, who assert that they're Establishment oriented or improperly influenced by politics, and too old and tired to do their work with the necessary dispatch. If there's a single theme to all these complaints, it's that the law is failing in its responsibilities — that it simply doesn't function well enough to meet our needs.

If this view is accurate, it's made all the more troubling by the growing popular awareness that we are surrounded by law. There is virtually nothing we do that doesn't have a legal element, whether it's buying or selling, living or dying, marrying or divorcing, breathing or polluting — even going to the ball park.

Many of us treat this universe of law as a mixed blessing. It does try to protect us from the risks of our complex, technological society. And it does safeguard our liberties and freedoms. The truth is that as a people Americans have more rights than any society on Earth. It's the law that gives those rights definition and vitality. Yet, the charge often is made that our society has become overregulated, that government red tape has had a stifling effect both on individual initiative and on the economy. Elements in the business community claim that "mindless" and "excessive" preoccupation with safety, the environment, privacy, affirmative action, and other concerns has destroyed American efficiency and our competitiveness with manufacturers elsewhere in the world.

But even if the more onerous and inconsistent aspects of our regulatory schemes were to be abolished — as the Reagan administration has promised to do — we still will be living in an environment permeated by law. There simply is too much of it for any reformer — even one wielding a broadsword — to eliminate.

Beyond our doubts and suspicions about the legal system is perhaps the most troubling aspect of all: The darn thing is incomprehensible! To the nonlawyer, it often seems an arcane and alien business presided over by priestly officials and practitioners who speak a private language, and who magically arrive at strange conclusions by means of an impenetrable mumbo jumbo. Examples abound: You borrow money from the bank, and they hand you a loan agreement written in what initially appears to be English, but which upon closer inspection proves to be convoluted, unintelligible, and interminable — it might as well be in Martian.

Indeed, we seem to be surrounded by fine print and legalese. When was the last time you read your "rights" on an airline or parking-lot ticket or a monthly credit-card bill? And then there are the mandatory safety notices slapped on things like stepladders. One needs good eyesight and the patience of Job to wade through them. There is also the growing phenomenon of the media trying to report on the latest Supreme Court case. If you're like many of my nonlawyer friends, you often may be baffled by how the Court came to what strikes you as an incorrect conclusion; or you may wonder why the Court got hung up on what seems like a technicality and didn't go even further than it did to remedy what you think is a clear injustice.

It's all really quite unfortunate. The truth is that much of the law need not be a mystery to you, and it's hoped that this book will help demystify part of it. The goal is to enable *you* to understand how the process works and why it operates as it does, and ultimately to allow you to form your own judgment as to whether it's really as gummed up as cynics claim it is. This doesn't mean you'll turn into a lawyer (a fate many of you doubtless would wish to avoid) or even start to love them, but you'll become an informed observer, someone who can make some sense of what previously may have seemed a great slough of confusion.

One doesn't learn how the law works by memorizing a set of rules or theorems. A misconception lies in the commonly asked question, "What is the law?" — since it presupposes that it's all laid out some- where on great stone tablets. The truth is that the answer often is, "It depends." As you'll soon discover, the legal system basically is a method of applying abstract rules or social policies to concrete situa- tions. To comprehend its workings, you have to get involved in the process — it's a little like learning to swim in that you've got to jump in and try to get the feel of things by splashing around a bit. It's not an unpleasant sensation, but it may seem a little strange until you get used to it and learn to keep your head above water.

More specifically, in order to understand how courts arrive at deci- sions of what the law is and how it's to be applied in given situations, you'll be taken step by step through the reasoning process that a lawyer or a judge engages in. You'll discover it's a bit like peeling an onion in that as you strip away one layer of complexity you find another one just below it, and it's akin to rotating a diamond and watching the light refract off the individual facets of the stone.

The governing legal principles will provide the tools for thinking about different "fact situations" taken from actual life or modeled on it. For example, how does the rule about self-defense apply to a woman being attacked by a mugger, or the constitutional prohibition against cruel and unusual punishment to imposing the death penalty upon a murderer? I'll tag along playing devil's advocate, trying to get you to think through the problem. From time to time I'll change the fact situation, and you will have to consider whether the basic principle still applies, and if not, what it should be in the new situation. Then you will be given a different set of facts to test the law, and so on — the onion being slowly peeled, the diamond rotated. As part of getting you involved, you may be encouraged to take a position and then asked to defend it in the light of competing values or changed circumstances. You may even find yourself being prodded occasionally. But don't worry, it's an invigorating process and all part of learning to think like a lawyer and about the law. Indeed, the "dialogue" you'll be engaging in is similar to the Socratic dialogue that students and teachers enter into in law-school classrooms. If you're a movie or television buff, it may remind you a bit of *The Paper Chase.*

This book is divided into fourteen chapters under four general headings. The chapters are followed by vignettes called Points of Law that enlarge upon some part of the preceding discussion. Each chapter deals with a separate area of the law, and can be read without the other chapters, although there are occasional cross-references. The subjects have been selected for their dramatic and emotional appeal, their contemporary relevance, and their value in illustrating various aspects of the legal process. The treatment is not meant to be exhaustive, either in the discussion of specific subjects (lawyers always have more to say!), or in the inclusion of subjects (the law is said to be a "seamless web," so there's always more to talk about). Considerations of time and space make "comprehensiveness" impossible. But the hope is that you will become sufficiently adept at thinking about the law to apply your skills to issues that aren't dealt with here, and will feel more comfortable whenever you encounter the law during your daily life — even if it's just ruminating about a Supreme Court decision you hear about on television or read about in the newspaper.

One bit of background before we begin, just to give you the lay of the land. The "law" that we're going to discuss has two basic sources — cases and statutes. By cases we mean the judicial decisions handed down by a court in resolving particular disputes. Once it has made up its mind, the court writes out its result, setting forth the facts (who the litigants are and what they're fighting about), then its reasoning on how the rules of law are to be applied to the facts of the dispute (or perhaps reformulated if the facts show that a change in the law is needed), and then its conclusion, which is the "result" of the case. Each case therefore is an example — or precedent — showing how one or more legal principles governed a particular set of facts. As such, each case "makes" law in that it influences the court in every subsequent case (especially those in the same state) involving the same or a similar principle, on the theory that if the same situation comes up again, the same reasoning and conclusion are called for. This process promotes the law's stability and predictability. That sounds highly desirable. But in times of social change or turmoil that very reverence for precedent often prevents the law from reacting speedily to new phenomena.

In addition to cases, there are statutes, which are legal rules enacted by a legislative body. They can range from a full-scale regulatory scheme or a tax code adopted by the United States Congress to a leaf-burning ordinance promulgated by a town council. Although our elected representatives have enormous discretion in passing statutes, the United States Constitution adopted by the Founding Fathers two centuries ago is the supreme law of the land. Thus any statute that transgresses its provisions must fall, as did some of the early New Deal legislation that was designed to fight the Great Depression.

Keep in mind that many court decisions involve interpretations of statutory provisions — indicating how the abstract, general rule enacted by the legislature is to be applied to the specific facts before a court. In that sense, cases and statutes operate in concert; they are not mutually exclusive elements of the law. Moreover, as we shall see, it is the special prerogative of the United States Supreme Court to be the ultimate interpreter of the Constitution. To the nine justices who sit on that tribunal falls the task of applying the document's often terse, seemingly straightforward statements to the myriad controversies that arise in our complex society and are brought to the state and federal courts of the land for resolution.

Now let's take a walk through the legal environment. Get out your map and compass, say good-bye to your loved ones for an hour or two (perhaps even longer, if you feel like a long hike), and let's get started. We have a lot of ground to cover. But don't worry, you'll find it an interesting and provocative journey, and when you get back you'll have some tales to tell and insights to share about a legal system that may seem far less forbidding and insensitive than it does to you now.

Freedoms and Rights

1

SCHOOL PRAYER:

Can Religion Be Kept Out of the Classroom?

THE PLEDGE OF ALLEGIANCE, which is recited daily by schoolchildren throughout this country, refers to the United States as "one Nation under God." Our coins are imprinted with the motto, "In God We Trust." When the president-elect takes office he swears upon a Bible, held by the chief justice of the Supreme Court, to uphold the Constitution of the United States "so help me God." Both Houses of Congress begin their work with a short prayer recited by a chaplain. And at the opening of each day's session of the Supreme Court, the crier says, "God save the United States and this Honorable Court."

In an opinion handed down in 1952, the Supreme Court stated: "We are a religious people whose institutions presuppose a Supreme Being." Yet within ten years the Court was to bar prayer from the public schools. Was this decision in keeping with its earlier pronouncement, or was it a radical departure toward a secularization of American society? How is it possible to have separation of church and state and still respect our religious and cultural heritage? These questions, as well as the role of precedent — the influence of past judicial decisions on the resolution of present disputes — will be examined in this chapter.

*   *   *

One of the basic principles upon which this country was founded was freedom of religion. Our ancestors were only too aware — sometimes from personal experience — of the tendency of a dominant religion or sect to seek to obtain official status from the government and then to use the state's power to persecute all those who hold different beliefs. Many of the colonists originally had fled Europe to escape religious persecution, and many had encountered — or themselves engaged in — similar persecution on this continent.

Thus when the framers of the Constitution drew up the Bill of Rights the problem of religion and government becoming entwined, to the detriment of each, was foremost in their thoughts. The very first sentence of the First Amendment states: "Congress shall make no law respecting an establishment of religion, or prohibiting the free exercise thereof." The two clauses of this sentence, which have become known, respectively, as the establishment clause and the free-exercise clause, are the basis for the separation of church and state in this country. Our discussion will be mainly concerned with the establishment clause, although — as we will see — how we interpret it may be influenced by the free-exercise clause.

The basic purpose of the establishment clause was to preclude the federal government from setting up or "establishing" an official religion, such as the Anglican church in England. The idea was to avoid the whole problem of religious persecution by not giving any one religion or sect the power of the national government to use against the others. At the same time, the free-exercise clause prohibited the government from interfering with the religious freedom of its citizens. As the Supreme Court later would say, the government's posture in regard to religion must be one of neutrality.

* * *

Now that you know what the framers wrote into the Constitution, let's jump 171 years to our recent past and see how the establishment clause was applied to the issue of prayer in the public schools. In 1962, in a case entitled *Engle* v. *Vitale,* the Supreme Court was presented with a challenge to the constitutionality of a nondenominational prayer recited daily in the public schools of New York State. The prayer, which had been composed by the Board of Regents, a governmental entity of that state, went as follows:

> Almighty God, we acknowledge our dependence upon Thee, and we beg Thy blessings upon us, our parents, our teachers, and our Country.

Recitation of the prayer was voluntary: Those students who didn't want to participate were not required to, and would be excused from the room while it was said if they had a note to that effect from their parents or guardian.

The question that the Supreme Court was called upon to answer was whether this seemingly innocuous prayer, recited on a voluntary basis, violated the First Amendment. More specifically, did the recitation of the prayer in some way tend toward the establishment of religion?

Before we go any further, you may well be asking how the establishment clause in the First Amendment to the United States Constitution has any bearing on what the government of New York State chooses to do. After all, the clause says, "Congress shall make no law," and by that the framers were referring to the United States Congress, not to the legislature of any state. The answer lies in a later addition to the Constitution, the Fourteenth Amendment, which was adopted in 1868 to preserve the civil rights of blacks in the South during Reconstruction. The Fourteenth Amendment provides, in part, that no state shall "deprive any person of life, liberty, or property, without due process of law."

The language of this amendment (which, of course, applies to all states, not just those of the former Confederacy) is extremely broad. Just what is the "due process" that the States must provide? Over the years, the Supreme Court has interpreted the due-process clause of the Fourteenth Amendment as incorporating certain provisions in the Bill of Rights. In effect, the more basic rights of the Constitution, which originally were guaranteed only by the federal government, gradually were extended through the medium of the Fourteenth Amendment so that the states also had to provide them to the people. As part of this process, in 1940 the establishment clause was interpreted to limit state actions that might form or encourage an official religion.

Okay, now that we know how the First Amendment applies to the states, we're ready to consider *Engle* v. *Vitale.* With only one justice dissenting, the Supreme Court voted that New York State had violated the establishment clause by having its pupils recite the prayer quoted earlier. They concluded that the practice was a religious activity, and found it to be constitutionally prohibited as part of a governmental program to further religious beliefs.

Do you agree with this decision? If you do, how do you deal with the argument that the prayer was nondenominational, and thus couldn't involve the establishing of any particular religion? The answer you might give is the one that has been provided by the Court: The establishment clause precludes the government from promoting any religious activity, not just its advancing any one religion or sect.

What about the fact that reciting the prayer was voluntary? The Court had an easy answer for that one: It said that you could have a violation of the establishment clause without coercion by the government. This is because it is possible for the government to take steps

to establish a religion without forcing anyone to do anything, so
these steps must be prohibited. Moreover, just how voluntary is a
prayer under these circumstances? Don't the children run the risk of
being branded different or odd by their classmates if they choose not
to participate in the recitation? And doesn't leaving the room make
that worse? Peer pressure could make any voluntariness largely
illusory.

How about the argument that the prayer was too general and brief
to endanger the separation of church and state in any serious way? In
response to this objection, the Court in *Vitale* quoted James Madison,
the author of the First Amendment, who wrote, "It is proper to take
alarm at the first experiment on our liberties." In other words, we have
to be careful not to permit even the smallest violation of the principle
set forth in the establishment clause, in order to prevent more serious
violations in the future. What it amounts to is, don't let the camel's
nose get in the tent.

Not all the justices agreed with this decision. Dissenting, Justice
Potter Stewart argued that the purpose of the establishment clause was
to prevent government from setting up or encouraging an official
religion, and that the voluntary recitation of the prayer in question was
a far cry from accomplishing that purpose. Instead, he characterized
the prayer as giving the children an opportunity to participate in our
spiritual heritage.

Was he right? A lot of people think so. After all, it's rather ludicrous
to think that the children in the New York public schools would be so
aroused by the prayer that they would rise up in righteous ferver,
march on Washington, and force the adoption of an official religion
upon the rest of us. Can't it be said that the "religious activity" in
question is so far from the evil the establishment clause is designed to
prevent that no violation worth paying attention to occurred? And the
truth is that despite James Madison's purist view, the law doesn't
always go to the barricades at the first hint of a violation; it's possible
to take the position that only a violation that offers a serious attack on
the principle involved should be censured. So why not use the same
approach with respect to the establishment clause and wink at such
small encroachments as the prayer involved in *Vitale?*

And what about the "spiritual heritage" that Justice Stewart referred
to, as illustrated by the examples of official invocations of a deity listed
at the beginning of this discussion? Isn't that worth preserving, indeed,
nurturing? Beyond that, we have the influence of religion on history,
arts, and literature. Thus one question raised by the *Vitale* decision is
to what extent religion can be eliminated from the public schools

without also eliminating extremely valuable parts of the educational curriculum.

* * *

Let's suppose that by some mathematically unlikely turn of events, one of your oldest friends — someone who has owed you a big favor for years — gets elected president of the United States. Soon after his inauguration, you read in the newspaper that one of the Supreme Court justices has retired, and shortly thereafter your pal the Prez calls you and tells you he will nominate you to take his place on the Court! You're not even a lawyer, but you're game; after all, it's a high-prestige job and pays reasonably well. Besides, nothing in the Constitution actually requires that Supreme Court justices be lawyers, so maybe it's about time someone else got a chance to tackle the job. So you show up at the Senate hearings where they interrogate nominees to the Court, because the Constitution requires the Senate to give its advice and consent to the president's selection. None of the senators can find any fault with your views on legal matters, probably because you don't have any. Publicly, the president calls you the "people's" representative on the Court; privately, he tells you that as far as he's concerned that old debt is paid off. To everyone's surprise, including your own, the Senate actually approves your nomination and in due course you're sworn in.

It's just your luck that the first case the Court is called upon to decide involves the establishment clause. It deals with a state law requiring public-school students to listen as the teacher or one of the students reads ten or so verses from the Bible, without comment, at the start of each school day. Since *Vitale* was decided before you were appointed to the Court, the law of the land is that school prayer is unconstitutional. So how do you decide the case before you? It's not exactly a prayer, but isn't it a "religious activity"? Not according to the school authorities who argue that the Bible reading has a secular purpose, that it's designed to promote moral values, to combat materialism, and to teach literature.

Remember, you're being asked to decide this as a Supreme Court justice. This means that regardless of your personal preferences or beliefs, two factors must control your decision. The first is the wording of the Constitution, the "law" that you swore to uphold and are called upon to interpret in this case. And it doesn't matter what you think the framers *should* have written into the Constitution; rather, you must deal with what they actually *did* include. Otherwise you'll be "rewriting" the Constitution to suit yourself, which isn't your job.

The second controlling factor is precedent — that is, how the Court has interpreted the establishment clause in its past decisions. Even if you agree with Justice Stewart and think that the prayer involved in *Vitale* should have been allowed, you have to keep in mind that the Court decided that case the other way. Of course, a court always can overrule one of its decisions (indeed, one of the prerogatives of the Supreme Court is to overrule the decision of any court); a famous example is *Brown* v. *Board of Education,* in which the Court in effect overruled one of its earlier cases when it concluded that school segregation is unconstitutional. If courts couldn't do that, the law would be unable to change to keep up with the times. But courts don't like to overrule themselves, since it promotes instability by calling their decisions into question. Many people rely on judicial decisions in planning their activities, so once judges start overruling their own cases, people will find themselves without clear or predictable legal principles to obey, since what is legal one day may become illegal the next and vice versa. These considerations cause courts to follow precedent — what lawyers call the doctrine of *stare decisis* — even when they'd rather not. And that's why law libraries are lined with shelves of books filled with old decisions. Thus, as a Supreme Court justice, you feel an obligation to stay on course, even if you think you're going in the wrong direction.

All right, you have the arguments for both sides in the Bible-reading case, and you've got the *Vitale* case firmly lodged in the back of your mind. So how do you vote? Now remember, you're supposed to make up your own mind, so don't be swayed too much by what the other members of the Court say is best. If you want to go down in history as one of our great Supreme Court justices, you'll have to show some independence. On the other hand, if you show too much independence, and get too far from the fundamentals that control these decisions, you'll go down in history as a screwball.

Mind made up? Okay, let's see how your thinking and vote stack up. In 1963, in *Abington School District* v. *Schempp,* the Supreme Court was faced with a case involving these facts and decided that the Bible reading violated the establishment clause. Rejecting the argument that the purpose was secular, the Court noted that the Bible reading had a "pervading religious character" and thus was prohibited in the public schools.

What else would be a forbidden activity? Suppose the teacher told the students to close their eyes and meditate. Would that have a pervading religious character? Maybe we need more information to come up with an answer. Let's say the meditating students were asked to think about (1) a Supreme Being, or (2) all the starving people in the world, or (3) the big basketball game the school team was playing that night.

The first appears to be religious in character, since a typical religious activity involves communication with or meditation upon a Supreme Being. As for the other two, it depends on precisely what the teacher is asking the students to do. If they are taking a moment to sympathize with the poor, or to contemplate the importance of school spirit, then they probably are not engaging in a religious activity. But if they are seeking the intercession of a Supreme Being in behalf of either the poor or the basketball team, then it seems their meditation has a pervading religious character and so is not permissible in a public school.

Let's stop for a minute and add a twist. Although the prayer and the Bible reading in *Schempp* were both voluntary in that a child who didn't want to participate didn't have to, the activities were mandated by the school authorities. Suppose the children, completely on their own, hold an election among themselves and a large majority vote to say a prayer before class. As a Supreme Court justice, would you tell these children that their praying under these circumstances violates the First Amendment?

If you would, you'd probably be in the majority on the current Court. Although this exact case has not come before the Court, its decisions in establishment-clause cases suggest that even a prayer voted for by the children would not be legal in the public schools. If this seems strangely undemocratic, remember that constitutional rights are so basic that they are not subject to majority vote. The people cannot vote in a general election to do away with free speech, the establishment clause, or any other part of the Constitution. (If they want a change, they have to do it by constitutional amendment, which must be approved by two-thirds vote of both houses of Congress and then ratified by three fourths of the states.) Similarly, if prayer in the public schools violates the First Amendment, a vote by the children cannot make it legal.

But doesn't preventing the children from praying violate their religious freedom? Remember that the free-exercise clause of the First Amendment prohibits the government from interfering with the people's right to worship as they please. The answer is that the children have every right to pray, but not in the public schools. The right to practice your religious beliefs is not absolute; you cannot, for example, kneel down and pray in the middle of traffic on Main Street during rush hour. And if prayer in the public schools violates the establishment clause, then perhaps it is not unreasonable — and not too serious an inhibition upon the rights protected by the free-exercise clause — to limit prayers to the students' nonschool hours. You might well wonder, though, what the Court would say in a case in which a student's religion required prayers at a time of day when he was in school. Would he be allowed to pray in the classroom? Would he be excused? It's hard to tell, since this particular case has not come before the Court — at least not yet.

*   *   *

Suppose you've been on the Court for a few years; you're getting used to the routine, and you think this business with the establishment clause and public-school prayer has been settled once and for all, when lo and behold it shows up again. It seems that at public-high-school graduation exercises in Pioustown, Pennsylvania, a short invocation and benediction are being given as part of the ceremony. The question has come up whether this practice constitutes a violation of the establishment clause.

How would you decide this case? Certainly the invocation and the benediction are prayers. The graduation is a public-school function. So aren't you compelled by *Vitale* to find a violation?

But that's not how it has turned out. The Supreme Court has not dealt directly with this issue, but the lower courts that have considered it have said that the invocation and benediction are not a First Amendment violation. And thus far the Supreme Court has let these decisions stand, which is an indication that either it agrees with the lower courts, or doesn't think the issue is important enough for it to consider, or is not yet ready to take the issue on, waiting, perhaps, for the "right" case or for more experience to build up in the state and lower federal courts. (The mere fact that the Supreme Court doesn't review a particular case doesn't mean that the justices approve the decision reached by the lower court. The Court's docket is so overloaded that it can consider only a small fraction of the cases brought to it. Sometimes the press fails to make that clear in reporting on the Court's work.) So, until the Supreme Court tells us otherwise, these graduation practices do not fall under the prohibition of *Vitale*.

The lower courts reasoned that the graduation exercises are ceremonial and not educational, and that the invocation — admittedly a prayer — is too brief to violate the establishment clause, since the graduation takes place once a year, whereas the prayer in *Vitale* was said every day. Also, the graduation exercises were voluntary: There was no compulsion to attend, and a student who stayed away still graduated and could simply pick up his diploma afterward. This is in contrast to *Vitale,* in which the prayer may have been voluntary, but daily school attendance was not. What these lower courts did was to "distinguish" *Vitale* — that is, they found differences between it (the precedent) and the cases before them. Thus they were able to reach the result they thought appropriate without going against *Vitale* as precedent.

Now, while you're still wondering about the graduation invocation, we'll give you a tough problem: What about Christmas carols sung by public-school children during a holiday assembly? This is not an imaginary case; a lower court has ruled that the caroling does not violate the establishment clause. Now the question is whether you and the other members of the Supreme Court should let the case stand or overrule it.

Do you think that singing Christmas carols is a religious activity, somewhat like prayer or Bible reading? No one could deny that these songs are religious in their origin and content — they commemorate a central event in the Christian religion. But when you sing one, do you think of yourself as praying? Or are you just singing a holiday song? On the other hand, maybe you do feel some religious stirring when you sing "Silent Night" as opposed to "The Twelve Days of Christmas," or perhaps other people do.

Moreover, the singing of carols is different from a graduation invocation, which as we have seen does not violate the establishment clause. First, the songs are not as brief as the invocation — the caroling could go on for an appreciable time. Also, the school assembly may not be as educational as activities on a normal school day, but it's less ceremonial than a graduation exercise. Finally, although the children weren't required to participate in the assembly, the absence of a child because of the religious aspect would be noticeable to his classmates and could mark him as "different."

So how did that court manage to decide that the carol-singing was not unconstitutional? It did so by concluding that the songs had become part of our cultural heritage, and that to prevent the students from performing them simply because of their religious origin would be to present a "truncated view of our culture." The court was careful to note that not every Christmas program involving the singing of carols would be permissible. In the case before it, the school board had required that the material be presented in a "prudent and objective manner," and not in such a way as improperly to stress its religious aspect.

The approach used by this court was similar to that of the Supreme

Court in an earlier case in which state "blue laws" that required the Sunday closing of stores and businesses were challenged as violating the establishment clause. Conceding that these laws had their origins in religion, the Court decided that they were not unconstitutional, since their present purpose was secular — that of providing a common day of rest. The approach is also consistent with remarks by Justice Tom C. Clark, writing for the Supreme Court majority in *Schempp.* In that opinion he noted that to the extent the Bible was taught from the standpoint of its literary and historical qualities, it could be a valid part of the public-school curriculum.

What's your reaction to this analysis? More specifically, would you let the lower court case stand and thus allow the caroling? Just how much of our culture is tied up in "Silent Night" and "Hark the Herald Angels Sing"? If you had never heard a Christmas carol, would your grasp of Western culture be seriously "truncated"?

But look at it the other way: Unless the cultural or historical content of "religious" material can remove it from the prohibition of the establishment clause, a great deal more than Christmas carols might be excluded from the public-school curriculum. Students might be prevented from singing the religiously inspired works of Bach, or from studying the art of the Renaissance because much of it centers around religious subjects or expresses religious themes. The Bible could not be read from the standpoint of literature, nor possibly such American classics as *Moby-Dick* or *The Scarlet Letter,* both of which are infused with religious imagery. In the study of history, the reading of the Declaration of Independence or of the Constitution itself might be banned because each makes a number of references to "the Almighty" or to "God" or other descriptions of a deity.

If you accept the need to allow religious content to be taught from a cultural or historical perspective, how do you draw the line between what is really religious and what isn't? Perhaps one element is how the material is presented: A reading from the Bible before class has the attitude of worship, while reading the Bible during English class, along with several works of Elizabethan prose, does not. Reciting a prayer addressed to Almighty God is religious, but reading a historical document that refers to God is not.

Indeed, the Supreme Court seems to have had this distinction in mind in a recent case in which it struck down a Kentucky statute that required the posting of the Ten Commandments on the wall of each public classroom. The state claimed that its purpose was secular, since the children were being reminded that the Ten Commandments had been adopted as the fundamental legal code of Western civilization.

(Indeed, there was a notation on the posting to this effect.) The Court pointed out, however, that the Ten Commandments were not being integrated into the curriculum as part of a course of study, but were on the wall to induce the children to meditate upon, and perhaps to venerate and obey them — a purpose it found to be "plainly religious in nature."

As for the Christmas carols, remember that a lower court decided that they were cultural so long as their religious aspect wasn't unduly stressed and the Supreme Court chose not to review the case. So if you hear caroling coming from the local public school, don't call the police.

*   *   *

We've been looking at variations on the Supreme Court decision in *Vitale* that prayer in the public schools violates the establishment clause. But all the prayers and readings and singing we've considered have involved religions in the Judeo-Christian tradition, with emphasis on the latter. That's only natural, since "traditional" Christianity always has been the dominant religion in the United States, and attempts by a majority to further its own religious beliefs generally have involved the promoting of Christianity, even if only in a nondenominational form.

Over the past few decades, however, there's been an increasing interest in Eastern, often nontheistic, religions, such as Zen Buddhism, Hinduism, and Taoism, as well as mystical and ethical systems derived from them. Moreover, the more liberal segments of traditional Christianity lately seem to have moved toward a belief in a system of ethics grounded in the nature of reality rather than on precepts handed down by a Supreme Being.

What happens when one of these systems turns up in the public schools? Suppose, for example, that the school offers an elective course in Transcendental Meditation. Let's further assume that it's taught by people from outside the school who teach only this course, that the instruction is based on a textbook developed by an Indian yogi, or Hindu monk, and that part of the instruction is an initiation ceremony during which the teacher engages in a chant in Sanskrit addressed to an entity known variously as "the Unbounded," "the One," "the Eternal," and "the Pure." Let's finally suppose that someone goes to court objecting to the course, and in particular to the chanting, as constituting a form of prayer or religious exercise prohibited by the First Amendment.

As you probably already have guessed, these are the facts of an actual case. And the decision by the lower court was that the medita-

tion course — in particular, the chanting — constituted a religious activity prohibited in the public schools by the First Amendment. The
supporters of the course argued that any religious effect it might have
was insignificant, and that it should be allowed just as the invocations
and benedictions were allowed. The court, however, rejected this argument, pointing out that a regularly scheduled course in the school's
educational program was involved, not a noninstructional commence-
ment exercise.

You're still on the Supreme Court — it's up to you to let the case
stand (which might be interpreted by lower courts all over the country
as indicating the Court doesn't strongly disapprove of the decision) or
to overrule it and allow the meditation. How do you vote?

Suppose you're leaning toward permitting the meditation. That
probably means you have a hard time seeing that a bunch of kids
listening to words recited in a language they don't understand really
tends toward the establishment of an official religion. But then how do
you answer the charge that the nondenominational prayer in *Vitale* was
a long way from establishing a religion? Remember Madison's advice
about drawing the line at the first violation of the Constitution? How
can you distinguish between a chant addressed to "the Omnipotent"
and the prayer in *Vitale* addressed to "Almighty God"?

Hold on, though. Before you decide against allowing the course,
consider the beneficial effects it might have on the students. In the
case, it was argued that the meditation had a secular purpose —
it would help the students relax and increase their "sociability and
educability." One also might note its value in exposing the students
to a different culture. Shouldn't its good effects be allowed to outweigh
the slim tendency it might have somehow to further religion?

Oh, but wait — that's the argument the school authorities made in
Schempp. As you recall, they said the purpose of the Bible reading was
to inculcate moral values and combat materialism. Aren't those good
purposes, too? So if you allow the meditation, shouldn't you allow the
Bible reading?

Try looking at the problem from a very different viewpoint. Consider whether the followers of the yogi would be protected by the
free-exercise clause of the First Amendment if the government tried
to suppress their rituals. If this species of Hindu mysticism isn't a
religion, then it's not protected from government interference. Assuming you think it should be a protected religious activity, which
clearly seems to be correct, then don't you have to say it's a religious
activity for purposes of the establishment clause as well? The word
religion is used only once for both clauses, so shouldn't it mean the
same thing for each?

Ah, but your years on the Court have sharpened your wits, and you think you may have a solution to the problem. Why not interpret the word *religion* broadly for purposes of the free-exercise clause, but narrowly for purposes of the establishment clause? That would mean that a wide range of beliefs — Hinduism, Zen, whole earthism, whatever, plus the more traditional Western religions — would be protected from government interference or suppression. At the same time, only the traditional, more established religions and activities associated with them, such as Bible reading, would be barred from the public schools. This approach would allow everyone freely to practice his beliefs, and at the same time it would allow the public-school children to derive whatever benefits would flow from exposure to the nontraditional religions.

If you think that's a solution, now you must face the argument that this dual interpretation of *religion* favors nontraditional faiths over traditional ones. According to you, it's okay to pray in Sanskrit but not in English, and the teachings of the yogi can be propagated but not those of Moses or Jesus. Is that really a sensible policy? Sounds more like the twisted — or desperate — logic of someone painted into a corner.

Keep in mind, too, that this approach could allow a lot more religious matter into the schools than Transcendental Meditation. What if a school board allowed the Moonies or the Hare Krishnas to proselytize the children? What if each school day started off with a black mass? Perhaps this is taking things to absurd lengths, but at least with the traditional religions you know what you're getting, and what "ethics" are going to be taught.

Yet, it's been argued that unless a dual approach is used, humanitarian government legislation or programs might be invalidated under the establishment clause. The idea is that as progressive ethical systems increasingly are accorded the protections of the free-exercise clause, government programs that have the same ethical ends will have to be deemed religious activities, and therefore prohibited under the establishment clause. For example, if a "protected" religion taught that in an advanced industrial society everyone should have a minimum income, then any attempt by the government to pass a law designed to achieve that goal could be challenged as constituting an improper establishment of religion.

Does this strike you as a real problem? Why is it that the ethical beliefs of the traditional religions, which often are indistinguishable from those of the more progressive religious systems, haven't required the invalidating of existing social legislation? Christianity always has taught the importance of charity and helping those in need, yet this

hasn't required that government welfare programs be declared unconstitutional. Perhaps the simple answer is that as long as humanitarian
legislation serves a legitimate government goal, the fact that it also
accords with a religious belief does not bring it under the establishment clause.

In any event, the Supreme Court has not provided a definite answer
to whether *religion* has the same meaning for both the free-exercise
clause and the establishment clause. However, in the case in which the
meditation course was barred from the public schools, the court
treated the establishment clause as embracing a nontraditional religious exercise. The case, which was not appealed to the Supreme
Court, thus suggests that a single definition may well apply to both
clauses. So, for now, if you're a public-school student who wants to
meditate on the teachings of a yogi, or to recite from the Song of
Solomon, it looks like you'll have to do it on your own time and not
during school hours. On the other hand, you'll be able to do so anywhere else without fear that the police will come knocking at the door
to haul you away for engaging in a proscribed activity.

* * *

Few decisions of the Supreme Court have promoted as much controversy as *Vitale* and its progeny. Critics charge that the Court's stance
regarding prayer in the public schools is antireligious, and has the
effect of promoting a religion of secularism. Others point out, with
Justice Stewart, that religion is part of our heritage, and that too strict
an interpretation of the establishment clause requires us to turn our
backs on the past.

There have been efforts to have a constitutional amendment
adopted that would allow prayer in the schools. Without an amendment, it is unlikely that *Vitale* will be overturned, since by now it
represents an established line of precedent. Even if a majority of justices were to come to disagree with the result of the case, odds are they
will leave it in place; as we noted before, courts do not like to reverse
themselves any more than individuals like to admit errors.

Also, in an increasingly pluralistic society, it may well be that only
the strictest separation of church and state is a workable policy. As a
nation, we are even more diverse today than we were in the past, and
many different religions — some less traditional than others — have
their followers. It would be a pleasant prospect if all these many forms
of worship could unite on a prayer that would satisfy each, but history
suggests that the only common ground among competing religions is
likely to be the battlefield. Under the circumstances, perhaps it's best
to keep prayer private and the schools public.

POINT OF LAW:

Cults and Family Rights

The phone rings. It's your daughter, who's just turned seventeen. She's been spending a lot of time away from home with new friends, but you haven't minded because she seems happy.

Now she says she's sorry, but she's not coming home again. She's going to live with her friends and work sixteen hours a day for their new messiah. Your child, like hundreds before her, has left home to become a "Moonie," a follower of the Reverend Sun Myung Moon's Unification Church. As a parent you are heartsick and enraged. Can the law do anything to get her back?

Several years ago, the parent of a child who joined a religious cult could turn to a "deprogrammer," who would arrange to spirit the child away from the cult and apply psychological pressure to wean him from its influence. But the law says that kidnaping is kidnaping, even when authorized by a parent, and deprogrammers now face the possibility of criminal charges and jail sentences.

Another tack was to convince a court to use its general power to appoint a guardian over incompetent individuals as a basis for arranging psychiatric treatment for a straying child. But judicial concern for a child's privacy and freedom of religion has limited the use of this technique. Let's face it, when a court orders a child to honor his parents' wishes on religious matters, it can be criticized for censoring and persecuting unpopular beliefs in a way that treads upon the free-exercise clause.

But there may be another possibility — suing the cult for damages. A New Hampshire man once was given a sizable damage award against the Unification Church on the theory that it had enticed his daughter away; its likely that other juries would sympathize with a parent's plight. If actions of this type become common, it could bring financial pressure to bear on religious cults and discourage some of their more zealous recruiting practices. But this legal path isn't an easy one to follow. Indeed, the New Hampshire jury verdict was later overturned by a judge because of some special factors in the case.

The roots of an action for enticing a minor out of the home go back hundreds of years. To make their case, parents must show that someone deliberately convinced the child to leave, interfered with parental education of the child, or encouraged the child to disobey the parents. In many ways, the theory seems tailor made for attacking the activities of religious cults. The problem is that the concept of enticement is so broad that it could encompass many innocent activities that we do not want to stifle — for example, the free exchange of ideas between a student and teacher encouraging intellectual independence on the part of the youth. Lively debate with others is an important aspect of a young person's development.

Damage actions against a so-called cult pose another grave difficulty. Consider this scenario. Your sixteen-year-old son isn't at home very often anymore. He's been spending all of his time with new friends across town in their church. One day he announces that he's joining their religion and won't participate in any other religious activities with you. You've raised him as a Lutheran, but now he's become a Catholic. Just about everyone's sense of religious freedom would be offended if a court penalized the Catholic church for encouraging a child to join that faith.

Remember, the very first freedom guaranteed by the Bill of Rights is that of religion. For two hundred years this has meant that as long as a religion appears genuinely founded on ethical and moral concerns, neither the courts nor the legislature can challenge its beliefs, stop its discussion in public, or regulate recruitment of new members.

Even laws that on their face seem not to apply to religion are thought invalid to the extent their vagueness or generality might pose a threat to religious expression in the hands of an unfriendly judge. This policy is so strong that religious freedom must yield only when there is a compelling state interest, and even then the government may use only the least intrusive method available to accomplish its purpose.

Given this background, courts find themselves in a quandary when children are unwilling to accept their parents' viewpoint on religion. Since the family is the basic unit of our society, judges are reluctant to turn children against parents in the name of a child's freedom to choose to pursue his own religious beliefs. Yet parental authority is not always benevolent, and courts occasionally feel obliged to step in to prevent some parents from stifling a youngster's freedom to decide what he will be, even if the choice is to become a Moonie.

Trying to walk the tightrope between religious freedom and parental authority is no mean trick. It requires judges to tread very lightly and limit their inquiry to those elements indicative of abuse by one side or the other.

One factor likely to play an important role in resolving future disputes between cults and families is the age and maturity of the child. Our fears of infringing a young person's religious freedom fade when the child whose beliefs are in question is only twelve years old.

Another potential line of judicial inquiry is to look beyond the cult's claims of religious freedom to assess the methods it uses to attract new converts. But to keep this kind of scrutiny from discriminating against unpopular but legitimate religions, courts must develop criteria to distinguish harmful proselytizing from acceptable recruitment methods. A proposal adopted by the New York legislature, but vetoed by Governor Hugh L. Carey, would have asked judges to focus on recruitment practices such as sleep deprivation, isolation, and bone-wearying work coupled with changes in personality, to determine whether a conversion was legitimate or not. Yet these factors also characterize many traditional adolescent activities, such as fraternity parties and cramming for exams. Do you have enough faith in judges to let them distinguish among the organizations that attract our children? But then, who else is there to do the job?

The struggle among family, state, and religion has been with us at least since the Christians first met the Romans. Early in our colonial history, Massachusetts Puritans expelled "heretic" cult members such as Roger Williams, who went on to found Rhode Island. And, after the Revolution, Baptists enjoyed a reputation similar to that of the Moonies today, as have a number of groups since then. It would be best if our courts could refuse to become involved in monitoring religious "deviance." But as long as parents choose to bring suit against religious cults, the courts will have little choice but to walk the thin line between their obligation to resolve disputes and their tradition of avoiding involvement in religious controversy.

2

FREE SPEECH AND CIVIL DISOBEDIENCE:

Are the Rules to Be Broken?

THE UNITED STATES was born out of a rebellion that began with protests against taxation and the curtailment of liberties. Today organized protest is an accepted part of American life. It is difficult to flip through the newspaper in any large city without coming across an account of one protest or another.

> WELFARE MOTHERS DEMONSTRATE FOR HIGHER BENEFITS.
> STUDENTS STAGE SIT-IN IN DEAN'S OFFICE.
> JEWISH GROUPS PROTEST OUTSIDE RUSSIAN EMBASSY.
> DRAFT REGISTRATION DENOUNCED BY SPEAKERS.
> NUKE FOES PLAN RALLY.

Many forms of protest, and many activities associated with demonstrations, are protected by the First Amendment's guarantee of freedom of speech. Let's explore when and why this sacred principle applies to protest situations. In the process we'll also look at civil disobedience, a particular form of protest, and try to determine what it is, why it's used, and whether it should be permitted.

Freedom of Speech

The First Amendment states, in part, "Congress shall make no law . . . abridging the freedom of speech." Those seemingly simple words have sparked a tremendous amount of controversy. Time and time again our courts have struggled to interpret these words and apply them to the difficult task of balancing the often competing interests of the individual and society.

Many believe that the freedom to say what we want is our greatest and most precious freedom. We exercise it constantly, whether we are saying who we think will win the Super Bowl, who should be elected mayor, or whether the president is doing a good job. It is a measure of how wide-ranging our freedom of speech is that we normally take it for granted: Few of us would feel compelled to choose our words carefully when voicing our opinions on registration for the draft or on nuclear energy.

Our Constitution and laws encourage the freest possible exchange of opinions, ideas, and information. In part, that recognizes our worth and dignity as human beings. To forbid us to speak our minds demeans us and makes us more like slaves or robots than citizens of a free country. But as important as freedom of expression is for us as individuals, it is perhaps more important to society at large.

Our democratic system of government depends upon our participation through voting. The free flow of ideas and information is essential to ensuring that we will not be making decisions in the dark. The assumption underlying this "marketplace of ideas" is that when presented with all the relevant information, people will be able to make the best possible choices. In order to ventilate and explore various positions on an issue we have a right and maybe even a duty to speak our minds. It's healthy for a minority to test the ideas of the majority; sometimes the majority may even be convinced to change its views.

When people don't feel that their message is getting across, they sometimes try talking a little louder. That simply might mean raising their voices a bit. Or they might wear armbands or buttons, hand out leaflets, carry placards, or hire a sound truck. They might even get hundreds of people who feel the same way together for a march or a rally, which they hope will be covered on the evening news.

Like all freedoms, though, freedom of speech has its limits. Society cannot afford to permit speech that will lead to chaos or serious harm. This is rarely a problem in day-to-day living, so we usually are unaware of the limits of freedom of speech. When protests become loud or insistent enough, however, those boundaries often are tested, and sometimes crossed.

As we will discuss more fully later on, a classic example of speech that does not come within the protective bounds of the First Amendment is falsely shouting "Fire!" in a crowded theater. This is an easy case, however, since the speech is likely to lead to injury or death and lack any possible benefit to society. Other situations present much closer, much tougher questions about the limits of freedom of speech, requiring the courts to elaborate, at great length, on the few simple words of the First Amendment.

In interpreting the amendment, the courts have not had much trouble extending its prohibition against infringing freedom of speech beyond the federal government. As we saw in Chapter 1, School Prayer, the United States Supreme Court has interpreted the due-process clause of the Fourteenth Amendment to extend the basic provisions of the Bill of Rights — including the First Amendment — to the states and to local governments. This is significant, since it would make little sense to prohibit one level of government from restricting a basic freedom while allowing other levels to do so. But that eliminates only a small fraction of the problems of interpreting the amendment. The more difficult questions remain: What is protected by freedom of speech and what constitutes its abridgment?

* * *

To begin to grapple with those questions, let's look at two hypothetical laws. The first prohibits the expression of support for handgun registration. The second forbids talking above a whisper in a public library. Few of us would disagree that the first law represents a more serious threat to freedom of speech. It discriminates on the basis of the ideas expressed, the content of the message, and it smacks of Big Brother–type censorship. From a constitutional point of view it is clearly a forbidden abridgment; it strikes at the heart of the First Amendment.

This is not to say that the government must be absolutely neutral regarding all ideas — it can take sides in a debate. For example, the First Amendment does not prohibit the president from making a speech urging us to conserve energy by buying smaller cars. Auto manufacturers can counter with ads extolling the virtues of large luxury sedans. But if they try to stop the president's message, there is no doubt that they will fail. Like anyone else, the government has a right to express its view. What it cannot do is cut off the debate by silencing one side. The purpose of the First Amendment is to keep the debate going. Thus the government will have no success suppressing the car companies' speech either.

The second law is simply designed to make the library a better place for reading. It is not aimed at content; whether you are for or against handgun registration, you can't let those in the library know your opinion with a bullhorn. We feel less threatened by the second law because it doesn't involve censorship. Those who favor handgun registration are not silenced — although they are reduced to a whisper in the library. They are free to take out a newspaper ad or address a rally in a public park. Unlike the first law, the second does not strike at the core of the right to express ourselves. It simply allows the government to draw up rules for the debate, without taking sides or preventing one side from speaking. As we will see, this does not mean that all content-neutral laws automatically will pass constitutional muster, however.

Because the first kind of law aims at controlling the message's central idea — *what* may be spoken, not merely where, or when, or how — it's reasonable to assume that it abridges speech and that a court would declare it unconstitutional. There may be a few instances, though, in which a law affecting content is valid. "Wait just a minute," you cry. "The First Amendment says Congress shall pass *no law* abridging freedom of speech. And, if it means what it says, a law like this abridges speech, is not valid, and always should be ruled unconstitutional by the courts." Well, as you might suspect, there is very little that is absolute in the law. The catch is that a statute may be valid if it prohibits speech that is not really speech. Confused?

To make the distinction a little easier to follow, courts have called speech that the First Amendment applies to "protected speech" and the not-really-speech "unprotected speech." The Supreme Court has defined unprotected speech very narrowly in order to give First Amendment coverage to the widest possible variety of messages.

One of the clearest examples of unprotected speech, an example used by Justice Oliver Wendell Holmes in defining the limits of First Amendment protection, is falsely shouting "Fire!" in a crowded theater. At least three factors go into pushing the word *fire* in this context into the area of unprotected speech. The first is that the speaker does not intend the word to communicate any idea. Rather, it is said in order to cause a panic; it is more a weapon than speech. (It is like sneaking up and screaming "Boo!" at someone you know has a weak heart.) Of course, if there really was a fire, we certainly would not punish someone for pointing that out, even if a panic ensued. Yelling "Fire!" in that situation would be communication. Indeed, if someone honestly thought there was a fire when there wasn't, we wouldn't want to prosecute him for trying to help.

The second factor is that shouting "Fire!" is quite likely to lead to serious harm as the audience rushes for the exits. If there is a fire, we'll take that chance rather than leave the audience to burn in their seats. But if there isn't a fire, the risk of people being crushed or trampled as a result of yelling "fire!" is unacceptable. If we can be fairly sure that no one will be hurt, the situation is very different: You're not going to land in jail for shouting "Fire!" — no matter how falsely — in the middle of a forest where no one can hear you.

The immediacy and unavoidability of the speech's harm is the third factor. There is no time to debate the question of whether or not there

is a fire before the panic starts. If there was, then the spirit of the First
Amendment calls on us to discuss the matter freely. Since shouting
"Fire!" cuts off discussion, it is contrary to that spirit and the freedom
to shout can itself be cut off.

Speech that compromises national security is another example of
unprotected speech. The Supreme Court once suggested that disclosing the sailing dates of troopships in wartime falls within this "national
security exception" to the First Amendment. The potential for immediate, grave, and irreparable harm from that kind of speech is obvious.
For many years it was thought that comparable harm might flow from
the dissemination of information about our nuclear weapons, which
meant that the government would have the power to prevent it. A case
testing that notion arose in 1979 when a magazine called *The Progressive*
announced it was going to publish plans for making a hydrogen bomb.
The magazine claimed that everything it would publish already was
available to the public. Nevertheless, the government sought an injunction barring the article. A United States district court granted the
injunction and the case appeared headed for the Supreme Court.
Before it got there, however, H-bomb plans were published by a small
Madison, Wisconsin, newspaper. With the cat out of the bag, the
government dropped its case against *The Progressive*.

Most scientists agree that the plans as published contained several
important errors, and that terrorists and foreign governments could
not use them as a simple recipe for whipping up a bomb. But assume
you didn't know that; how would you, as a judge, weigh the freedoms
of speech and press against the claim of national security? Would you
issue the injunction? Would you simply take the government's word
as to the gravity of the risk? After all, shouldn't a judge believe what
the government says? But what if you have learned that the government has tried to impair freedom of speech in areas having only a
tenuous relation to national security, perhaps by indiscriminately
stamping documents TOP-SECRET? But more of that later.

Advocacy of lawless action is another example of unprotected
speech. If Babyface, a mobster, is holding a gun to Dick's head and
Rocky, Babyfaces's partner, yells "Shoot!" Rocky cannot later claim
that he can't be prosecuted for participating in Dick's murder because
he simply was exercising freedom of speech. But if Babyface and Dick
are hockey players having a fistfight on the ice, and Rocky, at home
watching on TV, shouts "Murder the bum!" we're not going to worry
too much about Rocky's advocacy of a lawless act.

These cases are easy. But what if Rocky is at the ball park and yells
"Kill the ump!"? Should it make a difference whether he is sitting high

in the left-field bleachers or within a few feet of home plate? That the crowd is already in an ugly mood and some fans have thrown rocks and bottles that have narrowly missed the umpire's head? That Rocky is the official announcer and is speaking over the public-address system? That Rocky is a former ballplayer and holds a long-standing and bitter grudge against the ump?

In 1919, the Supreme Court attempted to distinguish between permissible and impermissible advocacy in *Schenck* v. *United States.* In that case, Schenck and others had been convicted for urging World War I draftees to resist the draft. Speaking for the Court, Justice Holmes said that advocacy can be forbidden or punished, if the words "are used in such circumstances and are of such a nature as to create a clear and present danger" that an illegal action will result. In that case, the conviction of Schenck and others for urging World War I draftees to resist the draft was upheld because the jury had found that Schenck's words were likely to cause obstruction of the draft and to interfere with the war effort. Since Schenck's speech was found likely to lead to the commission of a crime, his words could be forbidden and he could be punished for speaking them. In the case of our hockey fight, then, Rocky would be off the hook because there is no clear and present danger that any harm would result from his words. Ask yourself, though, whether the clear-and-present-danger rule makes the baseball example any easier to resolve. Just how clear and present does the danger have to be? And what other factors — such as the state of mind of the speaker or the magnitude of the harm that might occur — should enter into the law's calculation?

Fifty years after its decision in *Schenck,* the Supreme Court redefined the clear-and-present-danger rule in *Brandenburg* v. *Ohio.* That case involved the prosecution for criminal syndicalism of a Ku Klux Klan leader who, at a cross-burning rally, urged his armed listeners to "bury the niggers" and "send the Jews back to Israel." In reversing Brandenburg's conviction, the Court narrowed the advocacy category of unprotected speech to words "directed to inciting or producing imminent lawless action" and that are "likely to incite or produce such action." The second part of that test is similar to the clear-and-present-danger rule but with the added element that the harm must be likely to occur. How much more likely is a "likely" harm than a clear and present danger of harm? It's hard to say. To return to our baseball example, Rocky's screaming in the bleachers is unlikely to cause any harm, except to his neighbor's ear. Even a few feet from the plate Rocky will be little more than an annoyance. Umpire baiting is part of the ambiance of the ball park. Of course, if Rocky was the announcer and the crowd was in a violent mood, it would be much easier for us to agree that some harm was likely to occur.

The first part of the *Brandenburg* test speaks of words being "directed to inciting or producing imminent lawless action." By requiring incitement, the speaker's state of mind becomes relevant. The distinction between incitement and other forms of advocacy is hardly crystal clear. Again, extreme cases are easy enough. A speech persuades some listeners that our political leaders are corrupt and our laws unjust, so that two years later they rob a bank as a "revolutionary exercise." Nevertheless, the speech is protected by the First Amendment. At the other end of the spectrum, a speech denouncing Islam, linking Ayatollah Khomeini with Satan, and calling for "death to all Iranians" before a crowd that has just placed a noose around the neck of an Iranian student is clearly not protected. (If you're curious about whether there is a problem in proving the speaker's intention here, our law presumes that we intend the natural and logical consequences of our actions.)

Further, under the *Brandenburg* formula, the harm threatened must be "lawless action" rather than simply illegal action, as under the *Schenck* test. Once again, the Supreme Court has not fully spelled out the difference. By the use of the word *lawless,* however, the standard appears to be aimed at serious harm. Thus, we wouldn't punish someone for inciting another to jaywalk.

Perhaps you're wondering why the Supreme Court protected the speech of the Ku Klux Klan leader in *Brandenburg.* You might even be more perplexed when you learn that the courts allowed American Nazis to march in uniform in Skokie, Illinois, a predominantly Jewish suburb of Chicago, and refused to prohibit the publication of a viciously anti-Semitic newspaper in *Near* v. *Minnesota.* Surely the Supreme Court does not subscribe to these hateful ideas. Why, then, does it protect them? The answer is not that they are worth protecting but that other ideas are and we don't want to give some government "Ministry of Truth" the power to decide which ideas will be allowed to circulate and which suppressed. If the government did have the power to censor ideas, we might still believe that the Earth is flat, or that it is the center of the solar system. At the beginning of this century it was a crime in some parts of the country to teach the theory of evolution. Even today some would like to ban its teaching. Do we really want the government in the business of telling us what we should think and say and believe, or should we trust our own ability to screen out worthless and harmful ideas?

Let's go back now and have another look at our second law, the one prohibiting anything above a whisper in a library. Because this kind of law does not involve outright censorship — it does not regulate the content of what is said, but rather when, where, and how it is said — it does not have to meet as stringent a standard of necessity as the first type. Nevertheless, it does restrict expression, and any limitation is contrary to the ideal of free speech embodied in the First Amendment. So the Supreme Court has required that these laws meet two tests: The government must have a valid purpose for the regulation and it must use the method of achieving its purpose that inhibits speech the least.

Our library-silence rule passes both tests. Providing a quiet place for reading and research is surely a valid governmental objective, and permitting anything louder than whispering is inconsistent with that goal. It is often the case, however, that there is more than one way for the government to reach its objective, so although relatively few laws fail to meet the first test, many are invalidated on the second.

The Supreme Court's concern for placing as few restraints as possible on freedom of speech is illustrated by *Schneider* v. *State,* which involved an ordinance prohibiting distribution of handbills. The ordinance did not single out specific messages; all handbill messages were forbidden. The ordinance therefore was like our second law, and had to meet the tests of having a valid governmental purpose and being the least restrictive alternative. One of the major purposes of the ordinance was to cut down litter, to avoid the pileup of trash on the streets when those who receive the handbills throw them away. There was no question that this was a legitimate purpose. The second test, however, sunk the regulation. If the state didn't want litter, it could allow the handbillers to distribute the leaflets and simply issue summonses to those who threw them on the streets. Of course, the Court knew that alternative was totally unpractical, and that even if it was pursued diligently, some paper inevitably would find its way to the ground. By invalidating the ordinance, the Court was willing to impose a financial burden on the state, requiring it to prosecute litterbugs or clean up the mess itself. In effect, the Court was saying that freedom of speech is so important that the government not only must avoid interfering with it but must sometimes subsidize it as well.

* * *

Now that we've taken a look at how the Supreme Court has interpreted the First Amendment's free-speech clause, let's see if we can figure out how some problems arising during a demonstration should be resolved. Assume we're in Pleasantville, an imaginary small town that ten years ago became the host of a nuclear power plant. At first the residents were worried about the dangers of nuclear power. But the plant has had a perfect safety record — no leaks or accidents. In fact, everything is running so smoothly that the utility that owns the plant, High-Charge Electric, has decided to build a second atomic generating unit next to the first to replace two oil-powered facilities that are no longer profitable. High-Charge is the largest employer in Pleasantville.

Since the accident at Three Mile Island, the plant has become the target of several protests by antinuclear groups. Another protest — the biggest yet — is being planned by the Alliance for Safe Energy. More than three thousand demonstrators from a five-state area are expected to converge on Pleasantville for a day of speeches, marches, and picketing. It's rumored that a small fringe faction known as Nuke the Nukes intends to block the gates of the plant. Leaders of that group are claimed to have been behind a plot to sabotage a nuclear facility in California.

The town council understandably is not too pleased about all this, especially since police overtime to control the crowds at the last few demonstrations has taken a considerable bite out of the town budget. The council has asked you, as the town attorney, for your advice. How can the demonstration be stopped, or at least controlled?

Can the town pass an ordinance forbidding antinuclear demonstrations? Of course not; that's blatant censorship. But what about banning all public demonstrations? That way the town isn't favoring any particular point of view. Or is it? If the ordinance's purpose is to stop this particular demonstration, then it's just as bad as the first proposal. And in any case, it probably is just too restrictive of speech to be permissible. The ordinance would be totally inconsistent with any conception of a free marketplace of ideas. Thus, the courts most likely will require the town to find a less inhibiting alternative to achieve whatever purpose it may have.

May the town at least charge a fee to the demonstrators in order to cover the costs of crowd and traffic control? Probably not. As we saw in discussing the *Schneider* case, the government sometimes must shoulder some of the financial burden of people exercising the right to speak and protest.

Can the town at least prevent the use of bullhorns and sound trucks? That depends on the purpose of the ban. If it is simply to cut down on noise anywhere in town, or even worse, if it is to limit the number of people who can hear the speeches, then the ban won't stand up. But if the purpose is to reduce noise because there is a hospital right across the street from the proposed demonstration, then the ban probably will be upheld. Similarly, if the demonstration is held near a residential area, it might be permitted only during daylight or early evening hours so as not to prevent people from sleeping.

* * *

The town council has reluctantly accepted that it cannot prevent the demonstration. But the police chief has just received a call from the head of the Atomic Particles, a pronuclear group made up largely of nuclear industry construction workers, warning that any antinuclear demonstration will be met by a counterdemonstration. Fistfights have broken out, and some people have been hospitalized, in two other towns where pro- and antinuclear demonstrators have clashed. The police chief wants to know if that isn't enough to stop the demonstration.

This raises the problem of the "heckler's veto." It's when one group attempts to get the police to silence another group, in the name of preventing violence. For example, when American Nazis planned a demonstration in Skokie, Illinois, many of whose residents are concentration camp survivors, members of the militant Jewish Defense League vowed that the Nazis would not march. Authorities were afraid that if the Nazis were allowed to march fights would break out.

Should the threat of violence by others silence protesters? The answer in Skokie was no. Allowing one private group to silence a demonstration by another because of its distaste for the latter's ideas is not much different from having the government prohibit the protest from the outset. Thus, as in the *Schneider* case's treatment of handbills causing litter, the government is required to go out of its way to aid the protesters. In this context that means giving the Nazi demonstrators in Skokie or the Alliance for Safe Energy in our fictitious town of Pleasantville all the police protection necessary to prevent their being impeded.

Doesn't the situation present a clear and present danger that the laws will be broken, though? Yes, it might, but that isn't the test for separating protected from unprotected speech anymore. Under the *Brandenburg* test, the speech is protected unless it is "directed to inciting or producing imminent lawless action." Thus, if one of the demonstrators called for a physical attack on the counterdemonstrators, that would meet the test. What the town claims to be worried about, though, is the counterdemonstrators attacking the original protesters. You might think that demonstrators — especially the Nazis in Skokie — are "asking for it." But is that enough reason to ban the protest? In many cities a black walking through a white neighborhood (or vice versa) is "asking for it," but that could never be used as a reason to prevent people from walking in the area or for denying them police protection.

The controversy in Skokie ended peacefully enough, by the way. The Nazis eventually were told they could march, but decided to hold their demonstration elsewhere. Confrontations between opposing groups of demonstrators do not always end without incident, however. In Greensboro, North Carolina, a clash between Ku Klux Klan members and a Marxist group called Worker's Viewpoint holding a "Death to the Klan" rally resulted in a gunfight that left four dead and ten wounded. An incident like that raises the question of just how high a price we as a society are willing to pay for freedom of speech. In Greensboro it was far higher than cleaning discarded leaflets off the street.

* * *

Fortunately, the Pleasantville demonstration goes off as planned. There are a few arrests, mostly for disorderly conduct, trespass, and failure to disperse. One arrest clearly has First Amendment implications, though. A woman was arrested for wearing a T-shirt printed with the words "Fuck Nukes Before They Fuck You." She was charged under a state law that banned the display of obscene words. Obscene words are defined in the statute as "Anglo-Saxon words describing intimate bodily parts or functions." Is the law valid? Can the demonstrator be convicted?

In *Cohen* v. *California,* the Supreme Court said someone wearing a jacket inscribed "Fuck the Draft" could not be prosecuted under an obscenity statute. First, as we'll see in Chapter 4, Free Expression, the words on the jacket or the T-shirt are not obscene in the legal sense of the word; they are very unlikely to arouse anyone sexually. Second, the words are not "directed to inciting or inducing" anything illegal. If, in a face-to-face situation, words had been shouted impugning the honor of one's mother and questioning one's sexual preferences, we might say there was an incitement or an inducement to violence. Those would be "fighting words." But even though someone might be offended by "Fuck the Draft" and "Fuck Nukes Before They Fuck You," they are not directed at anyone in particular.

Perhaps more important, banning the use of particular words to express ideas might have the effect of cutting expression short. To some, substitutes like "The Draft Stinks" or "I Don't Like Nuclear Power" simply do not convey the same meaning; certainly they lack the same emphasis! How something is said, and maybe where and when it is said, can be inseparable from what is said. If that is true, nearly all laws and ordinances regulating demonstrations in a sense are abridgments of freedom of speech.

Civil Disobedience

Sometimes protesters deliberately cross the boundaries of permissible speech, protest, or other protected conduct by marching without a permit, for instance, or demonstrating on private property without permission. They may feel that they are justified because, as they see it, the harm that will flow from whatever they are protesting far outweighs any harm that might come from their demonstrations. Indeed, they may feel morally compelled to break the law, either because the law they are breaking is unjust or because they are trying to focus attention on some other injustice. For example, those who oppose registration for the draft might attack the laws directly by refusing to register. Or they might try to frustrate the purposes of the draft registration law by breaking trespass and disorderly conduct laws by blocking the entrances to post offices where registration is taking place. Or they might violate traffic laws by lying down in the street at the gates of an army base in order to focus attention on their objections. The protesters know they face possible arrest, fines, and even prison, but they hope by calling attention to the importance they attach to their cause and their willingness to sacrifice themselves that they may be able to sway public opinion.

In deliberately disobeying authority, they join a long and rich tradition in Western culture. In Sophocles' *Antigone,* the heroine defies the order of Creon, King of Thebes, that an attacking army's dead, including Antigone's brother, not be buried. Before she is put to death for her transgression, Creon asks if she knew of his decree and deliberately disobeyed it. "Yes," Antigone replies, "your law, but not the law of Justice who dwells with the gods." When Saint Peter was asked by the high priest why he and the other apostles persisted in preaching after being forbidden to do so and repeatedly imprisoned, he answered, "We ought to obey God rather than men." Saint Thomas Aquinas wrote that men must disobey earthly rulers when the state's laws conflict with those of nature. Sir Thomas More lost his head when he chose to follow the laws of his God rather than the command of his king. In this country, pacifist Quakers refused to pay taxes for war, and abolitionists resisted the fugitive slave laws by smuggling slaves north to freedom.

Henry David Thoreau is responsible for giving principled resistance to authority the name civil disobedience. In 1845, he refused to pay taxes because he strongly objected to the war against Mexico and to the federal laws requiring the return of runaway slaves. He would not permit others to pay his taxes for him, and insisted on spending a night in jail for his crime. Later, Thoreau wrote about his experience and about his reasons for breaking the law in an essay, "Civil Disobedience." "Under a government which imprisons any unjustly," he declared, "the true place for a just man is also a prison." According to Thoreau, our conscience tells us what is right, and we are justified in following its dictates because "any man more right than his neighbors constitutes a majority of one already."

Thoreau's essay profoundly influenced Mahatma Gandhi in his struggle to win India's independence from British colonial rule. To Thoreau's ideas Gandhi added the concept of *satyagraha* — passive resistance. Protesters would place themselves in such a way as to obstruct some government function. Then, when the police moved in, they would neither budge nor resist arrest — they had to be dragged or carried away. In India this brand of civil disobedience was employed on a massive scale, which tied up the police, snarled the courts, and filled the jails to overflowing. More important, the idea that thousands were willing to be roughly treated and punished for their beliefs lent a sense of tremendous moral strength to the movement, winning many converts to the cause of independence and even gaining the sympathy of many of the English.

As Thoreau influenced Gandhi, Gandhi influenced Martin Luther King, Jr., and other leaders of the civil rights movement in the United States. In the 1950s and early 1960s sit-ins were held in many Southern cities despite having been forbidden by state and local authorities; thousands were willingly arrested and jailed for violating Jim Crow laws, which legalized segregation. Those laws were later determined to be unconstitutional.

The 1960s saw a veritable explosion of protest movements. From civil rights demonstrations the tactic of civil disobedience gave birth to protests against the war in Vietnam. Sit-ins were held in government offices, draft cards were burned, some people, including Muhammad Ali, were convicted for refusing induction, and others went to Canada or Sweden to avoid the draft. Students occupied administration buildings at Columbia, Harvard, and many other campuses. Some demonstrations, like the one at Kent State University, that began peacefully, ended in bloodshed. American Indians seized buildings at Wounded Knee and Alcatraz. The Weathermen faction of the Students for a Democratic Society battled the police in Chicago during the "Days of

Rage." Daniel and Philip Berrigan and several others destroyed selective service records in Catonsville, Maryland. And bombs destroyed defense-related laboratories and caused a death at the University of Wisconsin.

Not all of these are acts of civil disobedience. On an intuitive level we probably would say that sitting in at a segregated lunch counter is civil disobedience while planting a bomb is not. But how do we know which is and which isn't? The truth is, there is no easy test, no set, universally accepted definition. And we have no established body of "civil disobedience law" as such.

Perhaps the closest thing we have to a definition of civil disobedience is a statement made by Martin Luther King, Jr., in accepting the Nobel Peace Prize. Using the words of Socrates to explain the strategy of the civil rights movement, he said, "We will not obey unjust laws or submit to unjust practices. We will do this peacefully, openly, cheerfully, because our aim is to persuade." Civil disobedience usually is peaceful, because the use of violence would result in alienation rather than persuasion. And nonviolence is often a part of the "higher law" that dictates that a civil disobedient break a statute or an ordinance. Civil disobedience also typically is practiced openly because others must know of the movement in order to be converted to it. In fact, in these media-conscious times, protest groups often will announce their intention to break the law in advance in order to generate extensive news coverage.

These characteristics are not necessarily prerequisites of civil disobedience, however. Under particularly exigent circumstances many might feel that the use of violence against corrupt and oppressive authority is an act of conscience in defense of moral principles. Might not the members of resistance movements who fought against Nazi-controlled regimes during World War II be thought of as having practiced an extreme form of civil disobedience? And, under some conditions, openly practicing civil disobedience might not be possible or appropriate. For those who ran the Underground Railroad, for example, conducting their activities openly would have meant not only exposing themselves to punishment but also jeopardizing the welfare of the runaway slaves they were spiriting to freedom. Generally we don't want to include violent or secret acts under the heading "Civil Disobedience," however. If we did, we would be including the clandestine acts of terrorism committed "on principle" that seem so prevalent today.

Perhaps the only universal characteristic of civil disobedience is that it involves deliberately breaking the law. Unless a person knowingly acts in an illegal fashion, we hardly can say that he is being disobedient. But even with so fundamental an aspect of civil disobedience as this, there might be some trouble with our definition. Consider the case of a black woman who deliberately drinks from a whites-only water fountain and is arrested. At her trial she admits to knowing that the law prohibits blacks from drinking from the fountain. She is convicted, but she appeals her conviction, claiming that the whites-only rule is unconstitutional. The appellate court — perhaps the United States Supreme Court — agrees and reverses her conviction. Has she really broken the law? Maybe we should simply think of so-called test cases as a special class of civil disobedience.

As for the civil aspect of civil disobedience, we probably would say that it contains elements of nonviolence and good motive. As Dr. King pointed out, the aim of civil disobedience is to persuade, and we are much less likely to trust or be persuaded by someone who is acting selfishly or maliciously. We might want, then, to distinguish between "civil" disobedience and "criminal" disobedience, and we might expect the law to draw the same distinction.

Our legal system historically has not treated those who are civilly disobedient differently from other lawbreakers, however. If a valid law is broken, the transgressor will be convicted whether he is acting on the basis of the highest moral principles or out of sheer greed. Of course, being human, the judge and the jury are likely to sympathize more with the former — who might receive a lighter sentence than the latter, or even be found not guilty.

*   *   *

Let's return to the site of our antinuclear demonstration to look at a few activities that might be going on there. Which are examples of civil disobedience and why? Which might justifiably receive special treatment from the law and why?

1. A man is standing near some demonstrators who are being arrested for disorderly conduct after failing to comply with a valid police order to disperse. The police think he is part of the group and arrest him too. At his trial it is shown that he was not a protester and that he had done nothing illegal.

An easy case, right? He didn't do anything illegal and he didn't intend to do anything illegal, so he couldn't have been disobedient. But what would you say if he had intended to join the group but arrived on the scene too late to be hauled away with the others? In other words, he intended to break the law if given the chance. Conversely, what if, instead of being just a bystander, the man was a protester, but had not heard the order to disperse and would have moved to another area if he had heard it? That is, what if he was arrested, but hadn't intended to do anything illegal? Are intention and lawbreaking both required, or is either alone enough to constitute civil disobedience?

2. A protester cuts away a section of the chain link fence of the plant and puts it in the back of her pickup truck. After the demonstration, she takes it home and uses it to patch an opening in the fence around her yard.

What do you think? It doesn't sound like civil disobedience, does it? She certainly has broken the law; she could be prosecuted for destruction of private property, theft, and conversion. And we have no trouble inferring that she intended to break the law. No physical violence was involved, and there is no evidence that she tried to conceal her actions. But we certainly would hesitate to label this civil disobedience. If the aim of civil disobedience is to persuade, then this misses the mark by quite a bit. If anything, this selfish action will turn us against the antinuclear position. It certainly is not calculated to win our sympathy, support, and admiration.

3. A demonstrator cuts a hole in the plant fence. A policeman steps forward to arrest him, but the demonstrator punches the policeman in the jaw, knocking him unconscious. The demonstrator flees and is never caught.

There are lots of problems trying to fit this into the mold of civil disobedience. Yes, he certainly did break the law; if he had been caught he would have been charged with resisting arrest and assaulting a police officer. Did he mean to do that? In the immediate sense, probably. But is that what we mean by intention in the context of civil disobedience? His actions were made on the spur of the moment and almost certainly not thought out in advance. We normally think of civil disobedience as something planned, and sometimes even announced, before the event. Further, by hitting someone and then running, he is unlikely to move us very far toward believing in the rightness of his cause. We might even think that if this fellow wasn't willing to be arrested for his part in the demonstration, then he didn't believe very strongly in his cause. And if he didn't, why should we?

4. Several demonstrators go through holes in the fence. They had announced their plans to do so at a press conference last week. The police are waiting for them and they are all arrested for trespassing.

Lawbreaking? Yes. Openness, willingness to be arrested? Apparently. Nonviolence? Check. Intention? Unquestionably. Looks like a pretty solid case of civil disobedience, right? But wait, don't we want to know more? For instance, what were they going to do once they got inside the fence? Would you think it was civil disobedience if the protesters intended to break into the plant and destroy equipment? If they planned to take over the control room and threatened to cause a meltdown? If they were going to form a peaceful picket line? Or if they wanted to swim in the pool on the other side of the site?

5. A dozen demonstrators sit in front of the plant gate, blocking the entrance. They sing "We Shall Overcome." The police chief gives them an order to leave the area, which they ignore. After a few minutes the police begin making arrests. The demonstrators do not actively resist, but they refuse to stand or walk and must be dragged to waiting police vans.

You breathe a sigh of relief. Here it is, you say, a pure case of civil disobedience. What makes you so sure is the fact that you've seen or heard or read about hundreds of cases just like it. And therein lies one of the keys to what civil disobedience is all about. Civil disobedience is what you recognize, and what you think it is. Whatever judges, juries, lawyers, and the law have to say about it isn't terribly relevant because the activity is aimed at *you*. It is trying to get your attention and your support.

* * *

You might be beginning to wonder why someone would want to be civilly disobedient. Surely only an idiot would invite punishment if there wasn't something to be gained. Probably those who are civilly disobedient feel that they are working to correct injustices and to help form a more just society. The question then becomes: Why, if faced with unjust laws, would someone have any reason to believe that the injustice could be righted? After all, laws are supposed to be a reflection of the majority's will, so the small minority that is civilly disobedient cannot hope to change them. Dr. King's answer was that the goal is to persuade: A person who is civilly disobedient must believe that society, or at least a majority of it, is basically good and simply needs to have the injustice pointed out. In a way, then, the reasons for an act of civil disobedience are like those for exercising freedom of speech — assisting the process of societal decision making.

Some injustices and errors of societal judgment are so serious that we might agree that working for change outside the law is justified. Racial segregation is an example. But does draft registration meet this standard? And what about the use of nuclear energy? How and where do we draw the line and who ultimately does it?

Our culture places tremendous value on individual thought and on acting according to one's beliefs. Many of our heroes became heroes by "bucking the system." Indeed, the founders of our nation were leaders of an armed rebellion that was unacceptable to most of the world at the time. Opposed to this notion of individualism is the idea that we need the stability and order of a system of obedience to laws. If each of us was to throw off the yoke of restraint and act only on the basis of our beliefs, the result would be chaos. This does not mean that, in order to stave off chaos and the collapse of society as we know it, we have to have a rigid and unchanging system of laws. As we have seen, our system allows and even encourages the public debate of issues by guaranteeing freedom of speech; in this way, public opinion may be changed and eventually the laws may be rewritten. What our system does not encourage is self-help — taking the law into our own hands. Too many innocent people have been the victims of vigilantes and lynch mobs for us to allow that.

If the law is changing too slowly, or not at all, and if the injustice the law insulates from change is serious enough, then self-help — in the form of civil disobedience — might be the only alternative. The problem is in deciding which problems are serious enough to justify proceeding against normal channels.

*   *   *

We've been trying to define just what civil disobedience is. As we have seen, it's not an easy task, precisely because civil disobedience is outside the law and thus not subject to exact legal formulation. Perhaps one approach to understanding it is to remember that it flourishes in countries that operate under the rule of law rather than the rule of men. For example, Gandhi developed the tactic of passive resistance in India, where, to a certain extent, the established procedures and safeguards of English law were observed by the colonial authorities (whether they wanted to or not). It's hard to imagine Gandhi, or anyone else, creating a similar resistance movement in Stalin's Russia or Hitler's Germany. When the government is truly oppressive, civil disobedience becomes virtually impossible: The severity of the state's response obliterates it, as the participants are executed or sent to concentration camps; the state's control of communications prevents the message from being heard; and, even if it is heard, the people are powerless to act effectively against the government.

So maybe our understanding of civil disobedience requires that we recognize that in a sense it is a creation of a tolerant and civilized legal system, and cannot exist without it. Moreover, the goal of those who engage in civil disobedience often is not merely to do away with an unjust law, but to replace it with a just law; after all, the ultimate triumph of the civil rights movement was the passage of laws safeguarding civil rights. Thus it is unlikely that genuine practitioners of civil disobedience would take actions intended to undermine the law as such; rather, they act to correct, rather than to destroy, the legal system, which they assume — and hope — will continue to function.

The close tie between civil disobedience and the law may explain the tendency of judges to be lenient with those who engage in it. Sensing perhaps that the refusal to obey a specific law on principle reflects an appreciation of the law as a whole rather than an appeal to anarchy, courts sometimes return the salute, and wink at transgressions that otherwise might be viewed as criminal.

POINT OF LAW:

The Pentagon Papers Case

In 1967, Secretary of State Robert S. McNamara commissioned a study called *History of United States Decision-Making Process on Viet Nam Policy.* The resulting forty-seven volumes, which have come to be known as the Pentagon Papers, detailed the entire history of our involvement in Vietnam from World War II to the beginning of the Paris peace talks.

Two years after it was completed, Daniel Ellsberg, an employee of the Rand Corporation, was given access to the study. Rand is a California-based think tank that held Defense Department contracts to analyze American strategy in Vietnam.

Ellsberg, who for years was a staunch supporter of this country's participation in the war, had become convinced our involvement was a mistake and that American forces should be withdrawn as soon as possible. Believing that the government study itself supported this view, in November 1969 he delivered a copy of it, along with other documents obtained from Rand, to Senator William Fulbright, chairman of the Senate Foreign Relations Committee. Ellsberg and others had secretly — and probably illegally — photocopied the documents in a Los Angeles advertising office. Neither Fulbright nor the committee made the papers public, and the war dragged on.

Under circumstances that have never been fully explained, the *New York Times* obtained copies of most of the documents and on June 13, 1971, began publishing a series of articles based on the study. The day after the second article appeared, Attorney General John Mitchell sent a telegram to the *Times* requesting that it halt the series. The *Times* refused, and when the third installment appeared the next morning, the government went to court to restrain further publication.

Judge Murray I. Gurfein of the United States District Court in New York City declined to enjoin the *Times,* but the federal appellate court, the Second Circuit Court of Appeals, reversed his decision and ordered the paper to halt publication. Meanwhile, the *Washington Post* had begun publishing articles based on the Pentagon Papers. The government proceeded to bring an action against the *Post* in Washington, but the United States Court of Appeals for the District of Columbia disagreed with the appellate court in the *Times* case, deciding not to prohibit the *Post* from continuing its publication.

The *Times* and the government petitioned the United States Supreme Court to review the two cases. On June 25, the Court agreed to hear them; argument was set for the next morning. Some idea of the importance of the matter can be gleaned from the fact that only eleven days had elapsed between the filing of the first action in the district court and the time the Supreme Court heard the case. Most suits never reach the Supreme Court, and those that do usually do so after years, not days.

This was the first attempt by the federal government to restrain the publication of a newspaper. In the 1931 case of *Near* v. *Minnesota,* which involved an attempt by a state government to block the publication of an anti-Semitic newspaper carrying on a smear campaign against local officials, the Supreme Court said that a prior restraint would be allowed only in the most exceptional cases. For instance, Chief Justice Charles Evans Hughes wrote, "No one would question but that a government might prevent actual obstruction to its recruiting service or the publication of the sailing dates of transports or the number and location of troops." The government alleged that the publication of the Pentagon Papers was a similarly exceptional case, one that threatened "grave and immediate danger to the security of the United States."

At stake, from the government's point of view, was secrecy in the conduct of foreign policy and the national defense. It argued: (1) Many of the documents involved were stamped TOP-SECRET. (2) The papers were stolen, and the *Times* and the *Post* had no right to have them, much less publish them. (3) Disclosure of the papers' contents, such as information on United States complicity in the assassination of South Vietnamese President Diem, would embarrass the nation in its dealings with other countries. (4) Release of information on the United States' approach to ongoing negotiations would hinder the progress of the peace talks and possibly prolong the war.

For the newspapers, the principles involved were (1) the freedom of the press guaranteed by the First Amendment; (2) the danger of allowing the government to censor the news; and (3) the public's right to know what its government is doing.

In a six-to-three decision, the Supreme Court declared that the government had not overcome the heavy presumption that all prior restraints on publication are unconstitutional under the First Amendment. But the Court did not definitely resolve the question of when prior restraints are permissible. In an unusual move, each of the justices wrote a separate opinion, reflecting the deep division within the Court on the subject. The six who voted not to allow a restraint differed in their reasons. Three — Hugo L. Black, William O. Douglas, and Thurgood Marshall — took an absolute view of the First Amendment, writing that a prior restraint would never be constitutional. The other three — William J. Brennan, Potter Stewart, and Byron R. White — held that a prior restraint would be permissible in cases when disclosure would lead to extreme danger, but felt that the government had not shown that publication of the Pentagon Papers would create a substantial risk of grave harm. Additionally, Justice Stewart was sharply critical of the government's practice of overclassifying documents:

> When everything is classified, then nothing is classified, and the system becomes one to be disregarded by the cynical or the careless, and to be manipulated by those intent on self-protection or self-promotion. I should suppose, in short, that the hallmark of a truly effective internal security system would be the maximum possible disclosure, recognizing that secrecy can best be preserved only when credibility is truly maintained.

The three dissenters — Harry A. Blackmun, John M. Harlan, and Chief Justice Warren E. Burger — felt that since the conduct of foreign relations and national defense is in the realm of the executive branch of the federal government, the decision of the president and his assistants that the disclosure of the information in question would harm the national interest should not be second-guessed by the courts. They also were concerned that the frenzied pace at which the case proceeded gave neither the government nor the courts the opportunity to give it the attention that so serious a matter deserves.

Two days before the Supreme Court handed down its opinion, Ellsberg was indicted for violation of the Espionage Act and theft of government property. Later, a federal grand jury enlarged the charges to include conspiracy and indicted Anthony Russo, who helped Ellsberg copy the documents, as a co-conspirator. If convicted on all counts, Ellsberg could have received a sentence of 115 years, Russo
35.

The government's own extraordinary misconduct proved fatal to its prosecution of the case. With the aid of the CIA, the White House "Plumbers" — the same group involved in the Watergate break-in — burglarized the offices of Ellsberg's psychiatrist. Wiretaps were used against Ellsberg and his attorneys. Presidential adviser John Ehrlichman held two private meetings with federal Judge Matt Byrne, who was presiding over the trial; although the meetings involved other matters, the press played them up in a big way. In light of these improprieties, Judge Byrne dismissed the case on May 11, 1973. "The totality of the circumstances of this case," he declared, "offends 'a sense of justice.' "

While these legal events were occurring, the events and subsequent disclosures of the Watergate cover-up were unfolding. Many of those who once would have trusted the government with the power to halt the disclosure of information in the name of national security had changed their minds. As was true of other aspects of our national heritage, free expression not only survived the crisis but, in the minds of many, was strengthened. It seems likely that to some indefinable extent, public attitudes toward the Vietnam War and the Watergate debacle had validated Daniel Ellsberg's civil disobedience.

3

THE RIGHT OF PRIVACY:

A Polemic: What's Left of It in Our Computerized, Information-Packed World?

HAVE YOU EVER applied for a credit card or insurance and been bothered by all those questions on the form? Or wondered how those companies check you out and what kind of "secret files" they have? And when you've applied for a job, have you felt some anxiety about whether your references will tell a "straight story"? What about applying to college? Are you sure your transcript, and not someone's with a name that sounds like yours, will go to the right school? Did you ever think that you'd like to look at your own files and make sure they are in good shape? Well, if you've ever had any of these thoughts, you have plenty of company! These days many people are worried about losing their privacy. It's something that's concerned people since the human race first began to keep records on itself, but today it seems to be bothering more and more of us.

There certainly is no reason to feel defensive about your concern. Privacy is important. It's essential to a person's sense of individuality and autonomy; that's a basic ingredient of life in a free society. At a minimum, I'm sure you think of your home as a sanctuary and your body as something uniquely private. And I'll bet you've had a personal secret or two that you didn't want to share with every Tom, Dick, or Harry. You're not unusual. Many people feel seriously diminished by the disclosure of personal information, even when it is accurate and they are not damaged professionally or socially. Small wonder that more than sixty years ago a prominent Boston lawyer who became one of our greatest jurists, Louis D. Brandeis, characterized the right of privacy as "the most comprehensive of rights and the one most valued by civilized men." The thought was echoed by the late Justice William

O. Douglas, who said, "The right to be let alone is indeed the beginning of all freedom."

Despite these deep roots, the law has given relatively little attention
to the development of a broadly based theory of privacy. The reasons
privacy has been treated with some indifference by the law and society
in general are fairly clear. To many, privacy is part of a Greta Garbo
or Howard Hughes syndrome or the refuge of those with something
to hide. Moreover, privacy is difficult to define because it is a subjective
value that is perceived differently by different people. What I want to
keep private, you may be happy to shout from the rooftops.

So until recently the subject has been left to be developed by the
courts on a case-by-case basis, which they have done by extrapolating
a few privacy rights from the existing doctrines of defamation, confi-
dential relations, trespass, and even property. It has really been a thing
of threads and patches, with various courts allowing privacy suits
against people who intruded on the seclusion or solitude of others, or
appropriated a person's name or likeness for commercial advantage,
or publicly disclosed embarrassing private facts, or did something that
put a person in a false light in the public eye. But the cases lack
uniformity and a focused theme; they look like a crazy quilt of rules,
exceptions, and inconsistencies.

But times change, and for more than a decade now, a privacy revolution has been under way in the United States. A concern that was once
rejected by many people as amorphous, almost paranoid, has become
a major social movement in this country. As a walker along the path-
ways of the law, I find the most interesting aspect of the privacy revolution to be the speed with which this concern has been translated into
legal action.

The catalyst for the privacy revolution has been the explosive
growth of computer technology. Recognition of the dimensions of
data collection in our society and the capacities of electronic record
keeping and its effect on "the right to be let alone" have galvanized
people's attention to the computer's threat to privacy. Revelations
concerning surveillance of Americans, commercial data banks filled
with hearsay and gossip, widespread nosing through school, medical,
and insurance records, the excessive zeal of the FBI and CIA, have
made some feel that our privacy is being assaulted from every angle
and that society today is at George Orwell's 1984 minus two and
counting.

* * *

Before exploring the law's reaction to privacy concerns, let's look at
the social phenomenon itself. Modern record keeping has generated

at least four anxieties about the state of our privacy. The first of these derives from one of today's most common clichés: "We live in an information-based society." What that means in real-world terms is that more and more institutions in our society today collect larger amounts of information about a wider range of facets of the lives of increasing numbers of Americans.

We are a highly scrutinized, watched, counted, recorded, and questioned people. Every time you file a tax return, apply for life insurance or a credit card, deal with the government, or interview for a job, a dossier is created under your name. Whenever you travel on an airline, rent a car, or reserve a room with a major hotel chain, you probably are leaving distinctive electronic footprints in the memory of a computer — tracks that, when collated and analyzed, can reveal a great deal about your activities, habits, and associations.

This seemingly never-ending upward spiral of data collection is made possible by the computer, which gives us the ability to store and process hitherto unimaginable quantities of information. It's all part of a computer-age variation on Parkinson's Law, that goes something like this: As technological capacity to handle information increases, a data-gathering organization will collect more information to fill that capacity. Then it will acquire more data-handling capacity and begin to fill that! In other words, information collection expands to meet the computer's ability to digest it.

An excellent example of today's escalating data gathering is the increased inquisitiveness of the basic federal income tax form — the notorious "1040" most of us fill out every April. Comparing this year's form with the one you filled out twenty years ago is a revealing exercise; it is incredible how much more information the government demands of us today. In addition to sources of income, a completed 1040 discloses a great deal about the taxpayer's medical situation, as well as his or her charitable, political, and philosophical orientation. Simply analyzing the deductions provides an excellent profile of many of the taxpayer's activities.

Almost all governmental questionnaires also reflect the marked expansion of data collection brought about by the computer. Several years ago, the United States Senate Subcommittee on Constitutional Rights, chaired by Sam Ervin, of Watergate fame, studied data gathering by federal agencies. The senator discovered that the executive branch had run riot collecting information. Although almost all the government's questionnaires seemed reasonable viewing them through a telescope focused on nothing but the agencies' policy objectives, the bureaucrats apparently were taking very little account of the intrusive aspects of their activities.

Not surprisingly, many Americans have begun to fear that the accelerating pace of information gathering is creating the much heralded "womb-to-tomb dossier" on each of us. People feel they are in what psychologists occasionally refer to as a record prison. After all, in an age of zip codes, area codes, and identification numbers, is it irrational to feel we have lost our independence, autonomy, and individuality and become the alter ego of a file whose existence, content, and use are beyond our control? It's this apprehension about uncontrolled data collection and the onset of an Orwellian age that has provided the initial impetus for the privacy revolution.

The second anxiety flows logically from the first. Ours is a crowded, complex world, one in which countless decisions affecting our daily lives are made by people we never see, using file information over which we have no control. Once this is appreciated, it becomes clear that to a substantial degree we no longer are truly masters of our own fate; we are at the mercy of files created and managed by others.

Are you insurable? creditworthy? employable? or eligible for government benefits? The answers to these questions increasingly seem to depend on how an anonymous administrator reacts to your file, rather than to you as a flesh-and-blood applicant. It's a reality of contemporary life. Our nation is no longer a network of small towns with everyone knowing everybody else in the community. In late-twentieth-century America, with its millions of people and the literally billions of decisions that must be made about them, most applications are processed impersonally, without the face-to-face dynamic of yesteryear.

A somewhat fanciful view of the admissions process at many universities and professional schools provides a useful example.

It begins with a vibrant, talented, active, expectant young man or woman seeking admission to, let's say, a law school, by filling out a lengthy application. Faced with thousands of applicants for a few hundred places, many prominent institutions, often with the assistance of the Educational Testing Service, take the raw college data and compute an adjusted grade-point average for each student. This often is a highly sophisticated process; certain undergraduate courses may be excluded, while others are weighted heavily. In addition, the overall scholastic average may be adjusted again to reflect the experience the professional school has had with students from the applicant's college. Once the adjusted grade-point average is computed — let's use 3.4 on a scale of 4.0 — it may then be multiplied by an arbitrary weighting factor — perhaps 200 — which produces a grade-point value of 680. To this the computer will add the applicant's score on any relevant standardized test, such as the Law School Aptitude Test — perhaps 650. The result is yet another number, an index score, which in our illustrative case would be 1330. Our flesh-and-blood applicant has now been reduced to a number.

The depersonalization continues. An admissions officer will mark a dot on a chart at the spot for those with an index score of 1330. So, metaphorically speaking, our aspiring student has been further reduced to a dot on a distribution graph.

Then, each spring, in what often has the trappings of a crypto-religious rite, two parallel lines are drawn on the chart. If the applicant's dot falls below the bottom line, a rejection letter issues. If the dot is above the top line, the applicant is accepted. If the dot is between the lines, the applicant is in a "hold" category, and, at last, someone will look at our applicant's record to distinguish it from the others whose dots fall between the lines. No matter where a dot falls, an automatic typewriter probably will produce the appropriate letter informing the individual whether he or she has been accepted, rejected, or is in a hold status.

This isn't all bad. It reduces the potential for racial or sexual discrimination. Moreover, given the numbers of people competing for admission to professional schools, this type of decision making may be inevitable. But it does put us at the mercy of the accuracy, currency, and relevancy of the files, and tends to foster a sense of dehumanization and helplessness that is the essence of the second anxiety about contemporary data gathering.

Let's face it, errors occur; they are bound to. The ever-present possibility of name confusion makes that obvious — a bittersweet cloud I have lived under since high school, when the *real* Arthur Miller's *Death of a Salesman* reached Broadway. Data-gathering institutions are not always to blame; they often are overwhelmed. Yet there's ample evidence that decision-making personnel frequently are not adequately trained in evaluating information, management does not emphasize the importance of maintaining privacy and confidentiality of individual data, information often is not sufficiently checked or updated, and hard questions as to whether certain information is relevant and should be gathered are not asked. Remember, computers rarely make mistakes, although companies blame the machinery all the time. Don't fall for that kind of scapegoating! It's the people handling the information put into the computers who make mistakes or errors in the data itself. One of the great truths of computer science is GIGO — garbage in, garbage out!

The third anxiety stems from the fact that technology has completely eliminated any space or time limits on the movement of information. It can be transferred anywhere on Earth and combined with other data in a matter of seconds.

When Horace Greeley remarked, "Go west, young man," he obviously was referring to the opportunities on the frontier a century ago. But he also may have been thinking of the anonymity it provided for keeping the past private and starting fresh by getting away from an eastern bankruptcy record, or an overbearing spouse. If a latter-day Horace Greeley advised someone to "go west" for a new start, it would be little more than a cruel joke. His electronic dossiers would arrive before he did!

The fear of transferring personal information from one place to another goes beyond losing the ability to escape the past. Exchanging or centralizing data often means taking data out of the context in which they were created and having different people use them at a different place for a different purpose. This creates serious risks for the subject. Information typically is gathered with a particular purpose in mind. It's unrealistic to think that users outside the collecting organization always understand what that original data gatherer's objective was or know how to interpret the information in terms of its standards and evaluative purposes.

To take an obvious example, an individual's army efficiency report is a radically different thing from a student's academic record at a college or professional school. They involve different performance scales and values. A rating of excellent in one is not comparable to an excellent in the other. Why should we expect a decision maker who is in an environment entirely different from the military or the campus to understand the nuances of interpreting data drawn from these two different contexts. The problem intensifies when the shadings are far more subtle than those in the illustration.

Among the most potentially damaging information circulating in the United States is criminal justice data, much of which is now computerized. Did you ever watch *The FBI,* a popular television series a few years ago? Then you may recall that Inspector Erskine frequently directed one of the agents to "check out the suspect in NCIC." The good inspector was referring to the National Crime Information Center, which is not a figment of Hollywood's imagination but an operating, sophisticated, computerized FBI criminal justice information system. NCIC contains raw data about arrests, prosecutions, and convictions drawn from law-enforcement agencies throughout the nation. Once this information is put into NCIC, it can be displayed on computer terminals in FBI offices and state and local police agencies throughout the country. But it has been estimated that almost 40 percent of the records that appear on NCIC terminals show nothing more than the arrest.

Remember, an arrest is simply a charge; it is proof of nothing. The Constitution presumes us innocent until proven otherwise. But do decision makers in government, business, or academe really understand the difference between an arrest — particularly an isolated one — and a conviction, and accord someone with an NCIC arrest record the presumption of innocence when evaluating them? Law-enforcement officials presumably do, and given the direct relevance of criminal justice information to their day-to-day duties, it probably is appropriate that arrest records circulate within the police community. But concern about this data has generated controversy even in this context. Civil libertarians and law-enforcement officials disagree sharply about the legitimacy of maintaining old arrest records, particularly those that show the accused was acquitted or do not indicate any prosecution followed the arrest.

The real problem is that in many states these records circulate beyond the law-enforcement environment, even beyond government, to employers, insurance companies, and credit granters. Moreover, the boards that control membership in various professions and trades often are required to check whether applicants have been arrested; indeed, some licensing agencies make these inquiries even without any statutory authorization, let alone obligation, to do so.

Do you really think administrators who license butchers in one state, beauticians in another, or taxicab drivers in a third understand the limited significance of an arrest or some of the police practices that lead to it? Is an arrest even relevant to cutting meat, styling hair, or driving a cab? How many decision makers understand that a significant percentage of the people in those files have never been convicted of anything?

The problem is real, and it may strike closer to home than you might think. Let's look at two examples of "rap sheets" drawn from a criminal justice record system. The details are fabricated, the situations are not.

> AARDVARK, ANTHONY K. Arrested, Philadelphia, Pennsylvania, June 5, 1943. Charged, felony. Tried, January 5, 1944. Convicted, January 8, 1944. Sentenced, three years Leavenworth. Served, six months. Released on probation.

Who is this felon, whose "record" probably will put off employers, insurance companies, and credit granters? He happens to be a nationally renowned scholar-teacher. His crime? Aardvark was a conscientious objector during World War II. An ironic twist is that he was convicted under a legal standard since declared an unconstitutional impairment of freedom of religion by the United States Supreme Court in a case involving Muhammad Ali. But for the rest of Aardvark's life, that "criminal" record will track him.

> DOGOODER, DIANA J. Arrested, Meridian, Mississippi, January 5, 1959. Charged, criminal trespass. Tried, June 20, 1959. Convicted, June 21, 1959. Sentenced, six months. Released on probation.

Troublemaker? Not really. That's the record of a civil rights worker, arrested and convicted under a criminal trespass statute for demonstrating — nonviolently — against segregation. How will it be interpreted by personnel managers who have come to believe that, in hiring, it's better to be safe than sorry? Will they probe behind the stark entries — "criminal trespass," "convicted"? Ironically, even though Dogooder actually was convicted, the illustrative record still is misleading; her conviction was reversed on appeal because, as you will recall from Chapter 2, by demonstrating she was legitimately exercising her First Amendment rights of free speech, assembly, and petition.

Using information out of context can even frustrate one social policy in the name of another. A good illustration is provided by New York's reaction when the pace of trading on the securities markets heated up so fiercely and became so hectic in the late 1960s that the brokerage firms could not keep up. In the confusion many stock certificates disappeared; perhaps they were misplaced, perhaps they were stolen. The state legislature passed a statute requiring that everyone working or seeking a job in the securities industry be checked out in New York's criminal offender record information system. The effect was to reduce the chances of anyone with an arrest record being employed in the securities industry.

Now, as a nation we supposedly are committed to equal opportunity in employment. But the reality is that if you are a nineteen-year-old black male living in one of New York City's ghettos, particularly Harlem or Bedford-Stuyvesant, the odds are extremely high of your having an arrest record — arrest, mind you, not conviction. In many cities these arrests may reflect little more than police "sweeps" designed to prevent troubles on the streets of the inner city, especially during the summertime. By reacting as it did to a legitimate concern about vanishing stock certificates, the New York legislature probably did not understand the risks of using arrest information outside the law-enforcement context. And, since the statute had a disproportionate impact on at least one minority group, it worked at cross-purposes with the nation's equal-access-to-employment policy.

The fourth and final anxiety stems from the belief that in a democratic society the government should not engage in surveillance of its citizens or maintain dossiers on them. As with the other three concerns, this one is a mixture of real and imaginary fears, but there are enough real ones to legitimize the apprehension. Watergate offers a graphic example of governmental information abuse, as evidenced by the Watergate bugging itself, the break-in at the office of Daniel Ellsberg's psychiatrist, and the compilation of the "Enemies List."

A more broadly based illustration is President Lyndon Johnson's activation of the domestic military intelligence network in the 1960s. This was a response to riots in several cities, including Detroit, Newark, and Washington, D.C. Like New York's reaction to the securities "crisis," the military operation was a well-intentioned and rational information effort, designed to use surveillance as a way of informing army units called in to deal with urban violence who the "enemy" might be.

Unfortunately the intelligence units were unleashed without sufficient direction or oversight. Within seven years, the army had collected information on seven million Americans, most of it worthless news clippings and trivialized gossip. Who were the people captured by the system? Were they all dangerous terrorists and radicals? No, only a minuscule fraction of them fit that description. It turned out that there was a good chance you were in the file if you had attended a protest meeting, signed a petition, written a letter to a major newspaper or magazine on a public policy issue such as Vietnam, or engaged in any form of dissent during those seven years. In short, it was a *Who's Who* of citizens who had exercised their First Amendment rights.

The lesson is clear. People who think they are in a crisis often overreact and are not sensitive enough to the rights of others. The effect can be quite insidious. Think of it in terms of today's issues. Suppose you want to go to a protest meeting, perhaps to hear what the Clamshell Alliance is advocating about nuclear power or to listen to the arguments against your son's registering for the draft. If you know that those attending will be photographed by government agents or that files will be opened on those signing a petition, you may be dissuaded from participating. By creating apprehension, the government has deterred you from engaging in constitutionally protected conduct. You have been victimized by what psychologists call the record prison syndrome and what constitutional theorists call the chilling effect.

The fear is not fanciful. After the Pentagon Papers were published by the *New York Times* and the *Washington Post* and read into the *Congres-*

sional Record by then senator Mike Gravel of Alaska, Beacon Press, which is a division of the Unitarian-Universalist Church, issued a multivolume paperback edition known as the Gravel Edition. The FBI announced it was going to analyze the financial records of Beacon Press and the Unitarian-Universalist Church to determine how the Papers reached the Press. Many people now believe the FBI actually knew all it needed to and that the whole business was something of a scare tactic.

What happened? Unitarian-Universalist Church attendance declined radically, as did contributions to the church. A number of Beacon Press employees quit. Although other explanations are possible, it's likely that by focusing its investigative muscle on the church and the publisher, the FBI caused many people, consciously or unconsciously, to distance themselves from the two organizations.

Stated starkly, the government's conduct amounted to behavior modification. If unrestrained, this type of conduct might lead to the frightening vision of society Orwell created for us in *1984,* in which everyone could be monitored on a telescreen and "you had to live . . . in the assumption that every sound you made was overheard, and, except in darkness, every movement scrutinized." Those who believe they are being watched will modify their behavior to be pleasing in the eyes of the watcher. Ironically, there need not actually be a watcher; all that's necessary is that people believe there is; one's imagination will do the rest. That is the most frightening aspect of the Big Brother image in *1984.*

These, then, are the concerns that have produced the privacy revolution, which has attracted support across the political spectrum. People on the political left have been activated by a concern for civil and constitutional rights. Those on the political right view data centralization as more big government and object to the diminution of individual and states' rights. Indeed, one major piece of federal legislation was produced by then congressman Edward Koch of New York, a liberal Democrat, and Representative Barry Goldwater, Jr., of Orange County, California, a conservative Republican. Strange bedfellows, indeed!

* * *

The legal system's response to this growing popular concern over privacy has been quite remarkable. This country's jurisprudence rarely changes overnight. Except in an emergency, neither Congress nor the courts operate quickly. The legal profession is populated by cautious, measured types who move at a deliberate pace to avoid the errors of

haste and the dangers of trying to foretell the future. In the copyright
field, for example, despite radical changes in the entertainment and
communications industries, the 1976 Copyright Act, which replaced a
hopelessly archaic act in effect since 1909, was the product of more
than twenty years of research, drafting, and industry negotiation.
Chapter 11, Landlord and Tenant, provides a further illustration of
how slow the law can be in reacting to new conditions.

Yet, uncharacteristically, the American legal structure has reacted
with comparatively blinding speed to the growing anxiety about our
loss of privacy. Privacy advocates, recognizing that the judicially developed right of privacy was far too restrictive and uncertain to meet the
threat of the new technology and that the respect for past precedents
meant that change in the courts would come at too glacial a pace,
realized that pressure for change would have to be put on Congress.
It responded. In less than ten years Congress enacted three major
statutes addressing privacy matters and included dozens of individual
provisions relating to privacy in other legislation; at the same time,
state legislatures enacted hundreds of additional privacy statutes.

A brief sketch of the three new federal laws illustrates the scope of
the legal changes that have occurred. The first — the Fair Credit Reporting Act — imposes some limits on what information a wide range
of consumer reporting organizations, most notably credit bureaus, can
collect and to whom they may disclose it. It's an attempt to eliminate
some of the abuses that result from the commercialization of personal
information by these companies. The statute also gives you the right
to know what's in the files these organizations maintain on you, provides a procedure for correcting any errors you find, assures that you
are notified when adverse decisions are made about you on the basis
of a consumer report, and places some restraints on the investigative
reporting conducted by these firms.

The act's premise is that an individual has a right to confront a file
containing information about him or her. If a neighbor with a mali-
cious tongue has been gossiping about you to a credit or insurance
investigator, shouldn't you be entitled to know about it? Maybe the
experience will make you think twice about what *you* say the next time
you're asked about another person. And if you have refused to pay the
bill for a new color television set because it doesn't work properly, you
can now find out whether the merchant has branded you "slow pay"
or "no pay" and get your side of the story recorded in the credit files.

All that certainly is sound. But many people, myself included, think
the statute isn't strong enough; moreover, its effectiveness really depends on your exercising your rights by going down and checking the

files. Try it sometime. You might find that the credit bureau has you confused with another person with a similar name, or has forgotten to record the fact that you have paid off a car loan.

Second, there is the Family Educational Rights and Privacy Act of 1974, commonly known as the Buckley amendment. This truly remarkable statute gives every student, or a parent or guardian of a student under eighteen, a federally guaranteed right of access to his school records, a right to know who has looked at those files, and a right to exclude anyone from using those records, except for educational and certain other limited purposes. The statute applies to all schools, public or private, receiving federal funds, whether they are primary, secondary, or higher. One of the amazing aspects of the Buckley amendment is the way it winks at the taboo about the federal government being involved in education, a field historically left to the states.

The idea is to maintain the integrity and confidentiality of school records. For example, it discourages, perhaps even forbids, teachers and educators from playing lay psychiatrist and dropping notes into the file saying such things as "Melissa seems quite upset and her mother strikes me as emotionally unstable," as was true in one case. Off the cuff items of this stripe serve no legitimate educational purpose, can scar a child badly within the school, and, if the record is maintained or passed along to the next educational level, can stigmatize the student for years to come. Congress also felt that outsiders, such as prospective employers, should not have access to educational records unless the student expressly consents.

Finally, there is the Privacy Act of 1974, which, like the other statutes, gives you the right to see *almost* any file the federal government has on you, to know who has been peeking at those files, and to challenge any errors you find. These principles, which really are notions of fair dealing, also appear in a number of state statutes that apply to governmental record keeping at the state and local levels. They even have been adopted by many private companies and professional associations.

Before these statutes, it would have been impossible for you to gain access to your credit file, let alone your FBI dossier, to tell prospective employers that they could not see your high-school or college record, or to fight with federal bureaucrats over the contents of a social security file. But today, with a little tenacity, you can do all these things.

Although legislation has been the focal point of the privacy revolution, the courts have been active in protecting your privacy concerning whom you associate with, what you think and believe, your home, marital relationship, and body. *Roe* v. *Wade,* for example, usually thought of as the seminal United States Supreme Court decision recognizing a woman's right to have an abortion (see Chapter 13 for a discussion of this subject), also serves as the first definitive recognition of the constitutional status of privacy. That right also underlies the Supreme Court's later decision protecting a citizen from being prosecuted for having pornography in the home. State courts have also breathed life into the right of privacy. The Alaska Supreme Court, for example, has concluded that a citizen cannot be prosecuted for smoking marijuana at home. And, as discussed in Chapter 12, the New Jersey Supreme Court has concluded that the constitutional right of privacy embraces the right to die.

In the 1960s and 1970s initiatives also came from executive branch agencies. Both the Census Bureau and what was then called the Department of Health, Education and Welfare appointed blue-ribbon panels to study the effect of their collection of personal information on privacy. President Gerald Ford established a national study commission, which held extensive hearings, published an impressive report, and made proposals for further legislation, some of which were pursued by President Jimmy Carter.

Now what does all this legal activity mean for us? At the risk of oversimplifying, the statutes, court decisions, administrative activity, and countless changes in information practices in the private sector that have been undertaken voluntarily can be synthesized into five principles.

First: The law has begun to insist that data collectors, handlers, and users be careful and recognize the potential damage that may be inflicted on file subjects. All of these people, be they in private corporations, banks, hospitals, universities, police agencies, or other government entities, are obliged to handle personal information fairly and honorably. At a minimum they must verify or otherwise ensure the data's accuracy and relevance. They owe what the law calls a fiduciary obligation to the people whose lives are recorded in their systems.

Second: There is growing recognition that certain kinds of information — such as data about people's political, religious, or charitable affiliations — should not be gathered. In addition, there is a belief that other categories of sensitive information, perhaps medical and psychiatric data, should not be collected, or at least not be made available, unless there is a strong showing of relevance and need.

Third: Information systems containing sensitive data about individuals must be subjected to rigorous administrative, human, and technological safeguards against uninvited intrusion or improper dissemination. Widespread data collection is less frightening a prospect when we are assured that appropriate steps have been taken to provide security and confidentiality for our personal histories.

Fourth: Although it still is a bit premature to think of this principle as firmly established in the law, we slowly are being given the right to examine files pertaining to us and to challenge inaccuracies or information we think is inappropriate for the data handler to maintain. When there is a reason to believe that disclosure might be detrimental to us, our access right may have to be exercised through a representative, such as a doctor in the case of medical data.

Fifth: Some of the legal developments recognize that data must be destroyed or its accessibility limited when the reasons for gathering it have ended. Certain types of data not only lose their utility with age but can become potentially dangerous — informational time bombs. Therefore, we must learn the virtues of forgetting, despite the urge to retain everything, a phenomenon that seems to plague all institutions. Thus, the Fair Credit Reporting Act bans the disclosure of such matters as bankruptcy and convictions a certain number of years after the event.

* * *

So ends the "good news" for privacy fans. It would be misleading to leave you with the impression that the picture is entirely rosy on this subject. The truth is that it is far too early to declare the revolution successful and to leave the barricades. Although the courts have done much to validate the right of privacy, some of them, notably the United States Supreme Court, have been reluctant to expand privacy rights beyond the protection of the body, home, and associations. Thus, for example, it has declined to bar governmental data collection about currency transactions that were "justified" by the Treasury Department as necessary in the war against organized crime. As this suggests, there are strong forces at work that are at odds with protecting privacy.

First is complacency. As the poet e e cummings noted, "progress is a comfortable disease." It's so easy to be anesthetized by the benefits derived from modern data technology — the instant airplane and hotel reservations, quick banking, and electronic record keeping — and overlook its deleterious side effects. This is especially true if we are gulled into believing that the law's work during the past decade sufficiently safeguards our privacy and gives us a protective umbrella that shields us from unwanted scrutiny. Unfortunately, neither proposition is true.

A second set of counterpressures to privacy is the quest for governmental accountability, cost-effectiveness, law and order, freedom of information, and the public's right to know. Not surprisingly, many think these objectives are more important than something as vague as the right to be left alone and therefore justify investigative work and intrusiveness that is antithetical to privacy values. For example, there are those who believe we must eliminate fraud and cheating in the administration of our welfare and medical payments systems. This, they believe, requires monitoring the records of individual recipients and crosschecking them against other files, such as social security and tax records. The question is: Are the deterrent effects and savings of money achieved by these procedures worth the psychological damage inflicted on significant numbers of our fellow citizens? What will be the feelings toward government of program beneficiaries when they learn that by accepting public largesse they become vulnerable to demeaning scrutiny of their finances, lifestyle, or medical history, an intrusiveness to which the middle class and wealthy are not subjected?

As in so many other contexts, the law's job is to strike a balance between competing social goals. To me, a modest recognition of our right to privacy does not represent an "ominous threat" to other social objectives, such as law and order and governmental accountability. Rather, it should be seen as a long overdue expression of the legal system's concern for the autonomy and individuality of each of us.

POINT OF LAW:
Privacy versus the Press

When ex-Marine Oliver Sipple grabbed the arm of Sara Jane Moore as she attempted to assassinate President Gerald Ford, did that make his sexual lifestyle newsworthy? Did that heroic deed, perhaps saving the president's life, suspend Sipple's right of privacy?

People involuntarily thrust into the glare of publicity pay a terrible price in terms of their right to be let alone. Oliver Sipple paid that price. So did the seven members of the Hill family who were held captive in their home for nineteen hours by three escaped convicts. Years after they had moved to a new community to put that event behind them, a feature story in *Life* magazine identified the Hills and associated their ordeal with the then new Broadway play *The Desperate Hours*.

Small wonder that privacy buffs and media people often don't mix. The antagonism has heightened recently as print and electronic journalists, flush from their successes during the Watergate years, vigorously try to fend off many of the legal protections growing out of the increasing sensitivity to privacy. These, they argue, chill the press's freedom to gain access to a great deal of information they think is of interest to the public. But does the press really need protection against popular concern over privacy, or is it the other way around?

Let's start by acknowledging that the nation's journalists have served as a bastion against governmental abuse throughout our history, as their performance during Watergate attests. But that doesn't mean that their rights are absolute or their eyewitness news teams, investigative reporting, and portable television cameras are beyond accountability. That ignores other social values, privacy among them. It's ironic that although the media have decried our loss of privacy at the hands of government and business, they assert an unfettered right to investigate our lives. Let's face it, disclosures by an excessively zealous newspaper, television network, or radio station about one's private life or the publication of "gossip," often in the guise of news, can be devastating.

Should we call on the law to protect our right of privacy against the threats posed by the media? Balancing competing values is a classic function of the law. Moreover, the contemporary imbalance between the right of privacy and press prerogatives in part is attributable to the extraordinary protection the judges of this country have accorded journalists in recent years. By expansively interpreting the First Amendment's provision for freedom of the press, which many journalists constantly invoke and conspicuously wallow in, media liability for defamation has been limited to fairly egregious cases such as Carol Burnett's thus far successful libel suit against the *National Enquirer*, the scope of executive privilege has been contained, and national security restrictions on publication have been overcome.

Despite these court victories, the press claims to be threatened by the concern for privacy and demands virtual immunity for publishing *anything* that is true, regardless of its sensitivity. Now why do journalists insist on pushing their prerogatives to the limits? Why do they react like terrified hemophiliacs to the slightest pinprick of criticism? Apparently journalists think they are engaged in a never-ending series of life-and-death cliffhangers. Challenged by one Goliath after another, media Davids must repeatedly sally forth to slay the enemy. The media also seem to feel that press freedom will come tumbling down like a house of cards and news gathering will be inhibited unless every competing social interest is subordinated to their wishes. But these concerns seem somewhat unrealistic and a bit paranoid. Not everyone is out to get the media. The nation's press is and can remain vibrant without a license to intrude on our privacy. The law affords it so much protection that tempering journalistic zeal by requiring a modicum of respect for people's privacy poses almost no risk that anything news-worthy will be lost.

The press begrudges the steps recently taken by the law to protect our privacy. For example, it would overturn the decision of several state legislatures to deny access — except under limited conditions — to certain criminal records. Perhaps these statutes will prevent journalists from seeing some law-enforcement files, but diligent re-porters can effectively monitor these agencies without examining the records of people who have paid their debt to society, who have met the stringent conditions of the statutes, and who deserve a second chance. If we believe that lawbreakers can be rehabilitated, then we must enable them to re-enter the mainstream of society by eliminat-ing the social and vocational barrier created by an ancient criminal record.

The press also is asking for prerogatives unavailable to anyone else. For example, some argue that it is justifiable for a reporter to trespass or use false pretenses to enter someone's home in order to get a story as long as the result "benefited the public." In short, the end justifies the means. How would you feel if a police officer entered your home without a lawful warrant? As a citizen you should be outraged by this violation of the right to be free of intrusion — even if the cop intended to "benefit the public." Vigilantism cannot be "justified." Shouldn't reporters be subject to the same sanctions for breaking the law as everyone else, however important they think a story may be?

In a legal cause célèbre some years ago, Ralph Nader brought suit against General Motors claiming that it had put him under surveillance by investigators who shadowed his every move. Before the litigation was settled, a judicial opinion was issued indicating that if the allega-tions were true, Nader's privacy had been violated. No one, to my knowledge, objected to the possibility of Nader recovering damages for General Motors' invasion of his privacy. From the perspective of social justice, isn't what's good for General Motors good for the na-tion's journalists?

To permit the press to justify intrusive conduct because it "benefited the public" is both vague and an open-ended invitation to mischief. It could lead elements of the press to intrude upon the activities and physical privacy of people and institutions with whom they disagree. Shouldn't we react with shock if media people engaged in the type of surveillance we object to when undertaken by the police and intelli-gence organizations?

The press argues that there is a difference between surveillance by a governmental agent and by a reporter. Of course there is, but isn't it one of degree, not of principle? Fear of official surveillance is based on our recognition of the government's power and the need to guard against its oppressive use. Putting legal distinctions to one side, the reality is that today media institutions are among the most powerful forces in America.

The media have a deep fear that allowing judges to weigh privacy against newsworthiness would amount to second-guessing editorial judgment. That's understandable. But in reality the risk is minimal, since judges always have presumed that "editing is for the editors." There is a limit, however. The First Amendment has never been interpreted to give the press unfettered discretion. In a variety of contexts courts have decided that certain values are worth protecting even if it means second-guessing journalists as to what is newsworthy. Our respect for property rights protects people from having their talents appropriated by the media. For example, the Supreme Court has concluded that the Constitution does not give a television station immunity to broadcast a circus performer's — the Human Cannonball's — entire act. In the libel field, courts have tried to achieve a principled accommodation between free speech and an individual's reputation. And under certain circumstances the law gives a rape victim's name a privacy-type protection and may close a courtroom door to shield extremely sensitive data.

If the courts left journalists completely unaccountable, it would validate the circular reasoning some of them use to rationalize gossip columns and "where are they now" articles: "When we publish it, people find it interesting and read it; that makes it newsworthy." But *interesting* is not synonymous with *newsworthy*. Nor is every truth newsworthy. Although we think Jacqueline Kennedy Onassis is interesting, a New York court decided that it doesn't make her every movement newsworthy and justify a photographer following her day in and day out. Nor does the "interesting" character of the drug difficulties of a senator's or governor's teen-age child make it news. And one doubts the newsworthiness, let alone the wisdom, of publishing the name and location of a robbery victim who had pleaded for anonymity because she was on a terrorist hit list in another country.

If the media had their way, they, unlike any other institution in society, would be unanswerable for their actions. The press responds by asking us to believe it is accountable to its readership through newsstand cash registers. Doubtful! People are captivated by gossip. Most of us revel in the latest pratfalls of celebrities of every description and derive vicarious pleasure from the intimate discussions of "Dear Abby" and the like. Pandering to the very reader appetites that promote press hyperactivity — morbid curiosity, desire for titillation, preoccupation with the sensational — is unlikely to lead to a withdrawal of patronage.

No one doubts that the public has a right to know. But like any platitude or cliché, it's only a generalization. The deeper questions are: Know what? And, what practices may the press employ to gather information? As things now stand, (1) the press may publish demonstrable falsehoods, subject only to a remote threat of liability; (2) the media have arrogated to themselves the right to publish any "truth," no matter how private it may be or how prurient the interests it caters to; and (3) journalists justify using improper and intrusive techniques in terms of the "benefit" produced by their stories. Does the press really enrich our lives by trespassing to get pictures of an accused's apartment — even that of David Berkowitz, the so-called Son of Sam, or Arthur Bremer, Governor George Wallace's assailant?

But if journalists continue to push the outer limits of the law and fail to exercise restraint, society, speaking through its courts, surely will expand the right of privacy. In our complex world, in which rights frequently collide, it is imperative that no institution assert its claims, let alone its special prerogatives, to the utmost. The press might well further its own long-term interests if it tried to balance individual privacy against the public's right to know and developed principles for staying the editor's hands when the former seems paramount.

4

FREE EXPRESSION:

Can the Government or the People Suppress It?

AS WE SAW IN CHAPTER 2, free expression is a right guaranteed by the First Amendment to the Constitution. But it's a right that comes at a price — we are constantly exposed to pornographic, suggestive, or otherwise offensive material. Let's examine the dilemma posed by the fact that abuses inevitably accompany the exercise of important rights, and focus on how the law walks the narrow path between regulating the exercise of a freedom and being repressive.

*   *   *

Let's start with a somewhat exaggerated example. Picture yourself as a hardworking American who has just come home from a tough day on the job. You could really use some entertainment, so you decide to go to a movie. A quick look at the newspaper tells you that a local cinema is offering an exciting double bill: *Orgy at Lill's Place* and *Teenage Sex Kittens,* featuring "buxom beauties and prepubescent pixies in nonstop, torrid action."

That's not your cup of tea, so instead you head for the corner newsstand to pick up a magazine. After you have worked your way past shelves full of magazines like *Hustler, Screw,* and worse, you find what you want in the space allocated to publications of a less prurient bent.

You settle for a copy of *Newsweek* and start home. To bolster your spirits you decide to stop for a beer, but all the family taverns seem to be vying to outdo each other with topless and erotic dancers. You escape by going straight home. There you read that a wave of "snuff" movies — films that purport to show the actual murder and dismemberment of women — is sweeping through the country's major metropolitan areas. Authorities in a number of cities have gone to court to try to prohibit any further showing of these films, but so far the courts have been reluctant to interfere with the film makers' right of free expression. You hope that none of these movies ever turns up in your town, but with the way things are going, you wouldn't be surprised if one did.

Depressed, you turn on the television only to encounter a suggestive tight-bluejeans ad featuring a Brooke Shields look-alike, which is followed by *Charlie's Angels,* who apparently are going to spend the next hour infiltrating a prostitution ring. You immediately switch to the local news, and see that Slim Brainpan, who lives down the street, is being interviewed about his antiobscenity campaign. Last month Slim proposed a town ordinance that would ban "all filthy, disgusting, degenerate, foul, and unclean books" from the town's libraries and public schools. When you first heard of Slim's proposal, you sympathized and even considered signing his petition to the town council; but that was before you learned that his list of objectionable material included some of the world's great literature. "All trash — nothing but French perversions and communist propaganda," Slim said when you objected to the inclusion on his list of Voltaire's *Candide* and Sir Thomas More's *Utopia.*

As you're listening to Slim explain to the interviewer that Mark Twain was a subversive, you hear shouting and chanting outside. Through the window, you can see there's a picket line in front of the house next door, which is owned by Billy Schlock, a famous movie director. It's a group of homosexual activists protesting Billy's latest project, a slice-of-life film containing a less than lyrical treatment of sadomasochistic practices among homosexuals. The homosexuals are pelting Billy's house with tomatoes and raw eggs and calling for an end to antigay bigotry.

You turn off the television, go upstairs to your bedroom, pull down the shades, and sit in the dark. It's quiet and you feel safe.

*   *   *

Each of these not entirely hypothetical tribulations involves an encounter with some aspect of "free expression." Chapter 2, Free Speech and Civil Disobedience, noted that Americans have historically taken the position that every form of expression should be tolerated in the interests of maintaining an open society. In a sense we've adopted a radical position. Perhaps no other country allows as much latitude to free expression as we do; but for us it has become a cornerstone of our political system, the key freedom from which many of our other freedoms are thought to flow.

In practice, however, free expression has not invariably been accepted, at least not when it has involved material viewed as porno-graphic, irreligious, or otherwise offensive to the sensibilities of the general community or a vocal segment of it. The modern law of ob-scenity — the legal determination that attempts to mark off a category of expression not protected by the First Amendment from government interference — has evolved over the past two centuries, and in particu-lar since 1957, when the Supreme Court first tackled the problem head-on in a now famous case called *Roth* v. *United States*. To some extent, the years since *Roth* was decided have proved an unhappy chapter in the history of American law, with many people upset at what they consider an overly permissive attitude by the courts, with others complaining that the legal standard should be even more liberal in a free society, and with the Supreme Court caught in the middle. But as we shall see, the question of what exactly is obscene is not easily answered, and a certain amount of unhappiness may be inevitable no matter what the courts do.

Government Restraints

Rulers and governments have a long history of censoring or destroying books and other forms of expression that they find objectionable. A book dictated by the prophet Jeremiah was burned by King Jehoiakim of Judah in 603 B.C.; and in the third century B.C. the Chinese emperor Shih Hwang-ti, who did things in a big way (he built the Great Wall), ordered the burning of *all* books, with the exception of those dealing with science, medicine, or agriculture. Even philosophers have been in favor of censorship: In the *Republic*, Plato proposed to censor "the writers of fiction" in order to keep "bad" works away from children.

In England, the advent of the printing press, with its potential for wide distribution of written material, led Henry VIII to require that all books printed in the country be licensed by the Crown. Additional control over printed matter was provided by the Stationers' Company, a guild of publishers who held a monopoly over printing under the Crown's direction. (Ironically, the modern law of copyright — de-signed to protect writers and artists — grew out of this arrangement, by which the Crown sought to protect itself against seditious writings.) Moreover, both the English common-law courts and the infamous Star Chamber, a special tribunal known for its disregard of the traditional rights of the accused, punished libelous and treasonous speech.

Most government censorship was not concerned with obscenity. The authorities were more worried about politically disruptive and irreligious utterances — forms of expression that might cause riots or topple governments — than they were about sexually oriented or pornographic materials that might corrupt morals. It is only in relatively recent times that governments have focused on controlling immoral expression. Perhaps the first recorded case on obscenity in England was in 1725, when a book entitled *Venus in the Cloister, or The Nun in Her Smock*, was suppressed.

The earliest prosecution for obscenity in the United States took place in Philadelphia in 1815, in a case in which the defendant was convicted of exhibiting a lewd painting. The judges, no doubt believing they were exercising sound judicial restraint, refrained from looking at the painting in order to avoid "wounding" their eyes. Six years later the Massachusetts Supreme Judicial Court concluded that John Cleland's famous *Fanny Hill*, already banned in England, was "lewd, wicked, scandalous, infamous, and obscene." Again, the trial judge protected his own morals by not reading the offending book.

These prosecutions were followed by the passage of a number of antiobscenity statutes, culminating in Congress's enactment in 1873 of the Comstock Law, which prohibited the mailing of "every obscene, lewd, lascivious, or filthy book, pamphlet, picture, paper, letter, writing, print, or other publication of an indecent character." The law was popularly named for the man who inspired it, Anthony Comstock, perhaps the greatest guardian of public morality this nation has ever produced. His zealous pursuit of vice, first as a private citizen, then as secretary of the New York Society for the Suppression of Vice (which became a model for many similar organizations), and finally as a special officer of the Post Office empowered to track down violations of the law that bore his name, made him famous on both sides of the Atlantic. Of him and his work, George Bernard Shaw said: "Comstockery is the world's standing joke at the expense of the United States. Europe likes to hear of such things. It confirms the deep-seated conviction of the Old World that America is a provincial place, a second-rate country-town civilization after all." In reply, Comstock is said to have referred to Shaw as an "Irish smut-dealer" and a "foreign writer of filth." Toward the end of his career, Comstock was able to boast, probably with some accuracy, that he had destroyed more than fifty tons of indecent books and (better yet!) had driven some fifteen purveyors of filth to commit suicide.

Comstock was no lonely eccentric waging war on impurity and bad morals; rather he was the head of a great crusade. The suppression of vice and obscene literature was one of many reformist movements that sprang up in the second half of the nineteenth century. The laws that were passed to suppress obscenity, and the societies that were formed to help enforce them, were benign in intent, for no doubt a lot of worthless material was in circulation. But the reformers weren't interested in preserving free speech, or with the effect their efforts might have on our traditional constitutional protections. Moreover, they were opposed to far more than what today we would consider pornographic. The list of books banned by the authorities at one time or another included Theodore Dreiser's *An American Tragedy,* Ernest Hemingway's *The Sun Also Rises,* James Joyce's *Ulysses,* and Sinclair Lewis's *Elmer Gantry,* while customs officials seized as obscene such works as Defoe's *Moll Flanders,* Rousseau's *Confessions,* and even the *Arabian Nights.* Not surprisingly, a "liberal" opposition began to build, and increasingly the reformers had to contend with constitutional objections to their methods and goals.

* * *

A basic constitutional question was raised by the antiobscenity statutes relied upon by Comstock and his imitators. Since the First Amendment protects speech and other forms of expression from government interference, weren't criminal prosecutions for obscenity constitutionally prohibited? The answer generally given by the courts (and eventually confirmed by the Supreme Court) was that obscenity was not "protected speech" under the First Amendment. Another way of putting it is that obscenity is not the kind of expression that the framers of the Constitution had in mind when they adopted the First Amendment. Or, if you like, it isn't speech at all, since it lacks communicative value.

Although this judicial approach permitted the authorities to suppress obscenity, it raised a second question for the courts to resolve, a question that has never been satisfactorily answered and that has been the cause of much of the confusion in the modern law of obscenity. The question is simply this: Exactly what do we mean by the word *obscene?* It had to be answered, since material that isn't obscene is constitutionally protected from government suppression. As sometimes happens in the law, a definition became the key issue.

* * *

When the Supreme Court first attempted to define obscenity, in *Roth* v. *United States,* a majority of the justices stated that the standard for determining if something was obscene was "whether to the average person, applying contemporary community standards, the dominant theme of the material taken as a whole appeals to prurient interest."

At first this seemed to be a useful definition. For one thing, it clarified that it was the effect of the challenged material on the "average person" that was critical. The older test, which went back to an 1868 English case, *Regina* v. *Hicklin,* was that you looked to the effect it might have on "those whose minds are open to . . . immoral influences." The *Hicklin* test had been criticized as "mid-Victorian" by Judge Learned Hand (certainly one of America's great jurists, who sadly never sat on the Supreme Court) in 1913 and had been rejected in 1933 in the famous case in which Joyce's *Ulysses* was ruled not obscene. But the old test was not fully laid to rest until the Supreme Court's opinion in *Roth.*

Another useful part of the *Roth* test for obscenity was the language "dominant theme of the material taken as a whole." This meant that the work had to be judged in its entirety, and not by bits and pieces taken out of context. In practice, it meant that the literary or artistic value of the work could protect it from suppression, since the "dominant theme" of such a work would not be pornographic, even if parts of it, taken alone, might give another impression.

So far, so good. But what did the justices mean when they said the material had to be evaluated by "contemporary community standards"? How do you determine what that standard is, since different communities may reflect varying views and tastes? Also, is there one standard for every place in the country? Do people in New York City have the same standards about what's offensive to them as the people in Walla Walla, Washington? But if you let each separate community make up its own mind, you end up with many different standards. In practice this might tend to let the least tolerant standard govern all others, since publishers, movie companies, television networks, and other distributors of "expression" who, for economic reasons, market on a national basis, would be tempted to shy away from anything that might offend the standard in any significant market in the country. Yet establishing a truly "national" standard would ignore regional differences in attitudes and mores, and tend to homogenize American culture to a degree that many people think is undesirable.

Worse yet, what does it mean to say that something appeals to "prurient interest"? Dictionaries define *prurient* (surely a word that a lawyer would use) as "lustful; lascivious; lewd." It sounds as if prurient interest involves an interest in obscenity. The definition seems circular, which is not how definitions are supposed to work.

In practice, the courts that had to apply the *Roth* test for obscenity often had difficulties in figuring out what the community standard was and what prurient meant. As confusion mounted, the Supreme Court reacted by *adding* to the definition, hoping that by elaboration they might arrive at clarification. As a result, the definition of obscenity began to grow like a weed. In addition to what we were told in *Roth,* we were informed in one case that obscenity involves "patent offensiveness," and in a second case (in which *Fanny Hill* was held not obscene), we were told that obscene matter can be recognized as being "utterly without redeeming social value." Justice Potter Stewart, dissenting from the majority in yet a third case, told us that what was really involved was "hard-core pornography," adding that while he couldn't define it, "I know it when I see it."

Unfortunately, policemen, prosecutors, and lower court judges did not always know it when they saw it. Moreover, pornographers found that by inserting a paragraph, or a scene, or even a single sentence, of reasonable comment in otherwise salacious material, they could claim the work was not utterly without redeeming social value, and thus was constitutionally protected. It became so hard to prove something was obscene, particularly in criminal cases in which the state had to prove its case beyond a reasonable doubt, that the Supreme Court was widely blamed for fostering pornography. Indeed, one pornographer even advertised his wares by proclaiming that you were able to see his hot merchandise only by virtue of recent Supreme Court decisions.

* * *

Finally, in 1973, the Supreme Court, now with what is popularly regarded as a "conservative" majority under Chief Justice Warren Burger, again tried to settle the question once and for all. Adding some words to the existing formulation, while subtracting others, the Court came up with the newest and still reigning obscenity definition. Pay attention, because in *Miller* v. *California* we learn that the definitive test for obscenity — at least for now! — is:

> (*a*) whether the average person, applying contemporary community standards, would find that the work, taken as a whole, appeals to prurient interest; (*b*) whether the work depicts or describes, in a patently offensive way, sexual conduct . . . ; and (*c*) whether the work, taken as a whole, lacks serious literary, artistic, political, or scientific value.

The language in subdivision (c) about obscenity being without "serious . . . value" replaces the language about its being "utterly without redeeming social value," which is no longer part of the test. The Court expressed the hope that this change would make prosecutions for obscenity less difficult. The Court also stressed that the community standard to be applied was *local,* not national, so that more conservative segments of the country could decide for themselves what was obscene.

* * *

Congratulations! You've just been appointed censor for your town under a new state law enacted to conform with the latest Supreme Court standards. It's your job to review various forms of expression and refer the obscene ones to the local prosecutor's office for possible legal action. You've been given a brand new Censor's Kit — it's a blue pencil and a copy of the Supreme Court's decision in *Miller* v. *California.* Now it's time to get started.

Three imaginary items are up for consideration: (1) a painting of a man and woman, both naked, embracing on what looks like a supermarket check-out counter; (2) the stage play *Follicle,* a sequel to *Hair,* which is being presented by a touring company at the local theater; and (3) an album of photographs of young boys, all nude, playing games or swimming or running through fields.

You don't know much about art, so you ask Mrs. Morris, your cleaning lady, who has lived in the community for more than fifty years, whether she thinks the painting appeals to prurient interest and is patently offensive. She says she doesn't know what prurient means, but (like Justice Stewart) she knows filth when she sees it, and that it's her opinion the painting is "low, dirty, and disgusting." But your next-door neighbor, Ms. Beacon, who majored in art at Radcliffe, tells you that the tone of the painting is "rather interesting" and that the composition is "extremely well conceived." She adds that it appears to be closely modeled after Boucher's *Venus Consoling Love,* which hangs in the National Gallery in Washington.

You should

A. censor the painting because Mrs. Morris is a long-standing member of the community and is older and wiser than you are;
B. not censor it because Ms. Beacon knows more about art than you do;
C. take an art appreciation course so you can make up your own mind.

(Answers to the Censor's Quiz appear at the end of the chapter.)

Next on the agenda is your evaluation of *Follicle.* You rush downtown and buy a ticket for the matinee performance. Lucky for you there's a big audience, so you'll be able to see firsthand how the local community reacts to it. As the play progresses, and as the actors and actresses appear in various states of undress and sing songs and participate in skits, you notice that the audience is about equally divided into two

groups. The members of the first group, who are mostly older and more conservatively dressed, are either averting their eyes from the nude skits or staring at them with expressions of horror or, in a few cases, with what might be taken as prurient longings. The other group, mostly younger, doesn't seem to be affected one way or another by the nudity, but is visibly moved by the songs calling for love and peace.
You should

A. take a poll of the audience to see which group is the larger and censor the play if you find the older group to be the majority;
B. watch the play instead of the audience so that you can make up your own mind;
C. try to have dinner or a drink with one of the actors or actresses in the cast and find out what he or she thinks.

Now you have the photograph album to consider. At first you aren't clear why it's been referred to you, but then you learn that the book is published by Pederast Press, which specializes in pictorial works for homosexuals. You also learn that the book is a hot seller in the part of town rumored to be heavily populated by "them." You look at the photographs carefully, but none of them means very much to you. When you ask Mrs. Morris for her opinion, she tells you that the children are nice, but that they shouldn't be allowed to run around without clothes on because they'll catch cold. Art specialist Beacon thinks the photographs are poorly composed and points out a number that are out of focus. She believes that from an aesthetic point of view, the photographs are "serious but essentially unrealized."
You should

A. not censor the photo album, because it doesn't appeal to the prurient interest of your community, which is predominantly heterosexual;
B. censor it, because deviant behavior, and anything that appeals to it, is patently offensive;
C. pass on this one because it's just too complicated to figure out.

Just as you're wondering if you really want to be town censor, you're presented with the biggest challenge of your young career as a blue-nose. On Friday the thirteenth, the coldest day anyone around can remember, a film we'll call *Snuff II* opens at your local cinema.

Snuff II, named after the infamous movie *Snuff*, is also about the mutilation and murder of young women. *Snuff* opened in New York City in early 1976 and immediately became the subject of outrage and protest. The film began with a scene of a young woman being held down while one of her toes was sheared off. It ended with another young woman having her hands and feet sliced off, after being slit lengthwise, from throat to pelvic area, and having her intestines removed in a parody of childbirth.

But the worst aspect of the movie lay not in the events depicted, but in the claim of its distributors that those events had been filmed as they actually occurred, and that they had been staged solely for purposes of the film. The promotion for the film stressed this aspect, with ads disclosing that it had been made somewhere in South America — "where life is cheap."

Apparently, it wasn't cheap enough, at least from the promoters' standpoint. It turned out that *Snuff* was a fraud, that none of the actresses had been harmed, and that the claims of the distributors had been a publicity gimmick. Indeed, the murders and mutilations were so clumsily staged that anyone who saw the film could tell it was a fake, and only the reluctance of most people to go see it had enabled the publicity campaign to convince people that murders had occurred. Once the truth became widely known, both the protests and any patronage dried up, and *Snuff* seemed to blow away.

But now *Snuff II* has appeared, and its distributors say that this time it's the real thing. The distributors — a small, fly-by-night company that specializes in soft-core pornography but also deals in low-budget experimental films — claim that much of the footage was shot by right-wing vigilantes in Buenos Aires, who had abducted three prostitutes one summer night and filmed their mutilation and death as a lesson for others who would ply that profession. Then, it is claimed, the film of the event fell into the hands of a group of left-wing film makers, who used it along with footage they shot themselves to make what the distributors call "a searing indictment of the psychosexual basis of capitalism."

Although investigations are under way into the circumstances of the film's origin, so far no one has been able to say for sure that it's a fake. According to reviews by those who have sat through it, the movie is technically uneven, with many of the more gruesome passages seriously underlit, but with a number of others sufficiently realistic to support the thesis that what the viewer is seeing is the actual torture and murder of three young women.

And it's your job to go see it! Your community is counting on you to protect them from obscene material, but at the same time to preserve the constitutional guarantee of free expression. So you reread the *Miller* decision to make sure of the standard (prurient interest, patently offensive, no serious artistic or political value), pass up lunch, and head downtown to the movie theater.

Outside the theater there are at least three demonstrations going on.

One is a group of women picketing with signs denouncing the film as sexist; a second group is picketing the film for being communist propaganda; and a third appears to be demonstrating in favor of the film, since they are carrying signs denouncing capitalism and American imperialism. Still, a surprisingly large number of people are lined up to get inside, ranging from well-dressed couples to solitary, lonely-looking characters.

The film starts and you brace yourself. It turns out that most of the movie is given over to bearded young men in green battle fatigues, who solemnly — and largely incoherently — address the audience on the evils of capitalism. They're supposed to be Argentine guerrillas, but in a couple of cases you'd swear you were listening to a Brooklyn accent, and at least one guerrilla's beard seems to be coming unstuck. Most of the snuff footage, as you had already heard, is badly underlit, so what you get is a lot of screaming and moaning coming out of what appears to be a murky pool of water. But a few of the scenes, which look as if they were shot separately, are better lit and technically superior. These show what could very well be the mutilation with knives and saws of a woman who is either unconscious or dead. You have a strong stomach, but these passages make you feel queasy. Your experience is made even worse by the audience, some of whom cheer and applaud the revolutionary speeches, while others do the same for the scenes of violence and torture, and still others denounce the film in toto. When the lights finally go back on, you find that a large number of people, including most of the solid-looking citizens, have already fled the theater.

You should

A. censor the film, because it meets *all three* parts of the *Miller* test for obscenity;

B. not censor it, because it doesn't meet *any* of the three parts of the *Miller* test;

C. give up the censorship business and get a job with less ambiguity to it.

* * *

Whether or not you've done well on this quiz, you might want to think about the present Supreme Court test for obscenity, as set forth in *Miller*. Is it clear enough? Keep in mind that one value we look for in a legal definition is clarity. After all, legal principles are supposed to be comprehensible; how else can we as citizens be expected to obey them? The vagueness inherent in the present test works a hardship on everyone, from the producers of "questionable" material (who can never be sure when they'll be arrested) to the Supreme Court justices (who can be absolutely sure that the Court's already overloaded docket will be burdened by obscenity cases, all waiting for the supreme censor to give the word).

At least two approaches have been suggested as a means of extricating the Court — and the rest of us — from difficulties raised by the attempt to define obscenity. They can be called, respectively, the public nuisance approach (a public nuisance is something that endangers or seriously upsets the community — for example, an open excavation, a house of prostitution or gambling parlor where that is illegal, or an unbearably loud, continuous noise) and the absolutist approach.

The Public Nuisance Approach. Remember that a lot of our difficulties have come from the idea that there are two kinds of speech: (1) protected speech, which is everything that isn't obscene; and (2) obscenity. It has been suggested that perhaps the Court should abandon this two-tier approach and try treating obscenity as something like a public nuisance. The idea would be to define *all* speech as protected by the First Amendment, but say that *some* speech can be suppressed, or at least controlled, if done in a reasonable manner pursuant to a legitimate state interest. The interests most often mentioned are keeping pornography away from minors and limiting the obtrusiveness of the offensive material so that people who don't want to be exposed to it needn't be. Regulations to achieve those ends would be valid. Thus the showing of pornographic movies might be restricted to certain parts of town, the men and women who appear on covers of magazines might have to be relatively fully clothed while those who appear inside would not, and any publication sold or readily available to children would be subject to greater control than material limited to adults.

But beware — this approach will require courts to wrestle with vague notions such as "legitimate state interest" and "reasonable restraints." Judges will have to balance competing interests, an often difficult process that may embroil them in a whole new set of definitions that don't define and tests that don't seem to have any answers. If nothing else, the Supreme Court's record as national censor has shown that complex social problems are not easily solved by verbal formulations.

The Absolutist Approach. One of the suggested answers for the last question in the Censor's Quiz was to "give up the censorship business and get a job with less ambiguity to it." At least one Supreme Court justice would have viewed this as good advice for the Court itself. The late Justice William O. Douglas, who retired from the Court in 1975, believed that the First Amendment precluded any government restraints on speech, regardless of how offensive it might be. Noting that what strikes people as offensive differs from person to person, he said that one of the most offensive experiences of *his* life was a visit to a nation where the only books available were on mathematics or religion.

The Douglas position is sometimes called absolutist, since it believes *all* speech to be protected without exception. The majority of the justices rejected the absolutist position in *Roth*, in which they held that only nonobscene speech was entitled to constitutional protection. But, as we have seen, this two-tier approach required the Court to define obscenity, which in practice has proved to be an extremely difficult task.

Wouldn't it make things a lot easier if the Supreme Court reversed itself and followed Douglas's advice? Certainly it would make things easier for the Court. No longer would the justices have to struggle with the definition of obscenity, since there would be no need to define it. No longer would they have to engage in a potentially difficult balancing of state interests in suppressing obscenity against rights of free speech, since the state's power over speech would be limited to the "inflammatory utterances" discussed in Chapter 2, Free Speech and Civil Disobedience. And best of all, no longer would their docket overflow with time-consuming and tedious cases about dirty books, revolting movies, and lewd photographs.

The absolutist position sounds great for the Supreme Court, but how would it be for the rest of us? Imagine a society in which anything goes as far as expression is concerned. How would you like the hardest of hard-core pornography to be sold in any bookstore; the most degrading practices pictured in any art gallery; the foulest of films exhibited at your local drive-in? Laws that try to keep pornography out of the hands of minors would either be struck down as unconstitutional or severely curtailed so as not to obstruct the free flow of protected expression. In like fashion, laws limiting the physical obtrusiveness of obscenity would be wiped away, or their effectiveness sharply reduced. Remember, even under a "liberal" Supreme Court standard, there still are laws against obscenity, even if they often are difficult to enforce. What we're considering now is a society in which anyone has an absolute right to express himself any way and any place he wants, without any legal interference. It's possible that nothing much would change under this standard, that in effect there's a saturation point for obscenity in society and we've already reached it. But we can't be sure of that, and it could be that the absolutist position would result in an even greater flood of obscenity, and in further erosion of the quality and civility of our life.

The absolutist position raises a basic question about the law's proper function. It's sometimes said that the law should not only regulate behavior directly but also establish or reflect society's norms — in other words, that the law should tell us what is acceptable in attitude and behavior. For example, proponents of the Equal Rights Amendment, in response to its opponents' charge that an amendment is not necessary because existing laws prohibit discrimination, have argued that it should be promulgated if only to *show* that women are to be treated equally in this society. One danger with this use of the law is that, taken to extremes, it can become paternalistic and even despotic. But as far as the law of obscenity is concerned, there may be some merit in announcing that certain forms of speech are not entitled to the law's protection, simply as an expression of society's distaste for it, even though we have a hard time controlling or even defining it. Moreover, the courts do provide us with a serious forum in which to "debate" this extremely tenacious and perplexing problem — a forum that will be lost if obscenity is placed beyond the power of the law.

*   *   *

What if you're one of those people who think that the present Supreme Court standard, as set out in the *Miller* case, goes too far in allowing free expression? You don't want to hear about free flow of ideas and constitutional guarantees — for you the plethora of offensive books, plays, and movies more than outweighs any supposed benefit to be derived from a liberal interpretation of the First Amendment. What can you do about it?

You could take a hint from the absolutism of Justice Douglas, who said that the only way offensive expression could be subjected to government restraints would be to pass a constitutional amendment. So there you are. All you have to do is draft an amendment and get it through Congress and ratified by three fourths of the states and you're home free.

Or are you? Assuming that you could get your amendment — no mean trick as the proponents of the Equal Rights Amendment have been finding out for years — what would you have it say? That the states can restrict anything they want? That's pretty broad. How about: The states can restrict anything that's obscene? Whoops, now you've done it — you're back to defining obscenity. Go back to the first idea: A constitutional amendment providing that each state can restrict anything it wants in any fashion it deems appropriate. After all, this just means that the majority will decide what can be suppressed. We're supposed to be a democracy, so why not rely on the judgment and good sense of the people to weed out those forms of expression that are worthless or potentially harmful?

Experience, that's why. The record of unrestrained censorship is a dismal one. As we saw earlier, many important works of art and literature were suppressed in this country prior to the development of the modern law of obscenity. Shaw's characterization of America as "a second-rate country-town civilization" might have become an accurate assessment if the courts had not acted to protect society from the unbridled impulse of many of its members to silence anything they disagree with or don't understand.

Keep in mind that the urge to suppress goes well beyond what we consider obscene. Works have been banned because of the ideas they contained (Bertrand Russell's progressive *What I Believe* was once declared to be in violation of New York's penal law) or because they are deemed to challenge settled custom or prejudice (a children's book called *The Rabbits' Wedding* was once suppressed in Alabama for allegedly fostering integration; the problem was that one of the rabbits was white and the other was black). Since there appears to be no limit to what people can find offensive, it seems we must place some limits on what they can get declared illegal. And for all the muddle about the definition of obscenity, the Supreme Court has drawn a clear line regarding culturally or politically offensive speech — the justices have consistently protected it, and thus have saved us from those who would suppress every new or unpopular idea.

The present legal standard may have its faults, but let's remember that it reflects a sincere and thoughtful attempt by the Supreme Court to come to grips with what one justice referred to as "the intractable obscenity problem." In fact, there may be no better approach. Perhaps it is inevitable that the preservation of free speech will involve occasional discomfort, disgust, even anguish, to the listeners. The notion that this is the price we pay for our freedom to express ourselves is not an empty one, for it truly is a *price,* one that will be exacted in the form of the constant testing, and downright abuse, of that freedom we value so highly.

But the direst predictions of the censors and their supporters have not been borne out: We have not become a society given over to sex fiends and ghouls, and thus far no one has conclusively shown a direct connection between permissiveness regarding speech and an increase in sex-related crimes. The more difficult question, however, is how it has affected the oft-cited but difficult to define moral fiber of the nation: What would we think if a real *Snuff* were made, and people flocked to see it?

Nongovernmental Restraints

We've seen how Anthony Comstock and his imitators took it upon themselves to cleanse society of impurity. The vigilante spirit he personified lives on today. A sampling of recent attempts by private groups to control or suppress what they consider offensive expression would include blacks objecting to the television miniseries *Beulah Land,* because the slaves are portrayed as insufficiently rebellious; women objecting to advertisements for Sidney Sheldon's *Bloodline,* because they depict a woman with her throat exposed, presumably for slashing; homosexuals objecting to the movie *Cruising,* because it shows the seamy side of gay lifestyle; and Orthodox Jews objecting to the movie *Wholly Moses,* because, among other things, it makes fun of God. The tactics of these groups range from petitioning and picketing to organizing boycotts all the way to physical disruption and violence.

Note that these are not government attempts at suppression. These are private groups relying on their own efforts, not on the police and the courts, to achieve their ends. Thus they are not subject to the restraints of the First Amendment, which applies only to government interference with free expression. The result is that their targets — the bookseller who finds himself boycotted, the movie company that has its offices picketed, the television station that is inundated with letters threatening not to buy the shampoo being hawked on its offensive soap opera — are unable to seek protection for their right to express themselves from the Constitution. Of course, they are not totally helpless. The courts will protect them from the type of forceful or violent obstruction the movie company shooting *Cruising* encountered in New York's Greenwich Village; they can prevent picketing on their own property; and in certain instances they can bring a lawsuit against a group that has organized a boycott against them. But apart from these limited responses they will not get much help from the courts, and they will get no help at all from the First Amendment.

The reason that the First Amendment applies only to government suppression of free speech is that the people who wrote the Constitution felt that the government is more powerful — and thus more to be feared — than any private group. Pressure groups do not have the police power of the state at their disposal; they are not in a position to seize and destroy offending material or arrest supposed malefactors and hustle them off to prison. The Constitution's framers were only too aware of how effectively governments can enforce their own views and suppress dissenting opinion, and it was this power that they intended to restrict when they adopted the First Amendment.

But that doesn't help the artist who finds his work being attacked as offensive by some puritanical pressure group, or the producer who is threatened with economic ruin if he goes ahead with the filming of a movie that upsets a militant segment of the community. The simple truth is that as long as the private censors stay within the law, they have just as much right under the First Amendment to object to what they find offensive as the supposed offender has to say it in the first place. And there is certainly no law against peacefully making your objections known about what offends you, or electing not to support economically those who finance offensive material. To have it otherwise, to allow the artist or producer — however noble and besieged he may be — to go to court to have the vigilantes silenced, would risk a constitutional violation of the latter's rights under the First Amendment. The First Amendment applies to everyone, even to those who try to deny freedom of expression to others.

* * *

Ironically, the Supreme Court's efforts to protect all but truly obscene expression from governmental restraints may be partly responsible for what appears to be a definite upsurge in both the vehemence and the range of activity by private pressure groups. First, much of what is now deemed protected speech under the First Amendment was subject in the past to government suppression, which meant that there was less occasion for private groups to resort to their own efforts. But now that the government has been forced to cut back on its role as censor, many in the private sector have felt obliged to take up the slack. Second, the willingness of the mass media to deal with themes that previously were not openly acknowledged has created anxieties about how these new subjects are to be treated. For example, if homosexuality can now be made the subject of a movie, then homosexuals naturally do not want to be portrayed in a derogatory or unflattering way. Thus the very broadening of the range of constitutionally protected speech creates a pressure to "regulate," by vigilante activity if necessary, what is said about the newly liberated subject matter. Ironically, broadening First Amendment protection may have contributed to the birth of the Moral Majority.

* * *

Let's pause for a moment, and consider if we're really being fair to these private pressure groups. Maybe it's wrong to call them vigilantes, with all the images of lynching and mob violence that word conjures up.

Let's look at it from another viewpoint. Suppose you're a woman, divorced and with a child to support, starting out in an executive position for a large company. You work very hard and you're good at your job, but you're concerned about your chances for promotion — you don't want favored treatment, but you don't want to work for years and then be passed over just because you're a woman. You know that in a highly competitive field like yours a lot depends on how your superiors see you; if they think of you as overly emotional or as unable to function rationally, or of *just having tendencies in that direction,* the odds are that you're never going to be admitted into the upper echelons of the company.

And every time you watch a television show or commercial or go to a movie or read a novel, you are bombarded with images of women as helpless clinging vines, who exist mostly to be rescued from dire straits by heroic, clear-thinking males or to solve the calamity of "ring around the collar." Oh, there are exceptions — sometimes women are portrayed as reasonably competent, but it happens so infrequently that it comes across as the exception that proves the rule. You don't want to be paranoid, but you can't help wondering what effect all this stereotyping is having on your male superiors at the company. If they see this sort of thing, and you don't see how they won't, they're going to form attitudes that will hold you back. Stereotyping is an insidious, often unconscious, process — no one means to do any harm, but when all is said and done you've lost the career opportunities you were counting on.

So when someone comes around with a petition to stop sexism in the media, you sign it. You don't see yourself as a censor or a vigilante for having done so; after all, it's your future these media people are tampering with, and it's time someone made them pay attention to your concerns.

Now let's change the viewpoint again. Suppose you're a writer who has worked for several years on a screenplay. The story is fictional, but you've drawn on your own experiences in writing it. A central part of the story concerns the emotional breakdown of a female intern who was unable to cope with the pressures of the medical profession. A number of agents and producers have told you it's a fine piece of work, but that they'd rather not handle it because of increasing pressure from a group that's out to stop media sexism. Maybe if you were a big-name writer they would take a chance on your screenplay, but you're new to the craft, and with the pressure group making such a fuss about any portrayals of women as weak, no one is willing to make a movie from your first work. You particularly resent the charge of a woman agent that the central character is unreal, because you are the woman on whom the character is based, and it is your breakdown when you were an intern that makes up the story.

Who is this pressure group, you wonder, and why are they tampering with your life? Shouldn't there be a law against their harassing you this way?

* * *

As these vignettes suggest, the self-appointed censors may have an argument to justify their activities, but it's not a very good one. The notion that certain forms of expression — such as dramatic presentations deemed to be sexist — should be suppressed has a seductive appeal to those who strongly oppose the message of the speech and particularly to those who feel personally threatened by its implications. But this is the same attitude that led to the banning of *Ulysses* and *The Rabbits' Wedding;* in the one case the censors opposed material that was sexually explicit, in the other they feared the prospect of racial integration. Our experience, especially in light of the legal struggle over government attempts at censorship, informs us of a guiding principle — namely that no one group, and no one set of values, has a monopoly on truth. We cannot trust others, or even ourselves, to decide what is and what isn't harmful to be seen, heard, or understood by the rest of society.

So far the power of the private censors, even all of them together, does not match the power of the government, and thus doesn't seem to call for the law's intervention to protect free expression. But if these groups should grow stronger, as the Moral Majority now threatens to do, and if the opposition to them from artists and writers and — perhaps more important — from producers, distributors, and advertisers should falter, then we will face the prospect of a society in which only expression that avoids offending any entrenched pressure group will ever be seen or heard. Culture by committee will give us what committees usually supply: the blandest, least imaginative, safest Pablum. And if we should fall into such a self-induced, semitotalitarian sleep, we soon may be unable to wake ourselves up and reverse the trend.

Answers to the Censor's Quiz (With a Bit of Tongue in Cheek!)

PROBLEM 1: *Painting of Lovers*

A is clearly wrong. The fact that Mrs. Morris has lived in the community for more than fifty years doesn't of itself make her representative of its standards. Also, she may be older than you are, but she isn't necessarily wiser — after all, she doesn't even know what *prurient* means.

B also is wrong, since the opinion of an expert doesn't reflect community standards, unless it's a community of experts, which yours isn't. On the other hand, Ms. Beacon's opinion could be useful in determining whether the painting has serious artistic value, except that you don't know enough about art to tell if she knows more.

C is correct, since everyone should know about art. But it's not clear how much use an understanding of art will be to you as a censor, since it's community standards that count and not individual taste. On the other hand, perhaps it will aid you in determining if something has serious literary or artistic value.

PROBLEM 2: *Follicle*

A is wrong, because this performance is a matinee and an entirely different audience (that is, community) might show up for the evening performance. Besides, what makes you think any particular audience necessarily represents the community? Maybe most of the community is turned off by the play and would never come to see it.

B is wrong, since it's by no means clear that you represent the community. Besides, we've already established that you don't know anything about art!

C obviously is correct, because censors lead notoriously barren social lives. Besides, someone in the play may have the best perspective for judging community reaction.

PROBLEM 3: *The Photo Album*

A can't be right, since it would allow free circulation of pornography directed at homosexuals in any community where heterosexuals were dominant. That would lead to the anomaly of the law's restraints on obscenity not applying to material prepared to appeal to one segment of the community while applying to that directed at all others.

B is also wrong. You may find deviant behavior patently offensive, but it's not per se legally obscene. As for material that appeals to a deviant group, the Court has indicated that the group's particular sensibilities can be considered in determining prurient appeal. But it would be absurd to suppress material like the photo album, which is not offensive to the normal community, just because of its supposed prurient appeal to a deviant group. (Note that this answer is inconsistent with the answer to *A,* whose logic requires that greater protection not be given to obscenity designed to appeal to homosexuals than that directed at the rest of us. But that's the way it goes in the obscenity business; very little seems consistent.)

C is correct, because it's the only thing left after reading the answers to *A* and *B*.

PROBLEM 4: *Snuff II*

A (censor it) and *B* (don't censor it) both arguably are correct, which is why *C* also is correct.

Whether *A* or *B* is correct depends on how you look at it, which is the problem with the obscenity standard. Let's take the *Miller* test step by step:

(1) Would the average person, applying contemporary community standards, find the film appeals to prurient interest?

He might conclude that it does. He could see the film as portraying extreme acts of sexual sadism. The fact that the appeal is to a deviant group wouldn't necessarily prevent this conclusion, since the perverse sexual element is manifest, even to nondeviants (this is why it differs from the photo album). As for the relevant community, he could refer to the demonstrators who protested the showing of the film and the people who fled the theater as indicative of community reaction.

Then again, he might conclude that it does not. He might see the film, taken in its entirety, as having no prurient appeal at all, even to deviants, either because of the extreme nature of the depiction or because it is essentially a political presentation. As for community reaction, he could point to those who demonstrated in favor of the film, and could argue that the other demonstrators opposed the film on political grounds. Also, the fact that the film was repulsive to much of the audience doesn't mean that it appealed to their prurient interest.

(2) Does the film depict sexual conduct in a patently offensive way?

Yes and no. If the film does portray sexual conduct, it could easily be concluded that it is patently offensive. But it's not clear that it does. Even if it's conceded that sexual conduct is involved, it could still be said that the presentation is not patently offensive, since its purpose is to illustrate the evils of the system that promotes such conduct.

(3) Does the film lack serious artistic or political value?

Again, it depends on how you look at it. All of the demonstrators take the film seriously, although each group sees it as involving a different issue. The film can be seen as raising serious questions, regardless of how well it answers them. In this light, it doesn't make all that much difference whether it's authentic.

On the other hand, the film can be seen as a simplistic fraud. Under the *Miller* test, the bogus insertion of "serious" matter into an otherwise salacious product should not protect it. Although it's a serious matter to commit (or even to pretend to commit) murder, that has nothing to do with the artistic or political seriousness of the film, which as "speech" must be judged independently of the "acts" surrounding it. Seriousness, in short, may lie in the eye of the beholder.

POINT OF LAW:

Censorship in the Classroom

Should assigned reading in the public schools be censored by school boards, so that the children are not exposed to "offensive" material? How about removing certain books from the school library or not letting them on the shelves in the first place? Or should a court step in and protect "academic freedom" and the First Amendment rights of the students?

We're all familiar with the famous Scopes — or monkey — trial, in which a schoolteacher was prosecuted for violating a Tennessee law that made it illegal to teach the theory of evolution. (A similar law was later found to be an unconstitutional establishment of religion — see Chapter 1, School Prayer, for a discussion of that subject.) But attempts to control what public-school children are exposed to go well beyond objections to so-called antireligious teachings. Often the controversy concerns books such as J. D. Salinger's *The Catcher in the Rye* and Joseph Heller's *Catch-22*, which are not legally obscene, but are thought by some people to be too sexually explicit, or otherwise objectionable, to be taught or even made available to high-school students.

The disputes arise in a variety of ways: A teacher may object to a school board's attempt to control the reading he assigns; an angry parent or organized group of parents may object to a book that is made part of the curriculum; or a student may claim the right to read a certain book in connection with his studies. Occasionally, an aggrieved party will go to court claiming that his First Amendment rights are being violated, and then it's up to the judge to decide if the court should get involved.

A preliminary question is whether the free-speech clause of the First Amendment applies to public-school classrooms. The answer is that it does. The Supreme Court has referred to the protection given to academic freedom by the First Amendment, and lower court cases have recognized the right of public-school students to receive educational information and of teachers to engage in classroom discussion.

But academic freedom has its limits, especially at levels of instruction below college. The Supreme Court has held that the material made available to minors can be restricted in ways that would be unconstitutional if applied to adults. Furthermore, by its very nature a classroom is a "limited" forum: Not everything can be taught in the time available, and space and budget considerations will prevent the school library's having anywhere near all the books it ideally should contain.

Given the fact that a selection process is inevitable, who should decide what the children are exposed to and what is kept from them? Virtually all states grant control over the public schools to local school boards, which usually are elected by the community they serve. Traditionally, these boards have had considerable autonomy in carrying out their duties, including selecting the curriculum. One of the benefits of this system is that the educational process is democratically controlled by the local communities, giving them the opportunity to maintain a school system that reflects their particular needs and values.

But the power of the school board is not absolute. As with every other governmental body, from the United States Congress on down, it is subject to the First Amendment. The problem is deciding under what circumstances a court is justified in overruling the school board's judgment in the name of that constitutional mandate. Not surprisingly, especially in view of the lack of a Supreme Court case dealing directly with this question, the lower courts that have tackled the problem have not established clear guidelines.

One court found it permissible for a school board to remove a number of books, including Anthony Burgess's *A Clockwork Orange,* from a school reading list, even though the judges acknowledged that the decision was "a political one influenced by the personal views of its members" (what those views were wasn't stated in the opinion). Similarly, another court found that a school board's placing Piri Thomas's *Down These Mean Streets* — a book objected to by parents because of "obscenities and explicit sexual interludes" — on a limited-access shelf was not a violation of the First Amendment. The court reasoned that the same authority that had selected it for the library in the first place could later remove it.

However, in a third case, it was decided that a school board could not remove Kurt Vonnegut's *Cat's Cradle* and Joseph Heller's *Catch-22* from the school library. The court said that once the state and the board had established the school library, conditions could not be put on its use based solely on the "social or political tastes of school board members." Again, it was not clear why the board decided to remove the books, although a hint was supplied in a general reference in the minutes of its meeting to "the drivel being pushed today."

These and other cases reflect the courts' uncertainty about how to strike a balance between First Amendment rights and the right of the community, through its elected board, to determine what its children will be taught. So far, a clear standard has not evolved, and it may well be that one won't until the Supreme Court rules on the issue, and more than one ruling undoubtedly will be necessary.

There's an old saying about the education of the young: As the twig is bent, so grows the tree. The dispute over censorship in the class-room indicates the difficulties involved in determining how, and under whose direction, the shaping of the twig is to take place. Perhaps all the courts can do on such a sensitive subject as the bringing up of the young is try to keep the school boards from going to extremes and bending the First Amendment out of shape.

Law and Order

5

SELF-DEFENSE:

Can You Protect Yourself and Avoid the Slammer?

SELF-DEFENSE FLOURISHES in periods and places in which the law is weak or nonexistent. In ancient China, Buddhist monks, harried by bandits beyond the control of the central government, developed the techniques that were to become karate and kung fu as a means of unarmed self-defense. And in the American Old West, where the law stopped at least one town back toward the east, men wore Colt forty-fives strapped to their sides as part of their normal dress.

The right of self-defense, however, becomes severely restricted as civilization closes in. In a modern, law-abiding society, you do not have the right to "settle affairs" for yourself; rather you must look to the official organs of the government — the police and the courts — for protection from the lawless behavior of others. Indeed, Thomas Hobbes, one of the more morose English political philosophers (in a line worthy of comic Rodney Dangerfield, Hobbes once wrote that life is "poor, nasty, brutish, and short"), conceived the formation of the state as taking place when each man relinquishes his sword to the king, who then becomes the sole possessor of power and the source of justice and safety for all.

Unfortunately, as we all know, the cops can't be everywhere at once. So the law will let you take certain measures to protect yourself and your property. Just what you can do — without ending up in the slammer — is the subject of this chapter.

* * *

Imagine you're a woman living alone in a big city. Lately, a number of people in your apartment building have been mugged right in the neighborhood — the worst place is an unlighted section of street near where you get off the bus from work. Since you often stay late at the office, you have no choice but to walk there after dark. A neighborhood committee has approached the police about getting more protection, but the police say that they already are spread thin and can't spare the manpower. To make matters worse, the city is in financial trouble and will be laying off officers, so in the future you can count on even less protection.

It's becoming clear to you that the neighborhood isn't going to get any safer, so you begin thinking about what you can do to protect yourself. Your thoughts grow more serious when you learn that the woman who lives across the hall was badly beaten by a mugger near the bus stop. Now you're really determined, but what's the first move? Should you learn karate, or buy a gun or a can of Mace? Are any of these measures illegal — will they get you into trouble? Now that you're actually considering self-defense, you realize you really don't know what you're allowed to do.

So the first thing you do is ask a lawyer friend what your rights are. He tells you that the law differs from state to state, but that the basic rule is that you can use reasonable force to repel a real or apparent attack. The amount of force that is "reasonable" differs according to the circumstances, but you're generally justified in using the same amount of force against your assailant as he is using, or proposes to use, against you. And you are allowed to use deadly force (which is force likely to kill, even if it doesn't succeed) against an attack that could kill you or cause you serious bodily harm.

In some states, however, there is a duty to retreat before resorting to deadly force: You must make an effort to escape, if it appears that you can do so safely, before you are entitled to use it. The classic case is the fight at the local saloon, in which the aggressor pulls a knife on the other man, who responds by pulling out a gun. Can he shoot if the knife wielder advances upon him? Not in a duty-to-retreat state if there's a back door to the saloon and he can safely run away. As you can see, the duty to retreat places a higher premium on human life than on human dignity. Thus it is not surprising that the states that allow you to "stand your ground" are generally found in the South and West — regions where the notion of "a man's right to be a man" is more deeply rooted than it is in the East.

Even in states that require you to retreat before using deadly force, there's an exception to the rule: You're generally entitled to stand your ground in your own home if you are menaced by an intruder. This stems from the old idea that your home is your castle, and that you should not have to retreat from the one place that is indisputably yours. But even in this context, society's desire to preserve life and discourage "frontier justice" has led a few courts to limit the defense of the home by force.

So now that you know the rules, what do you do next? You enroll in a self-defense class given especially for women. You learn how to chop throats and gouge eyes and stomp insteps and throw all sorts of exotic punches and kicks. You work out diligently, practice hard, and after eight weeks you're given your diploma, which officially declares you a mistress of unarmed combat.

Now, let's suppose a week after graduation from self-defense school, you get off the bus late one night and start walking home. Suddenly a man comes up and grabs you and starts to wrestle you to the ground. You use your newly acquired expertise to knock him flat on his back. Obviously you can't be convicted of assault. This is a clear case of self-defense, since you acted to protect yourself from physical attack. A court most likely would conclude that you used reasonable force to repel the attacker, especially since you did not employ deadly force.

Let's say that when you knock him down he hits his head on the pavement and dies. Does that change anything? The answer is that it probably doesn't, since his death was not a result that could reasonably have been expected to follow from the amount of force you used in the course of legitimate self-defense. In other words, you did not use deadly force, even if death in fact resulted. Assuming that your use of force was justified, the law won't hold you responsible for any unforeseen injury to your opponent.

But what if the man hadn't actually gotten close enough to grab you? What if he had suddenly emerged from the shadows, and without waiting for more, you had delivered a kick that sent him sprawling? Suppose it turns out he's a perfectly respectable citizen who just wanted to ask you for directions?

The rule is that you can use force against what reasonably appears to be an attack, even if you were mistaken and weren't really being threatened. For example, if someone points a fake gun at you as a practical joke, you can use force, in this case even deadly force, if under the circumstances you reasonably believed that the gun was real and that the person was about to shoot you. Similarly, if you reasonably believed that the man approaching you was about to attack you, then you would be entitled to protect yourself, even if it turned out that your "assailant" only wanted directions. The key, of course, is whether you were reasonable in believing you were under attack. You are not allowed to let fly every time someone comes near you, or bumps you, or says something unpleasant.

So what happens when you flatten the man who wanted directions? If he did no more than walk toward you, you probably were not justified in using force. He would have had to have done more for you to say you believed he was about to attack you — for example, if he had said something, or had made a threatening gesture, or followed you for a ways before approaching you. But unless you can supply some reason for your "belief" that you were under attack, you can be charged with the crime of assault, and also can be sued by the man you knocked down for money damages to compensate him for his injuries.

How do you react to that? Not surprisingly, you might say that you are an unarmed woman and that if you wait for a potential assailant to make his intentions clear, it may well be too late for you to defend yourself. There may be some truth to your argument, but in addition to your safety, the law has to consider the well-being of innocent people who might want to use the city streets. Suppose that you weren't the woman who was approached on the street, but were the wife or close friend of the man who wanted directions? How would you feel about his being clobbered by someone who was so jumpy she struck him before even attempting to find out what he wanted?

*   *   *

Thus far we've considered unarmed resistance. But what about weapons? And under what conditions can you use deadly force?

Let's say you've been going to self-defense school for eight weeks, but so far the most you can break with your mighty chop is a Hershey bar. Worse yet, your instructor tells you that it takes up to two years before most people can be considered proficient in unarmed combat, and that in your case he thinks that's an extremely optimistic projection. You begin to doubt you'll ever be a mistress of unarmed combat. So you decide you'd better get a weapon. There's an old penknife under the sink; it's rusty and the blade just falls open, but it's the best you've got, so you drop it into your handbag.

The next night you have to work late at the office, and it's past midnight when you get off the bus and have to walk through the same dark stretch of street. A man comes out of the darkness toward you. You increase your pace, but he keeps coming. He grabs you by the hair and neck and starts to drag you into a vacant lot. In a panic you reach into your bag, pull out the knife, which drops open, and stab blindly at the man. He lets go and staggers away. You run to the nearest telephone and call the police. When they come, you lead them back to the vacant lot, where your assailant is found lying dead of knife wounds. At the police station he's identified as a convicted rapist, out on parole, who is suspected of having attacked two other women in the past month.

Justified self-defense? The answer is not absolutely clear. There's no question that you were entitled to defend yourself from the attack, but the question is whether you were justified in using deadly force. As stated earlier, the general rule is that you can resort to deadly force only if you reasonably fear your attacker will kill you or cause you serious bodily harm. In our imaginary case, it is not definite what he intended to do, since you killed him before he got very far. It's possible that he only intended to rob you, which would not have justified your using deadly force unless he threatened serious harm to you in the course of the robbery.

You argue that if you wait for him to prove he's making a deadly attack, it may be too late for you to make any defense at all. You say it's one thing to require you to wait to see if he means to attack you, but quite another to expect you to "evaluate" the seriousness of an assault that's under way. You point out that as a woman confronted on a dark street by a man, who usually will be significantly stronger than you are, you don't have the luxury of testing out the ferocity of his attack — you have to act forcefully and quickly if you are going to have any sort of chance. You also point out that the man's history indicates that rape, not robbery, was his purpose.

Maybe so, but the law treats the use of deadly force as a very serious matter and permits it only in extremely limited circumstances. Your relative physical weakness does not automatically justify a quick resort to deadly force, although it can be a factor in determining if you acted "reasonably" under the circumstances. One difficulty with your case is that you responded with deadly force to an unarmed attack, and there is an old rule that an attack with fists or hands threatens only an "ordinary assault," and thus does not justify a defense with a weapon.

By now you may be a bit annoyed at the law's concern about the attacker rather than the victim. How do you respond? Well, you might say, (1) a man can do serious harm to a woman with just his fists, and (2) the man's prior record, plus the nature of the attack, indicate he was going to rape you. But let's face it, you didn't know anything about that record. Should that make a difference? Unfortunately — for you — it does. The attacker's history of rape technically cannot help you, since the question of whether you used excessive force has to be determined according to what you knew at the time of the attack. This is the other side of the rule that an apparent attack, even if not real, justifies resistance: Only appearances seem to count. Thus you cannot claim to be exonerated on the basis of facts you didn't know at the time.

Of course, his being a convicted rapist may help you in that the prosecutor probably will not bring a criminal action against you. The prosecutor is not obliged to charge everyone he thinks might have committed a crime; he uses what is called "prosecutorial discretion" to select which of the many potential cases should be taken to criminal court. Indeed, this discretion may be the reason why there have been relatively few cases in which a woman has been prosecuted for killing a man who tried to rape her. One result is that there is very little law on the question of whether rape constitutes serious bodily injury for purposes of allowing defense with deadly force. Although it's generally assumed that it does, there can't be a definite answer until more cases are decided (thus establishing clear precedent to be followed in other cases) or statutes are enacted to codify this assumption. Of course, even if it were determined that rape alone doesn't justify resistance with deadly force, the victim usually could claim she had no way of knowing her assailant wouldn't go beyond the sexual assault and seriously injure her.

But enough theory — let's get back to your case. What would happen if the prosecutor decided to bring you to trial? There's a good chance you'd be acquitted. In light of all the circumstances — a woman alone at night in a dangerous part of the city, the superior strength of your attacker, and the violence of the assault — a jury could easily conclude that you were justified in using deadly force. But be warned: Juries are notoriously unpredictable; moreover, they probably won't be told about the man's rape record, since it's not relevant to how you reacted. Thus there's a chance they might decide that you were too quick to resort to deadly force, since the assailant was never definitely shown to have threatened you with death or serious bodily harm, and you could end up convicted of manslaughter.

Keep in mind that in only slightly different circumstances you would not be entitled to use deadly force — for example, if the man had threatened only to take your purse or knock you down or even to molest you. These assaults may be met with force, but not force likely to kill. Remember also that in many states you have a duty to retreat, if it appears you can do so in safety, before using deadly force. In an urban environment, the duty to retreat, which is really a duty to avoid deadly confrontation regardless of right or wrong, might take a different form from fleeing the scene of the commotion. Thus if the attack we've been considering had taken place in daytime on a crowded street, a court might say that you had an obligation to yell for help or physically resist before stabbing your assailant, since it is likely that someone would have helped you or that he would have been frightened off.

Finally, the use of deadly force is particularly risky in cases in which the assailant's acts are ambiguous. Earlier we concluded that you could be charged with assault if you knocked down a man who just wanted directions. Your case would be much worse if you had stabbed him, not only because you would be up for manslaughter — or perhaps murder — instead of assault, but also because you would have a harder time justifying your apprehension as excusing your acts. If the law hesitates to let you assume that a man who walks up to you at night on a deserted street means to assault you, it will be even less inclined to let you assume he was going to kill you or cause you serious bodily harm. The fact of life is that if you're going to use a weapon, you'd better be sure you really have to.

* * *

The imaginary case illustrates the problems in applying the traditional law of self-defense to cases involving women. The law has grown up around quarrels between men, and assumes the defender and his assailant to be of roughly equal size and strength. It also assumes that an attack without a weapon is not likely to result in death or serious bodily injury, which has given rise to the rule, already mentioned, that deadly force usually is not justified against an unarmed attack.

All this ignores the fact that a woman may be unable effectively to resist an attack by even an unarmed man without resort to weapons, and that she may be seriously injured by a man using only his fists. Still, the policy of severely restricting the use of deadly force makes changes in the law unlikely, although it is possible that the disparity in strength between attacker and defender will be considered more carefully in the future in deciding what was "reasonable" resistance under the circumstances.

Indeed, one recent case suggests that women should not be held to the same standard as men in deciding if they responded too quickly or with too much force, on the theory that they are prone to be fearful of attack because of the passive role traditionally assigned to them. It is questionable, however, that courts will accept this subjective analysis, since the law feels more comfortable with objective standards, which often rely on notions of "reasonableness."

Moreover, pressure to establish a separate standard for women is seen by some as inconsistent, at least psychologically, with the current movement to secure a constitutional amendment guaranteeing equal rights for women. It's somewhat analogous to the ambivalent reaction that greeted the United States Supreme Court's decision upholding the constitutionality of male-only draft registration.

Let's go back to the point at which you had just returned to the vacant lot with the police and found your assailant lying dead of knife wounds. Let's say that everyone agrees you acted in justified self-defense. Are you free to go home? Not necessarily. You could find yourself charged with carrying a concealed weapon. Every state regulates the possession or carrying of certain weapons. In New York, for example, it is illegal to own a gravity knife — one that opens by the weight of the blade. Since that old knife of yours opens that way, in New York you could be charged with a crime.

But everyone agrees that you used the knife in justified self-defense, so how can you be charged with breaking the law? The answer is that the law considers defending yourself and carrying the knife to be "severable transactions," which means they are looked at separately in judging whether you have committed a crime. As to stabbing your attacker, you acted in justified self-defense. But carrying the knife, whether you use it or not, is illegal, and you can be prosecuted even if it's agreed that you needed the knife to protect yourself.

The law on what weapons are illegal to possess or carry differs from state to state; local governments, such as cities and towns, may impose additional restrictions. In general, weapons such as gravity knives, switchblades, blackjacks, and especially firearms, are prohibited or strictly regulated. And you can't count on soft treatment just because you're a law-abiding citizen — at least one state has passed a law making a minimum jail term of one year *mandatory* for anyone caught with an unlicensed firearm. So be careful — before you acquire any sort of weapon, you should find out if owning it is a crime or if it must be licensed.

* * *

We've considered what you can do to protect yourself. Now let's consider what you can do to protect your property. The general rule is that, as in the case of your body, you are entitled to use reasonable force to protect your property from someone who is, or appears to be, trying to steal or destroy it. But since life is considered more important than property, you are never entitled to use deadly force to defend property. The exception is that in certain circumstances, which vary from state to state, you can use deadly force to protect property in your own home. These include cases in which the intruder threatens serious harm to someone in the home, or to commit a felony there. Keep in mind, though, that if you resist someone's taking your property, and he responds with force to your person, you can use force back. If he increases his force, so can you, up to using deadly force if he attempts to use it. Thus it's theoretically possible to kill someone who initially tried to steal your lollipop and have it be justified self-defense.

* * *

Let's say you live alone in the city, and you're concerned about a rash of burglaries that have broken out in your apartment building. The burglars seem to be highly professional, because so far no system of locks has stopped them. You can't sit home all day long and guard the place, so you rig up a trap: a spear gun (you're a skin diver) pointed at the door and set to go off if the door is opened while the device is electrically armed. Next day you come home and find your superintendent lying dead on your doorstep with a spear in him. It turns out he was just checking the steam pipes in the apartments on your floor when he ran afoul of your apparatus.

Are you guilty of a crime? You sure are. The rule is that since you personally couldn't have shot him with a spear gun to protect your property, you can't do it indirectly through a mechanical trap. You can do indirectly only what you could do directly.

Suppose that instead of the superintendent you find your device has killed a man who is soon identified as a professional burglar. His tools are found lying beside him, and he got into your apartment — and set off the spear gun — by picking your lock. Justified defense of property? The answer depends on whether you could have used deadly force had you been there, and this in turn depends on the law of your state. Some states allow you to use deadly force to defend your home against a burglar, so there you would be all right. But others require that the intruder in some way threatened to harm someone inside. Since there was no one home when the burglar got speared, he couldn't have been threatening any physical harm to anyone, so you would be guilty of having used excessive force. (A number of states make setting a spring gun illegal under any circumstances, so you still could be in trouble even if you acted in justified defense of property.) Indeed, as crazy as it sounds, there have been cases of homeowners being sued success-fully in a private, civil action for damages by burglars who were injured by spring guns or other mechanical devices designed to protect the home while the owner was away. The irony is that if the burglar wins, the homeowner may have to sell his house to pay the damage judg-ment; the burglar even may recover enough to buy it, or to lay down his tools and retire!

* * *

Perhaps what is most striking about the law of self-defense to the nonlawyer is how restrictive it is — you really are limited in what you can do to protect yourself. The reason is that the law sees self-defense as a temporary measure to be used only when the normal processes of the law aren't available to help you; thus it is not designed to settle things once and for all or as a means to obtain justice. When you see a thief drive off with your car, you simply are not permitted to use a rifle to stop the robbery, even if that is the only way you can prevent it. You are expected to call the police and have them catch the thief. Similarly, if you are a woman who is punched by a man, you cannot use a knife to prevent his "ordinary assault" against you; you must resist with ordinary force to the extent possible, take the beating, and then call the police.

Or course, the premise is that the police will capture the criminal and the courts eventually will punish him. In many places in this country, particularly in the cities, this is no longer a very realistic prediction, both because the police have more than they can handle and because overloaded dockets and overcrowded prisons make plea bargaining and lenient sentencing almost a necessity. If this trend worsens, there may be more and more cases in which people resort to self-defense and to vigilantism to protect themselves and their property. If this happens, the law will have to contend with the difficult question sure to be put to it by the people charged with crimes for resisting criminals: If the law won't protect me, why should it limit me in my efforts to protect myself? Or as Hobbes might have put it: If the king will not offer me safety, shouldn't I get my sword back?

POINT OF LAW:

Rape — A Short Study in Legal Schizophrenia

Rape is a crime that calls up confused, almost schizoid images in the public mind. To the hardened male chauvinist no woman is ever raped, or at the very least, nice girls don't get raped. At the other extreme the radical feminists see rape as a deliberately invoked political tool by which men keep women in their place. Even the more moderate have mixed feelings: They view rape as an abhorrent crime and sympathize with the victims, yet at the same time they worry about innocent men being convicted on the basis of false charges.

The law also has been schizoid in its approach to rape. Historically, penalties have been severe. Sixteen states permitted the imposition of the death penalty for rape in 1972, when the Supreme Court decided that the death penalty for this crime was constitutionally prohibited as cruel and unusual punishment. (There's a discussion of capital punishment in Chapter 7.) A majority of states currently allow for life imprisonment for a convicted rapist, while others permit sentences of up to fifty years.

Even though the law resorts to draconian penalties for rape, it has created a number of procedural and evidentiary rules that make it difficult to convict someone charged with that crime. These all reflect a concern over the possibility that the purported victim is not telling the truth as to the incident's having occurred, or to her having been forced to engage in a sexual act. For example, the law traditionally has allowed the following cautionary instruction to be given to the jury by the judge (taken almost verbatim from the writings of Sir Matthew Hale, Lord Chief Justice of the English Court of King's Bench from 1671 to 1676): "An accusation of rape is one which is easily made and, once made, difficult to defend against, even if the person accused is innocent." The effect, of course, is to make the jury think twice about whether the alleged victim is being truthful and, inevitably, to cast some doubt upon her veracity.

Another roadblock to a rape conviction is the rule that the victim's chastity, or lack thereof, is relevant to whether she in fact consented to the sexual act that allegedly constituted the rape. The idea is that a "loose woman" is more likely to have consented than to have been forced into it. This rule could mean that the victim has to go through a grueling examination in open court by the defendant's lawyer that delves into her private life and sexual habits. The anomaly is that although her past was deemed relevant, the fact that the defendant may have been previously convicted of rape usually is not admissible to show he raped her, because of the established rule that an accused's prior convictions don't show a tendency to commit the crime again and allowing the jury to know about them would be prejudicial.

Some jurisdictions have required corroboration of the victim's testimony concerning the rape. This means that there must be other evidence, such as a third person's testimony, to support some part or all of the victim's story. Since there often isn't anyone else around at the time of the rape, it may be impossible to get corroboration, and so the result of this rule is to make a conviction difficult or impossible, no matter how strong the case is otherwise.

In addition, the rule developed that to support a conviction for rape, the victim has to "resist to the utmost," which often means she has to show signs of physical mistreatment before she can claim she had been forced into the sexual act. No doubt one basis for the requirement is that it is easier to believe her story if she has bruises and broken bones to back it up.

A modern trend in reforming the law of rape is to treat it like any other crime. One approach is to divide it into different degrees, depending on the circumstances, and to allow lesser penalties for the less serious offenses, such as when the defendant erroneously believes that the victim has consented and no violence occurs. This in turn may make it easier to get a conviction when the case doesn't fit the stereotype of the brutal ravaging of an innocent. At the same time, some of the procedural and evidentiary roadblocks described above are being eliminated in a number of states. The result is to let the jury decide for itself, pursuant to the usual rules of evidence and standard instructions on the credibility of witnesses that are given by the judge in other criminal cases, whether the alleged victim is telling the truth.

6

SPORTS VIOLENCE:

Should the Law Intervene or Has Everybody Assumed the Risk?

MANY PEOPLE THINK the law can solve any problem. If they see wrong-doing, whether by oil company executives, gangsters, student protest-ers, or whoever, they want the culprits hauled off to court. But it's not always that easy; sometimes the law is too blunt an instrument for handling human affairs. One area in which the law has rolled up an unimpressive score is sports violence.

* * *

It's a warm summer afternoon at the baseball park. The home team is at bat with two outs in the ninth inning and the score is tied. The local hero is up, and sure enough he hits a home run to win the game. Everyone goes home happy; it's the end of a perfect day. Or you're at a college football game and the running back for your alma mater suddenly breaks away for a long gain. The crowd, including you, is on its feet, yelling wildly. Or you're at a hockey game cheering the incred-ible moves and skating of Montreal's Guy Lafleur.

Sports give us something special. There's a drama, a heightening of sensation, an opportunity to see a real-life test of nerve and skill. In a sense sports give us a morality play, in which values such as tenacity, hard work, courage, and teamwork are shown to overcome obstacles and achieve victory. Thus it's not surprising that the most skillful and successful of sports figures — people like Joe DiMaggio, O. J. Simp-son, and Bobby Orr — have become national heroes. Indeed, some have termed the appeal of sports in America as mythic or religious, and have likened sports heroes to gods.

But there's a troubling tendency in professional sports, particularly in the more physical games such as football and hockey. We're witnessing an alarming increase in sports violence, incidents in which a player's use of extreme force has resulted in serious — even permanent — injury to another player. The level of violence seems to go far beyond the traditional boundaries of what is permissible even in the roughest of contact sports. Moreover, the violence is spreading from the players to the fans; incidents of hoodlumism in the stands are becoming commonplace.

Sound alarmist? Consider the evidence. On August 12, 1979, in a preseason exhibition game, Jack Tatum, a safety for the Oakland Raiders football team, tackled Darryl Stingley, a wide-receiver for the New England Patriots. As a result of the tackle, Stingley is permanently paralyzed from the neck down. Another player for the Oakland Raiders, George Atkinson, once hit Pittsburgh Steeler wide-receiver Lynn Swann so hard on the back of the head that Swann suffered a serious concussion. As a result of this and several other similar injuries he had suffered, Swann, one of football's most graceful and acrobatic performers, considered giving up the game for a less dangerous line of work.

Nor is the violence limited to football. On October 25, 1978, in a hockey game between the Colorado Rockies and the Detroit Red Wings, a Red Wings player named Dennis Polonick hit opponent Wilf Paiement in the face with his stick. Paiement responded by swinging his own stick like a baseball bat across Polonick's face, dropping him to the ice and leaving him lying semiconscious in a pool of blood. The physician who treated Polonick called it the worst nose fracture he had seen in eighteen years of handling hockey injuries. The incident recalled for many the time in 1969 when Wayne Maki hit Ted Green of the Boston Bruins on the head with his stick in retaliation for Green's hitting him with the back of his glove. Green suffered a concussion and massive hemorrhaging, and despite two brain operations he has never completely recovered.

Even a traditionally noncontact sport like basketball has its share of incidents. In a brawl that erupted during a game between the Los Angeles Lakers and the Houston Rockets, Laker Kermit Washington punched Rocket Rudy Tomjanovich as he charged down the court. As a result of one punch, Tomjanovich suffered fractures of his nose, jaw, and skull, as well as facial lacerations, a brain concussion, and leakage of spinal fluid from his brain cavity.

The violence also has involved the fans. After a hockey game between the New York Rangers and the Boston Bruins, played on the Rangers' home ice on December 23, 1979, an argument broke out between the Ranger goalie and a Bruin forward over an incident of rough play. The fans reacted by throwing debris onto the ice. Then a fan reached over the partition separating the spectators from the players, punched a Bruin, and tried to grab his stick. This precipitated a general brawl, with a number of Boston players going up into the seats to fight with the fans. Although no one was seriously injured, one fan was immortalized on national television as a player beat him on the head with his own shoe.

*   *   *

Sports violence involves acts both within and without the rules of play. An example of legal play causing serious injury is Tatum's paralyzing tackle. Much of the violence, however, occurs outside the rules. Polonick's jabbing Paiement with the end of his stick was an infraction of the hockey rule prohibiting high-sticking, while Paiement's retaliatory swing was penalized as an intentional causing of injury to an opponent. Of course, any act of violence that occurs outside formal play, such as Washington's punching Tomjanovich, or altercations involving the fans, are not sanctioned by the rules.

In reality, certain acts in contact sports that are prohibited by the rules are viewed by the participants as part of the game. For example, George Atkinson's forearm chop to Lynn Swann's head is not a permissible way for a defensive back to cover a receiver, but it happens so often that receivers have come to expect it. Similarly, the bean ball or "purpose pitch" (the purpose is to terrify the batter) has long been illegal, but it continues to be an accepted part of baseball, which isn't even a contact sport. In hockey, the line between truly illegal and accepted illegal play is fairly close; many would say Polonick's use of the stick to jab Paiement's face was acceptably rough play.

The point is that the rules themselves don't necessarily provide a basis for distinguishing rough but clean play from overly violent play. As the Tatum-Stingley affair amply demonstrates, legal play can involve the most atrocious violence and lead to the most serious harm. Nonetheless, one purpose the rules do perform is to keep rough play within bounds and to protect the players from injury; thus acts that go outside the rules, such as high-sticking in hockey, leave the player who commits the infraction with less ground to stand on in defending his conduct.

*   *   *

There are a number of causes of sports violence. An influence often cited is the intense media coverage, particularly by television, which tends to focus on the more violent aspects of the game, either because these elements are more "photogenic" or because they will appeal to the largest audience. Often it's the crushing tackle or the bone-rattling fore check that gets emphasized by the television commentators and the replay technology, rather than the perfectly run pass pattern or the superb display of skating. By giving so much attention to what is only one part of the game, the media impose a subtle pressure on players, coaches, and owners to live up to the violent image of their sport.

The media, and society in general, impose a much less subtle pressure toward rough, violent play in the emphasis they place on winning. One of the sad facts of life is that an "intimidating" style of play often wins games. One of the most successful National Football League teams of the past decade was the Pittsburgh Steelers, whose symbol was its murderous defensive front four, led by the massive "Mean" Joe Green. In hockey, the Philadelphia Flyers, a team not noted for having the best personnel, were for a number of years Stanley Cup contenders through the use of tactics that earned them the sobriquet "Broadstreet Bullies."

Finally, it has been argued that there is a growing thirst for violence in our society, and that more and more people seek to alleviate their frustrations by watching paid gladiators batter each other senseless. This sanguinary analysis of what motivates the sports fan may overstate the case, and it may be less true today than it was during the turbulence of the 1960s, with its social disruption and the Vietnam War. Still, certain sports, such as boxing, auto racing, and hockey, have gained an aura — they are fast and they are violent — and only someone who is totally tuned out from present American culture could miss this element, and the sense that it's satisfying an urge. Perhaps a trip to the stadium, where you can hear the calls for blood and see the faces of the fans, is all that is needed to confirm the existence of the dark side of sports in America.

*　*　*

But who cares if a bunch of overage children want to bash each other for the pleasure of a violence-hungry crowd? Is it really that important?

For one thing, if you're a sports fan who wants to see some finesse and skill, and who has invested the time and effort to learn enough about the sport to appreciate its nuances and fine points, you may find that the game you studied is not being played. Hockey in particular seems to have been affected by the violence, with play constantly interrupted by brawls and with goon tactics substituting for good skating.

Sports violence also may affect the actions of the fans. There have been numerous instances of fans abusing or assaulting other fans, or throwing debris onto the field or otherwise harassing the players. It's hard to say how much of this is a reflection of violence during the game, but incidents like the brawl at the Bruins-Rangers game suggest that the actions of the players serve as an unfortunate model for the fans.

The brutalizing effect of sports violence may extend well beyond the fans. In Canada, a government study found that the violent style of play in professional hockey had a direct influence on the way boys as young as twelve play in the amateur leagues. It found coaches looking for players willing to take and dish out physical punishment as preparation to their stepping up to the National Hockey League. The same phenomenon may affect the football programs at American colleges, or even at the high-school level, with youngsters taught the rough pro game right from the start, on the theory that a reputation for aggressive play or being a hitter helps the aspiring athlete qualify for that big bonus contract when the time comes.

Aside from its detrimental effect on organized programs for children and teen-agers, sports violence may have a corrupting influence on society as a whole. Just as there may be a reciprocal brutalizing effect between players and fans, so there may be a similar relationship between sports and the general community. It is the very specialness of sports, their immense attraction and the interest they generate, that gives them the power to affect our behavior and values. And we in turn bring our attitudes to bear in deciding how we want our sports played. Thus it is hard to avoid the unpleasant conclusion that sports violence bespeaks and promotes a streak of brutality in ourselves.

* * *

But even if sports violence is a serious problem, you might well wonder if the legal system should intrude. After all, no one forces the players to participate or the fans to watch. The courts already are overloaded with cases involving violent acts committed against people who by no means volunteered to get hurt. They certainly don't need more business! Shouldn't we first look elsewhere for a remedy for sports violence? Unfortunately, the two most often cited alternatives to hauling the players into court don't offer any great hope.

The first would be to let the leagues police themselves. Every major professional sport has procedures to deal with disputes, including incidents of violence. The problem with relying on these procedures is that the sanctions — fines and suspension — are not invoked with sufficient consistency or severity to deter the violence. A player, particularly one who uses intimidation, perhaps to make up for a lack of physical skills, might well be willing to risk an occasional fine for illegal play in return for staying on the team. Moreover, it's not clear that the sports establishment is all that interested in curbing the violence. For example, rough play often is taught the players by the coaches, who are presumably under the control of the owners. Also, the National Hockey League has refused to amend its rules to give extra time in the penalty box for the aggressor in a fight, even though this change might cut down on brawls. The possibility is not wholly remote that the owners subscribe to the theory that violence sells tickets and brings in big television contracts.

Since the sports establishment can't be counted on to police itself, it has been proposed that someone else should act as cop, or super-ref. There have been a number of proposals over the last few years that Congress create a government agency with broad regulatory power over sports. The agency could be empowered to intervene in cases of sports violence, review the evidence, and impose penalties. The advantage of a sports agency is that it can develop expertise in its area and can mold its rules and procedures to fit the controversies it will handle. It also would provide uniform treatment, and penalties, for acts of violence, so that the players would be forewarned of what to expect.

But the creation of a national sports agency has obvious drawbacks. First, we taxpayers would be faced with the expense of staffing and running yet another bureaucratic agency. Perhaps a more serious objection — and no doubt the reason no agency has been created — is the feeling that sports are a special area of American life and one that the government should stay out of. With a growing feeling that we are already an overregulated society, it is unlikely that the heavy hand of Big Brother will fall on sports, at least not in the near future.

*　*　*

Since the alternatives don't offer much hope, let's consider what help the legal system — in particular, the criminal courts — can provide in clamping down on sports violence.

Imagine you've been selected for jury duty. You're a little nervous, also a little excited. You hope you get something interesting. When you get to the courtroom you find it all very impressive, with high ceilings and dark wood pews and a raised jury box and an even higher bench for the judge. The prosecutor is talking with a very large man whose face is scarred and who you later notice walks with the help of a cane. The opposing lawyer, who represents the accused, is sitting at a table with a young, clean-cut-looking man, who sits very quietly with his hands folded in front of him. You know that the young man is the defendant, that he is the one who is on trial and whose guilt or innocence you and the other jurors will decide. You wonder what he could have done to be prosecuted for a crime, and what he has to do with the large man with the scars and the cane.

You soon find out. In his opening address to the jury, the prosecutor explains that both men are professional hockey players, on opposing teams, and that during a game three months ago, the young man hit the other man in the temple with his fist, knocking him cold and sending him to the hospital with serious and irreparable brain damage. The young man is on trial for assault and battery, a charge that carries a penalty of up to five years in prison.

It seems hard to believe that the defendant, who has the innocent look of a choirboy, would do such a thing. But the prosecutor shows a portion of the television tape of the game, and it's clear that he's telling the truth: The tape shows a melee involving a number of players, and then suddenly there's the young man throwing a tremendous punch at another player who falls and strikes his head on the ice.

That's enough for you. As soon as you see the tape your mind is made up. This sort of thing can't be allowed — it's no different from a mugging on a public street. You find it particularly reprehensible that this blatant assault was witnessed by a huge television audience, including a large number of children and teen-agers who are likely to mimic the actions of their heroes.

Then the defense presents its case. The young man's lawyer doesn't argue that the event didn't happen, or that there has been a case of mistaken identity. He concedes that what was shown on the tape is true. But he reminds you that this is a criminal trial, and that the issue is whether the defendant, who is twenty-one years old, will be sent to jail for up to five years and, even if he gets a much lighter sentence, will have to bear the stigma of a criminal conviction.

The defense lawyer tells you that the incident must be taken in context. He points out that the man who was injured is a nine-year veteran of professional hockey, known as "Gorilla" Guy Gaspaux. The Gorilla is widely recognized around the league as a cement head or hockey goon, a player of modest skills whose principal job is to intimidate players of superior skill and, if all else fails, to start fights with them so that each will be sent to the penalty box, thereby eliminating a skilled player in return for one whose talent is primarily pugilistic. The defendant, on the other hand, is in his first year in the National Hockey League and is considered a superb skater and stick handler. During the game he was repeatedly "tested" by the Gorilla, who constantly harassed him with rough, often illegal, play. The defense lawyer runs the game tape again, and this time he has the jury focus on the various acts of intimidation by the Gorilla. Sure enough, it's all there — even a nonfan like you can see how the older player is using his stick, his elbows, even his fists in close against the defendant.

Now the defense lawyer brings forth various theories on why the defendant is not criminally liable. First, he claims his client did not have the requisite criminal intent to harm the Gorilla. He tells you that to find the defendant guilty, it is necessary to show not only that he committed the act, but that he consciously meant to do it. He then points out that the defendant did what he did in the heat of an extremely rough game in which he was manhandled and provoked by his opponent. A witness is put on the stand — a "sports psychologist" — who testifies that hockey players are trained from when they are small children to stand up and fight back against the aggression of opponents, so much so that over the years such action becomes instinctive.

The defense lawyer also claims that his client is innocent by virtue of what the law calls the defense of consent. He notes that hockey fights are an accepted part of the game, and argues that the Gorilla — certainly no stranger to the hockey wars — consented to the risks inherent in the sport when he chose to go out on the ice and play. He calls the Gorilla to the witness stand and asks him if he expects to get into fights during the game; the Gorilla nods his head and says, "Yeah, sure. All the time. That's the game."

By now you're a little confused. You can't help thinking that the Gorilla got what was coming to him. Of course, he didn't deserve the severe injuries he received, but he was a bully and took the risk that someone would stand up to him. But at the same time you have some doubts about this "consent defense." You wonder if, by becoming professional athletes, Darryl Stingley consented to getting paralyzed and Ted Green consented to having his head split open.

With all the evidence in, it's time for both sides to give their closing arguments. The prosecutor goes first. He says that the defendant did have criminal intent, since he meant to punch his opponent, which is all that the crimes of assault and battery require, and that it is not necessary to show he intended the injuries that resulted. He adds that "provocation" is not a defense to the crime, since society cannot allow violent acts to be justified except under extreme circumstances, such as self-defense. The fact that the defendant may have been goaded can mitigate the severity of his sentence, but it doesn't alter the fact of his having committed the crime.

As for the notion that the Gorilla consented to what happened, the prosecutor states that in the case of certain violent crimes, such as murder or the more extreme forms of assault and battery, consent by the victim is not a defense. Again, society's interest in preventing outbreaks of violence overrides any claim that the assault was consented to and thus not a criminal act. The prosecutor tells you that he will ask the judge to instruct you as to that being the law.

He concludes by saying that sports violence is a serious problem in this country and that the only way to stop it is to crack down when it occurs. He argues that for all the complaints about the violence, nothing will be done unless the players who commit illegal acts are held responsible under the criminal laws. By bringing in a verdict of guilty, you, the jury, will be sending a clear message to the sports establishment that society no longer is willing to tolerate acts of public mayhem masquerading as sporting events.

Now defense counsel gives his closing arguments. He reminds you that the prosecutor must prove his case beyond a reasonable doubt, and maintains that he has failed to meet this heavy burden of proof with regard to the question of whether the defendant acted with criminal intent. He cites the testimony of the psychologist that an athlete acts reflexively in these situations, and he reminds you of the circumstances of the incident — the provocation by the Gorilla, the heat of the game, the sudden melee — and argues that taken together they indicate the defendant acted instinctively and without any specific intent to harm his opponent. He goes on to say that it is unfair to single out one player and make a scapegoat of him. He concludes by suggesting that if the sport is too violent, it should be changed through either rule amendments or internal league procedures or legislation, but that it is wrong to punish the defendant for doing his job the way he was taught to do it.

The judge gives you his instructions on the law. Among other things, he tells you that the prosecutor is correct in saying that the victim's consent is not a defense to criminal assault and battery. Although in some jurisdictions consent is a defense, he has concluded that the law of your state does not permit the defendant to so excuse his acts. Thus you are to disregard the Gorilla's testimony about his expecting to get into fights. Then you are all led to the jury room for your deliberations. You take a poll, and four jurors want to convict, four want to acquit, and four don't know. Into which group do you fall?

* * *

Before discussing how the case might be decided, let's consider a couple of variations on the facts. First, would it make any difference if the role of victim and defendant were reversed, if it was the skillful player who had been injured by the cement head or goon? Should it? Should people be held to different levels of criminal accountability on the basis of their athletic skills? That doesn't seem right, does it? The defendant may be a better player than the Gorilla, but that alone shouldn't make him any less liable if he commits an assault.

The few cases of sports violence that have reached the courts indicate that state laws may differ on whether consent by the victim is a defense. Suppose you were in a state where it is. Do you think the Gorilla consented to getting slugged? If you say that he did, do you also think he consented to permanent injuries? All right, suppose you change your mind and say his consent didn't extend to his being seriously harmed. But isn't that a little hard on the defendant, and doesn't it make the application of the law completely fortuitous? After all, it's impossible to foresee which of the many blows struck during the ubiquitous hockey fights will result in serious injury. Under your theory, the defendant will be punished if he's unlucky enough to throw the punch that causes real harm.

What if the case had involved violence whose capacity to cause serious harm is more easily foreseen, such as a hockey player swinging with his stick instead of his fists? One problem with answering this question is that the scope of consent expands according to what the player can expect will happen. Thus, as the game grows rougher, the player may be said to have consented to increasingly violent acts. Still, it seems reasonable that certain acts are so egregious that they cannot be excused by any notion of consent. This is particularly true if the act constitutes a flagrant violation of the rules. The attack by Maki on Green is a perfect example, since this type of violence is offensive even to the roughest hockey player. Another example is a clip — a block from behind — thrown in a football game after the play is over.

But how do you deal with the Tatum-Stingley situation, where truly horrendous violence is done within the rules, if not the spirit, of the game? Well, it's always possible that the category of unacceptable violence could extend even to legal play. For example, a court might decide that when a tackle is delivered with the intent to cause serious injury and succeeds, the victim has not consented. The problem is showing that the tackler intended to harm his opponent. Although Tatum boasted of his destructive prowess in his book *They Call Me Assassin,* most players probably would claim they had no specific intent to hurt anyone, and it would be difficult to prove otherwise.

Suppose the defendant had argued that he was only defending himself? As we saw in discussing self-defense, the general rule is that you can use reasonable force to repel a real or apparent attack. Both Maki and Green were tried for criminal assault for the stick fight in which

Green was almost killed, and both were acquitted on the basis of self-defense. Do you think this defense would apply in the case you have just heard? It depends on the facts. If the Gorilla had skated after the defendant to attack him with his fists or stick, the defendant could have fought back. But if the defendant was the instigator of the fight, or if he willingly joined in, then he probably can't prove self-defense.

* * *

The case involving the rookie and the Gorilla is difficult to decide. Whether the defendant acted with criminal intent is unclear. If it had been a street brawl, it would be easy to say that he did; but the issue is complicated by the brawl's taking place in the middle of a professional hockey game, a rough contact sport with its own special norms and code of conduct. The case is simplified if the consent defense is eliminated, but remember that in some states consent by the victim is a defense, which means that questions concerning the scope and nature of what the victim consented to will further confuse matters.

The prosecutor and the defense counsel had conflicting opinions about whether the young hockey player should be punished as a means of reforming the way the sport is played. The prosecutor saw it as the only effective way to pressure the sports establishment into making changes. The defense lawyer argued that it was unfair to make one player the scapegoat for an entire system. Who do you think is right? We've already seen how unlikely it is that the defense counsel's suggestions — rules changes, strict league enforcement, government regulation — will be put into effect. On the other hand, it does seem unfair to make the poor player bear the brunt of reform, unless his actions were so far beyond what is acceptable that punishing him was justified.

In the imaginary case we've examined, the difficulties of meeting the heavy burden of proof in a criminal trial, plus the natural reluctance of a jury to convict someone who is only playing the game the way everyone else seems to play it, very likely would lead to an acquittal of the defendant or possibly a hung jury (a jury that can't make up its mind one way or the other). At least that has been the result in a number of actual cases involving criminal prosecutions for sports violence. The record presented by these cases makes the criminal courts look like the wrong place to try to solve this problem, at least as long as juries are going to hesitate in finding athletes guilty of what clearly would be a crime in any other context.

* * *

What if instead of the state bringing a criminal action against the player who has committed a violent act during a game, the victim brings a civil lawsuit — a tort action — against the player who injured him? There are a number of differences between a civil lawsuit and a criminal prosecution. First, the defendant would not be threatened with jail or the stigma of a criminal conviction; instead, if he lost, he would have to pay money damages to compensate the victim for his injuries. Thus a civil suit may offer a more realistic approach to sports violence, since it would (1) deter violent behavior by making players pay for the injuries they cause; (2) compensate, as far as money can, the athletes who are injured; and (3) avoid the problem of treating players as criminals.

A second difference is that the victim, who would now be the plaintiff (and who would replace the prosecutor, since in a civil case the injured party sues for himself), would have a lesser burden of proof than a prosecutor: He need only prove his case by a preponderance of the evidence. This lesser burden of proof could give him a fighting chance to overcome the argument that the defendant lacked intent to injure the plaintiff. Also, even if intent can't be established, the injured player still can sue on the basis of "negligence." Many tort claims turn not on the fact that the defendant intended harm, but rather that he was so careless in causing injury to another person that he is liable for the results of his negligent conduct.

Another advantage of a private action is that the injured player could sue not only the opposing player who injured him, but also the team for which he plays. It is well established in the law of negligence that an employer can be held responsible for the negligent or intentional acts of his employees. For example, a bus company can be sued by someone who is run down by one of its drivers. Suppose, for example, Stingley sued the Oakland Raiders football team for the injuries caused him by Tatum, an "employee" of that team. The suit might charge that the Oakland management created a dangerous situation by not adequately supervising or restraining Tatum's proclivities toward mayhem. Since the Raiders have a lot more money than Tatum (and are in a position to insure themselves against loss), a lawsuit against them could allow Stingley to recover large money damages. Also, it might encourage the owners to restrain their more aggressive players, since the threat of being liable for the harm caused by sports violence might make them think twice about promoting it for fun or profit.

A private action, however, would run into some of the same impediments as would a criminal prosecution. The player sued could argue that, by participating in the game, the injured player had consented to the possibility that he might get hurt. In tort law, particularly in the context of claims based on negligence, the consent notion often is phrased as "assumption of the risk." For example, if you go to a baseball game and get hit by a foul ball, you'll probably lose if you try to sue for negligence. By going to the park you will be considered to have assumed the risk of being injured in a way that you might reasonably have expected to occur; getting hit by a foul ball probably falls into that category. Similarly, Tatum and the Oakland Raiders could defend themselves by saying that Stingley assumed the risk of any injury caused by a legal tackle. Moreover, in a civil action, unlike a criminal prosecution, consent or assumption of the risk is a valid defense in all jurisdictions. This is because the state is not directly involved in a civil suit, and so its interest in preventing violence — consented to or not — will not override the defense.

Perhaps a more serious drawback to relying on civil suits as a deterrent to sports violence would be the reluctance of the injured player to sue his opponent. He might come under considerable pressure from fellow players, as well as from coaches, owners, and league officials, not to take private disputes outside the sports family, and might risk being branded a crybaby or even a traitor if he did so. However, circumstances might overcome this reluctance. If the injury was serious and had resulted from a blatant violation of the rules, or had occurred outside the limits of play, the injured player might feel morally justified in seeking compensation through a civil action. This especially would be true if he was hard pressed to pay for the costs of treatment himself, or if the injury had prematurely ended his career as a highly paid professional athlete. Some of these concerns undoubtedly led Rudy Tomjanovich to take his grievance to court. He successfully — at least at trial — sued the Los Angeles Lakers for injuries that resulted from his being punched by Kermit Washington. But note, Rudy didn't sue Kermit!

* * *

No less an authority on sports in America than Howard Cosell has remarked: "Sport is indeed Camelot. Each evening from December to December, before we place our heads upon the cot, let's think back to all the games that we remember, because they're Camelot. Tatum may have made a quadraplegic out of Stingley, but that's Camelot . . . We have been taught that sport is so important in this country that it is our greatest escape, that we're not to ever be told that anything is wrong with it."

If you recall, Camelot was destroyed when Lancelot ran off with King Arthur's wife, Guinevere (clearly against the rules of the game), which precipitated a big brawl between King Arthur's team and Lancelot's team. When the brawl was over, so was Camelot. Let's hope Cosell's analogy doesn't prove to be all that appropriate.

POINT OF LAW:

Fan Violence — The Case for Legal Intervention

Fan violence is becoming as prevalent as sports violence. As previously mentioned, there have been numerous instances of fans abusing or assaulting other fans. In some places, particularly in cities where racial or other tensions may add to the problem, parents won't let their children go to the ball park or stadium and hesitate to go themselves, since they feel that there's a good chance of trouble.

Although the courts may not be well designed to deal with sports violence, they *can* help deter fan violence. The impediments to finding an overly rough player guilty of criminal assault or liable for damages don't exist in a legal action against an unruly fan. For example, there should be no problem in showing that the fan who punches another fan or throws a bottle at him acted with criminal intent. The fan is a spectator, not a participant, and cannot say he lacked intent because he was caught up in the game or acted instinctively.

Moreover, the unruly fan can't argue that his victim consented to or assumed the risk of being assaulted by coming to see the game. In a civilized society, no one should expect to be the target of bottles or punches or even verbal abuse at a sporting event. The fact that people do fear such treatment at a number of arenas and stadiums in this country does not mean that the law will say they assumed the risk, since the courts would then be accepting an intolerable condition.

Finally, the two subjective impediments to a legal action in cases of sports violence — the reluctance of a jury to convict a player, and the reluctance of the injured player to sue his opponent — won't be a barrier. A jury should have no hesitancy in punishing a fan as severely as they would anyone else, and a fan who is injured by another fan has no special reason not to bring a civil action for assault.

Perhaps the most effective legal action to curb the violence would be one brought not against the unruly fan but against the stadium operators. The people in charge of the facility where the game takes place have a legal duty to provide a reasonably safe environment for nonviolent fans, and can be liable for damages to one who has been injured because of their failure to do so. The fear of being sued should be a spur to them not to neglect this duty. They might, for example, be deemed negligent if they don't provide enough security — in the form of stadium guards and regular police — to control troublemakers in the crowd. They also might be found negligent if they fail to limit the consumption of alcoholic beverages at sports events, since drinking by fans has often led to hoodlumism. Unfortunately, enforcing rules against drinking may require that fans be searched as they enter the stands. Although searches might be subject to legal challenge as an unreasonable invasion of privacy, it is likely that a court would conclude that they are justified under the circumstances. To avoid legal objection, however, the searches must be conducted in a reasonable manner, and fair notice should be given that anyone coming to the game is subject to search.

These and other precautions, coupled with prompt criminal and civil actions against fans who commit assaults, should help to stop violence in the stands. The law may be an unwieldy instrument with which to deal with excessive roughness by the players, but it's an appropriate one to discourage spectators from too literal an emulation of their heroes down on the field.

Yet one hopes that the law will have to be invoked rarely, if at all. It would be nice to feel that we didn't need it, in part because it would be a mark of our own civility and in part because holding athletic contests under the gaze of the law can have a dampening effect on the venture. Grandstand searches, the presence of large numbers of uniformed police, and constant public-address-system warnings are bound to spoil the atmosphere of the stadium or field house. And since reaction tends to breed overreaction, what restraints would come next? Limits on free expression? What would baseball be without a fan bellowing "Kill the bum!"?

7

THE DEATH PENALTY:

Legitimate Sanction or Legalized Murder?

ON A CHILL JANUARY MORNING in 1977, convicted killer Gary Mark Gilmore was shot to death by a Utah firing squad. Thus ended a ten-year moratorium on capital punishment in the United States — a moratorium that had been imposed by the Supreme Court while it grappled with the question of whether the death penalty was unconstitutional as cruel and unusual punishment. Six months earlier, the thirty-six-year-old Gilmore had shot in the head at pointblank range a Brigham Young University student working his way through school as a motel operator. Within days of that killing, Gilmore murdered another student in exactly the same manner. Each victim left behind a wife and child.

After his conviction, Gilmore asked to be executed without delay. Yet even he may not have been prepared for what was to happen when he was escorted to the prison warehouse to be killed. He was strapped into a chair on a makeshift platform facing a cubicle behind which a squad of marksmen hid, their rifles aimed through five-inch holes. Then a black hood was placed on Gilmore's head, and a black target with a white circle marking his heart was pinned to his T-shirt. He was asked if he had any last words. He paused, then said, "Let's do it!" A signal was given and Gilmore was shot through the heart. Two minutes later he was dead.

Opinions differ sharply on the propriety of the death penalty. You may be among those who think that Gilmore deserved death. For you, and for many others, the death penalty serves as an expression of society's outrage at particularly heinous crimes, a way of permanently removing the worst criminals from our midst. Perhaps you think the threat of death even may make a potential Gary Gilmore think twice before he pulls the trigger; the death penalty is an effective deterrent to crime, you say. Or you may be someone who opposes the death penalty. To you, Gilmore's execution was legalized murder. Capital punishment brutalizes our sensibilities, and it serves no socially desirable purpose; a stiff jail sentence is a sufficient deterrent to crime.

Most people fall into one category or the other. It's hard to be neutral in the debate. After all, it is a matter of life and death. Still, precisely because the death penalty is such a serious — and irreversible — punishment, even those of you strongly in favor of it may think twice before imposing it. And because the penalty applies only to the most serious crimes, those of you against its use may pause in horror once you find out what a convicted murderer — like Gary Gilmore — actually did to land him in court. Let's explore why we resort to the death penalty, and what limits the law — in particular the prohibition in the Eighth Amendment to the United States Constitution against "cruel and unusual punishment" — places on its use.

* * *

The two justifications that always have been given for imposing the death penalty are deterrence and retribution. As a deterrent, capital punishment is designed to reduce the incidence of the most serious crimes by making it clear that severe consequences will follow a conviction for committing one of these acts. Historically, death sentences were carried out in public to make sure that the point was clear, with grisly methods of execution used to make the punishment especially terrible. Convicted criminals were subjected to exotic penalties like flogging, impaling, boiling in oil, breaking on a wheel, and sawing in half. Early on, the English appear to have favored drawing and quartering: The criminal was hanged, disemboweled while still alive, his entrails burnt before his eyes; then he was decapitated and quartered. After the execution, the remains of the criminal often were put on public display to reinforce the message. The corpse might be hung in chains and left to rot in them or the head stuck on a pike.

As to retribution, Sir Edward Coke, probably the greatest English jurist, justified drawing and quartering as the most appropriate punishment for traitors "not worthy any more to tread upon the face of the earth" and "unfit to take the benefit of the common air." As you can surmise, Sir Edward was not overly forgiving of those guilty of treason. In a similar vein, Sir William Blackstone, the most renowned English legal commentator, noted that the practice of hanging the corpse of a murderer in chains for all to see was "a comfortable sight" to the relatives and friends of the victim.

Today, of course, the method of execution has changed. In an effort to avoid brutality, we try to make death as quick and painless as possible. Electrocution or the gas chamber is used in most states, and Texas recently came up with what it considered an even more "civilized" technique — death by lethal injection. In addition, we hold our executions out of the public eye, with only representatives of the state, perhaps the media, and any witnesses who may be required by law present.

We also have different ideas than did our ancestors about what crimes merit capital punishment. One big change is that we do not execute people for their political or religious views. This was not always so; for example, after Henry VIII's break with the Pope, more than five hundred persons a year were executed in England, many for their political views. In a speech in 1791 to the National Assembly after the French Revolution, one representative declared that "there must be terrific spectacles in order to control the people"; the Reign of Terror followed, in which scores of Frenchmen were decapitated at the guillotines. The number of executions in Russia rose dramatically in the years immediately after the Bolshevik revolution as the new government entrenched itself in power. Even today, outside a relatively small number of liberal democracies, the death penalty remains an accepted method of silencing political opposition and promoting national stability. We got a graphic glimpse of this form of justice not too long ago when the front pages of American newspapers were emblazoned with a photograph of a Vietnamese soldier holding a gun up to the head of a suspect and pulling the trigger. No trial, no jury, just a swift and sure execution. The truth is that the technique, and kangaroo court variants on it, are far more prevalent in the world than we care to admit.

Even when the targets of the death penalty are common criminals, opinions have differed over the years as to which of them should be put to death. For example, in 1800 England's so-called Bloody Code listed some 223 crimes punishable by death, including stealing turnips, associating with gypsies, poaching, and cutting down a tree. If you think we Americans were any less sanguinary, consider that in 1641 the Massachusetts "Capitall Lawes," citing the Old Testament as authority, ordered death for blasphemy, idolatry, and witchcraft. And during the infamous Salem witchcraft trials, women accused of sorcery were executed and one man was crushed to death by placing him between boards weighted with stones. We also used the death penalty to maintain the institution of slavery. In many Southern states before the Civil War, it was a capital crime to harbor an escaped slave or to incite slaves to rebellion. Moreover, the color of your skin could determine your fate; the "Black Codes," which were the laws in Southern states relating to crimes committed by blacks, listed ten times as many capital crimes as did the regular criminal codes. As we shall see, the charge that the death penalty has continued to be applied discriminatorily against blacks was to become an important factor in challenging its constitutionality.

* * *

Over the years, the pendulum of American public opinion has swung back and forth between abolition and retention of the death penalty. In the 1850s, antigallows societies grew up along with antislavery groups. By the end of the century, several states had abolished, albeit only temporarily, the death penalty for any crime. Then in the 1920s and 1930s, when the likes of Bonnie and Clyde, John Dillinger, and "Pretty Boy" Floyd robbed banks, shot up towns, and made headlines, the national mood swung back in favor of it. By the 1960s, when so many of our institutions and practices were being questioned, the death penalty again came under attack.

Its most recent opponents went further than arguing that the sanction was inhuman or ineffective; they claimed it was outright illegal. More specifically, they charged that it violated the Eighth Amendment's prohibition against "cruel and unusual" punishment. The debate over this issue became so fierce that in 1967 the Supreme Court, knowing it eventually would have to resolve that question, refused to allow any more executions until it was prepared to make a decision one way or the other. In effect, a moratorium on all executions was called, and it wasn't for another ten years — until that cold January day in Utah in 1977 — that any one of the hundreds of people living on the death rows around the country actually died.

* * *

Do you think capital punishment is unconstitutional? In thinking about this as you read the pages that follow, try to divorce yourself from your personal views of the death penalty. Legally, its constitutionality depends on the meaning of those two words in the Eighth Amendment: *cruel* and *unusual.* With a clear eye and a cool head, step back and try to look at the words like a lawyer or judge would. Of course, you can't be completely detached — that wouldn't be human. Also, what *cruel* and *unusual* mean depends to a large extent on public opinion. Legal analysis is not done in a vacuum. Remember, though, that you're just one person with one opinion. Your fellow citizens' views count too.

Okay, let's take a try at it. First, do you think the death penalty is cruel? Remember, we're not talking about drawing and quartering or boiling in oil, or any of the other exotic methods used by our forebears. We're talking about the modern forms of execution — the electric chair, the gas chamber, or possibly the firing squad used in the Gilmore case. Do we satisfy the prohibition on being cruel simply by not inflicting pain in the process of the execution? Death by lethal injection apparently is no more painful than the many immunization shots we get throughout our lives. Blackstone was of the opinion that drawing and quartering was not cruel because the disemboweling of the criminal occurred only after he had been hanged and lost all feeling. (What a break for the criminal!) But even if he was right, isn't there the horror of seeing one's entrails being burned before one's eyes? How much psychological pain renders the execution cruel? Or do we evaluate the cruelty by how quickly death comes? The guillotine, which was the official technique in France until that country abolished the death penalty in the fall of 1981, is quick, but isn't there something barbaric about cutting off heads? (Indeed, isn't there something barbaric about thinking in these terms?)

Still, quickness and absence of physical pain seem to be significant elements mitigating against declaring the death penalty cruel. It was these considerations that led the Supreme Court, around the turn of the century, to uphold the constitutionality of the electric chair. The Court praised the new method as being more "humane" than hanging, the form of execution that it replaced in many states.

The Court was later to hold, however, that the quantum of pain inflicted was not the sole test for cruelty. In 1946 it said that Louisiana could take a second try at executing a man who had been strapped into the electric chair but had not died because of an apparent equipment failure. A witness said that during the first electrocution attempt the condemned man's lips "puffed out and he groaned and jumped so that the chair came off the floor." Despite his plea that to put him through the ordeal again amounted to torture, the Supreme Court said that the Eighth Amendment is not violated by suffering that is "necessary" to bring about death. Cruelty is the "wanton infliction" of pain, not pain resulting from an unfortunate accident.

Maybe the question of a punishment's cruelty depends on why it is being imposed; it has to "fit" the crime. Since the death penalty is the most severe of all punishments, it should be reserved for the most dastardly of deeds. But which are those? None of us would approve of condemning a man for stealing turnips or associating with gypsies. But how would you feel about imposing the death penalty for train wrecking, forcing a woman to marry, desecration of a grave, or statutory rape? At one time in the not too distant past, each of these crimes was punishable by death in different states. Certainly capital punishment would be a cruel penalty for jaywalking or shoplifting. But is it cruel for certain crimes that do not necessarily cause the death of another — like arson, rape, kidnaping, or skyjacking?

Even assuming we can agree about what *cruel* means, how do we define *unusual*? When the electric chair was introduced, it was unusual in that it was new; however, the Supreme Court did not find its use unconstitutional. Suppose a state law called for death by drowning? This also would be new. Would the fact that drowning is not an improvement in terms of the speed or painlessness of death mean that its "unusualness" would make it unconstitutional?

Do you agree with certain opponents of capital punishment that by its very nature the penalty is unusual in itself regardless of what technique is employed? Yet how can a penalty that's been part of our criminal justice system for so long be unusual? From the standpoint of history, the death penalty is certainly not new. Wait a minute! That raises the question of from whose perspective we decide what is unusual. We could put history aside and judge the death penalty against our own contemporary experience. Or we could go back in time and try to imagine what the framers of the Constitution had in mind.

Certainly, what was foremost in the framer's minds when they drew up the Eighth Amendment was the particularly bloody history of the death penalty in England. Drawing and quartering and hanging corpses in chains to rot were still fresh in their memories, and they wanted to make sure these practices were never revived and brought to the United States. If that's all the Eighth Amendment forbids, then it seems that our relatively humane forms of execution would not be constitutionally prohibited.

The Court doesn't always focus on just what the framers actually had in mind, however. Rather, they treat the Constitution as a "living document" and try to apply it to today's circumstances. The words *cruel and unusual* are especially subject to this sort of dynamic, updated interpretation, since their meaning can change according to what the Court has termed "evolving standards of decency." Assuming we've all become more humane and civilized over the past two hundred years, then it's possible that a punishment that was acceptable to our ancestors no longer is so today. But that leaves the question: What are our present standards of "decency" and does the death penalty comport with them?

* * *

Some answers to these lines of inquiry emerged from the debate that raged in the late 1960s and early 1970s over the constitutionality of the death penalty. By this time, the members of the Supreme Court had begun to wonder if it was constitutional in any form. They also started looking beyond the method of execution; they focused on why capital punishment was imposed, how juries decided upon it, and against whom the punishment was applied. A significant issue for their consideration was the possibility that capital punishment was being imposed in a discriminatory manner on blacks. Statistics seemed to indicate that it was. For example, more than half of the 3859 persons executed between 1930 and 1968 were black. Of the 455 persons executed for rape, 405 were black.

These concerns were reflected in *Furman* v. *Georgia,* a 1972 decision in which the Court struck down two state statutes that gave juries absolute discretion to impose or not to impose the death penalty. The justices who composed the majority, however, gave different reasons for their conclusion. Justice William O. Douglas was especially concerned that juries would discriminate against the poor and members of minorities. Justice Potter Stewart saw the penalty, as applied, as cruel and unusual because those who die were "capriciously selected" — there seemed no basis for telling why juries gave the death sentence to one defendant and not another. He likened being sentenced to death under these circumstances to the fortuity of being hit by lightning. Justice Byron White worried that juries assessed the death penalty so infrequently that it lost much of its deterrent force, and therefore its justification. Justice William Brennan, joined by Justice Thurgood Marshall, argued that the death penalty was unconstitutional no matter what procedure was used to impose it, no matter how gruesome the crime. It is "offensive to human dignity," they said. The remainder of the Court wanted to stay out of the debate. They said that it was up to state legislatures, not the Supreme Court, to decide whether the death penalty was good or bad and how it was to be used.

Three years later, in *Gregg* v. *Georgia,* the Court went beyond the question of juror discretion and finally addressed the main issue: Does the death penalty violate the Eighth Amendment so that its use under *any* circumstances would be wrong? First the Court set up a two-pronged test for deciding whether punishment was cruel and unusual. According to the Court, a punishment was excessive and thus unconstitutional if it (1) serves no legitimate purpose, and (2) is "grossly disproportionate" to the crime. Then the Court applied the test to the death penalty and concluded that it did not transgress the Eighth Amendment as long as it was imposed according to certain guidelines.

As to the first prong of the test, the Court said the death penalty served the twin goals of retribution and deterrence. "The instinct of retribution is part of the nature of man"; if it is not channeled, "there are sown the seeds of anarchy — of self-help, vigilante justice, and lynch law," wrote Justice Stewart for the majority. Although the Court saw the case for deterrence as inconclusive, it decided that the death penalty in some situations might make a violent criminal think twice before acting. As to the second prong of the test, the Court concluded that the death penalty was not grossly disproportionate when the crime was particularly severe.

In *Gregg* and a number of companion cases, the Court also addressed the problem raised in *Furman* of giving juries too much discretion to impose the penalty. In the years between the two cases, states with the death penalty had responded to *Furman* by revising their laws in an effort to conform to that decision. In reviewing several of these attempts, the Court in *Gregg* approved those that required the jury, before imposing death, to weigh aggravating circumstances — factors that make a crime worse — against mitigating circumstances — factors that make a crime less terrible. A sampling of aggravating factors listed in the state statutes includes a prior conviction for a crime involving violence, murder of a policeman, murder for profit, a crime that posed a risk of death to many persons, and one that was especially atrocious or cruel. Among the mitigating circumstances are a defendant's youth, a history of mental illness, intoxication, and no significant history of prior criminal activity.

Yet the Court struck down as unconstitutional a state statute that had been revised to make the death sentence mandatory for certain crimes. The Court felt that although juries should not be completely free to sentence an individual to death, neither should they be absolutely powerless *not* to do so; too much discretion was bad, but *no* discretion was worse. Mandatory death statutes for certain crimes forced juries into a corner. They could end up acquitting an obviously guilty criminal just to save him from the electric chair.

* * *

Do you agree with the Court's resolution in *Gregg* of the problems raised by the various justices in the *Furman* case? Does it provide adequate protection against prejudice given the statistical data indicating that the death penalty is disproportionately imposed on blacks? Race, of course, is neither an aggravating nor a mitigating circumstance under any state statute, and it would be unconstitutional to try to make it one. But isn't it possible that the prejudices of the individual jurors might affect their decision despite the restrictions on what they may consider? This fear of prejudice is one reason that both Justice Brennan and Justice Marshall continue to believe the death penalty violates the Eighth Amendment and should be totally banned. On the other hand, a majority of the justices were satisfied that the procedure of having the jury look to aggravating and mitigating circumstances would avoid the problem of arbitrary or discriminatory death sentences.

How about the Court's conclusion that capital punishment was justified from the standpoints of deterrence and retribution? The justices didn't sound very positive about its value as a deterrent. Remember, the question isn't whether a criminal is deterred from acting because of the death penalty, but whether he is any more deterred by it than he would be by life — or a long term — in prison. It raises an interesting question of perspective. Under the circumstances, would it be a sound policy to require clear evidence that criminals are deterred by capital punishment before holding the penalty constitutionally permissible? Or should it be the other way around: Should the opponents of capital punishment have to prove that it has no special deterrent value before it is declared unconstitutional? The Court apparently has taken the latter view and, as lawyers would put it, placed the burden of persuading the Supreme Court on those who wish to abolish the death penalty.

Now, what about retribution? Justices Brennan and Marshall think we have — or should have — risen above a visceral and vindictive response to crime. Keep in mind that the death penalty is unique, for it eliminates any possible rehabilitation of the criminal. Punishment is total and final. On the other hand, isn't outrage at certain particularly horrible deeds and a desire for retribution something that is perfectly natural and not to be ignored? Perhaps a majority of the Court was right in believing that the possibility of anarchy and vigilantism is reduced by allowing the instinct for revenge to be channeled. Or wouldn't a long prison sentence — perhaps a mandatory life term — satisfy this urge?

Look at it from another angle: A majority of states currently have laws imposing the death sentence. These provisions appear to reflect the view that most people in this country think capital punishment serves a legitimate purpose. Do you think the Supreme Court should attempt to nullify this determination unless it's patently clear that it is wrong? But to use an analogy, the Court didn't look to public-opinion polls when it decided that a woman has a right to an abortion. Nor did it feel obliged to honor the fact that most states had laws making it a crime. Should constitutional rights — like the Eighth Amendment's ban on cruel and unusual punishment — depend on majority vote? Or should the justices look to their own consciences to decide what those rights mean when the wording of the Constitution is ambiguous?

* * *

The *Gregg* case decided that capital punishment was constitutionally valid when applied to the most reprehensible crimes. Premeditated murder fits that description, since that is what was involved in *Gregg* and its companion cases. But these cases didn't tell us what other crimes, if any, fall into that category. Presumably it doesn't include stealing turnips or consorting with gypsies, but what about rape, treason, kidnaping, or skyjacking?

The answer was supplied in 1977, when the Supreme Court held that the death penalty could not be imposed for rape. The Court reasoned that since the victim of a rape survives the attack, death as a punishment was disproportionate to the crime — therefore excessive and cruel. The decision implies that capital punishment never can be constitutionally imposed for anything other than a crime resulting in death. That's certainly eye-for-an-eye thinking in its narrowest terms. Do you think the Court is being overly mechanical in its reasoning in limiting capital punishment to murderers? Were the male justices being insensitive to the terror and psychological harm inflicted on the female victim — harm that in the case of a brutal rape arguably could make the effects of the crime as serious as murder?

What about crimes like treason or skyjacking that may not result in immediate death to any single person, but can put many people in danger and perhaps cause death indirectly, perhaps through a delayed physical or emotional reaction? With skyjacking, the threat is quite imminent; not only are the passengers on the plane put at risk, but so are people on the ground who could be killed in a crash. With treason the threat may not be quite so imminent, especially in peacetime, but it may involve everyone in the country. Consider, for example, the risks currently posed to Americans because of past transfers of atomic defense secrets to the Soviet Union. Does the Supreme Court's approach necessarily preclude the death sentence in these cases? The answer simply is unclear, since there have been no cases since 1977 clarifying the issue.

* * *

Okay, we've been exposed to a lot of law about the death penalty; now let's try applying it. Consider the following three imaginary cases, and as you do, ask yourself if capital punishment would serve the purposes of deterrence and retribution. Then think about what aggravating and mitigating circumstances are involved, and decide if you, as a juror, would vote to impose the death penalty.

CASE 1

Jill married her high-school sweetheart, and they have a five-year-old son. Her husband, however, has turned out to be something less than a sweetheart. He's a poor provider, plays around with other women, and at least once a month goes out, gets drunk, and comes home and beats her. Jill has suffered countless black eyes, three broken noses, and a fractured jaw. She solves her problem by gradually, over a two-month period, adding increasing amounts of rat poison to his morning coffee. He gets weaker and weaker, as if suffering from a strange, intractable ailment (as she planned) and finally dies. But a suspicious relative convinces the police to conduct an autopsy, which leads to Jill's arrest. At her trial, Jill makes it clear that she feels no remorse at his death, but her little boy tearfully tells the jury that he loves his mommy and begs that she come home soon.

CASE 2

Fred and his friend Bill were drinking heavily and playing cards one night at the Dirty Hog Saloon, when Bill accused Fred of cheating. Outraged, Fred attacked Bill only to be knocked down by the larger man. In a drunken fury, Fred went outside to his pickup truck, took a double-barreled twelve-gauge shotgun from the front seat, returned to the crowded bar, and blasted Bill with both barrels, killing him and injuring numerous other people with stray buckshot. Horrified at what he had done, Fred immediately turned himself in to the police. At his trial, it is disclosed that he has two prior convictions for assault.

CASE 3

John was serving a life sentence in the state penitentiary for armed robbery, rape, and kidnaping when he escaped for the second time in a year. In his few hours of freedom, he broke into a young couple's home, pistol-whipped the man unconscious, and raped the woman. He also tortured her by burning her flesh with a lighted cigarette and beating her. He left the house assuming both his victims were dead. The couple survived, although the man lost the sight of one eye, and his wife required plastic surgery and needs continuing psychiatric care. At John's trial following his recapture, prison officials testify that he is a menace to inmates and prison guards alike.

* * *

Let's apply the Supreme Court's two-pronged test to the three human beings before us in the prisoner's box. First, look at the legitimate goals — deterrence and retribution. Would any of our three defendants have been deterred by the prospect of death as opposed to a long prison sentence? Perhaps Jill would have. After all, she poisoned her husband over a long period, so she had plenty of time to think about the consequences. On the other hand, she was very careful to try to make the death look natural, and may have thought she could get away with it. Therefore, it is possible that no threat of any punishment could have prevented her from going ahead with the crime. One can't help feeling, however, that if Jill is executed it might deter others who find themselves in comparably desperate circumstances and encourage them to seek less drastic means of safeguarding themselves.

As to the other two, Fred is a poor candidate for deterrence. He murdered in a drunken rage, and it seems unlikely that anyone in such an irrational condition would weigh the prospect of being executed against serving a long prison term. But John offers a strong argument for imposing the death sentence as a deterrent. Since he already is serving a life sentence, there is no other significant punishment that can be inflicted upon him. Thus, unless he is subject to execution, he has little to lose by killing prison guards, inmates, or those unfortunate enough to encounter him if he escapes again. It can be argued, however, that habitually violent criminals like John are not influenced one way or the other by the threat of execution; in effect, they are just as irrational as Fred was when he blasted Bill. Still, shouldn't the mere possibility that the threat of death will prevent him from hurting anyone else be enough to justify its imposition?

Also, suppose a habitual criminal like John held up a fast-food restaurant and the only witness was the cashier. In a state without the death penalty, but which provides for a possible life sentence for armed robbery, or for repeated violent felonies, the penalty structure would encourage him to kill the cashier. After all, having nothing to lose, it makes sense for him to eliminate the witness and thus improve his chances of escaping conviction, or so the argument goes.

What about retribution? Again, John seems to offer the strongest case of the three, since his acts were so cruel that we may feel he doesn't deserve to live. Also, he left two victims — the couple he mutilated — who may well want John dead. Remember that Justice Stewart wrote that the urge for retribution should be satisfied by society, or people might resort to self-help or vigilante acts. This argument has the most weight when there are victims, or families and friends of the victims, left behind to seek vengeance.

How about vengeance against Fred or Jill? In some ways, Fred doesn't seem like such a bad person. After all, he killed while out of control, and as soon as he realized what he had done Fred was remorseful and turned himself in. But don't forget that he was stupid, or weak-willed, enough to get into a drunken brawl. Should there be retribution for stupidity and character flaws, as well as viciousness? Does it make any difference if Fred's victim, Bill, had a wife and six children? Should their loss be vindicated with a death sentence for Fred, or should the family's desire for vengeance be ignored? Yet the fact that Bill has a family doesn't make Fred any worse a person, since he was out of his head when he killed and couldn't have considered what he was doing to Bill's wife and children.

Do we want vengeance against Jill? She poisoned her husband, but it's also true that he beat her. But are we sure that's why she killed him? Maybe it wasn't the beatings but the fact that he fooled around with other women that caused her to murder him. Or maybe she wanted the proceeds of a large insurance policy on her husband's life. Our judgment of whether Jill deserves to die could depend on what motivated her; yet, in some cases, there may be a variety of motivations — some perhaps less culpable than others — and it may be hard to tell which was the real one, or what combination of motives led to the murder.

What about the way she killed him? She was certainly cold-blooded about it — she planned and carried out the murder over a relatively long period of time. Doesn't that make her worse than Fred, who didn't plan anything? How about the possibility that her husband had living parents who want Jill punished as severely as possible for what she did? Does the fact that Jill's son pleads for her life offset the vindictive desires of his own grandparents? Has any of that much to do with how bad a person Jill is?

You'll have to answer these questions yourself, since they're mostly matters of personal judgment. That's really what the legal system expects of jurors in this context. What we do know is that the Supreme Court has expressed its judgment by deciding that the death penalty can serve the legitimate interests of retribution and deterrence, and that our analysis of our three cases doesn't indicate that the Court necessarily was wrong in that conclusion. So let's go on to the second prong of the Court's test: Is the crime serious enough to warrant death or would that punishment be "grossly disproportionate"? If it is serious enough, we have to ask ourselves two more questions: Does the law of the state where our imaginary criminals are tried categorize their acts as capital crimes? And finally, would we as jurors, balancing aggravating and mitigating circumstances, sentence them to die?

John's case is the easiest. The Supreme Court's decision rejecting the death penalty for rape strongly suggests that he cannot be sentenced to death because he didn't kill anyone — he only raped, beat, and tortured! Any state statute that allowed the death penalty in John's case would be unconstitutional, since it would permit a grossly disproportionate punishment. Yet all sorts of aggravating circumstances are present: He has prior convictions for violent crimes, his acts involved considerable savagery, and there is every reason to believe he will act in a similar fashion whenever he gets the opportunity. But no matter how much we as jurors might feel he should be executed, we can do no more than sentence him to another prison term.

Fred did kill someone, so capital punishment would not necessarily be disproportionate. What does state law say should be done with him? In a state like Texas, Fred faces only a prison term, since a capital crime there generally is limited to murder committed during the course of another serious crime, and all Fred did was kill. Still other states limit the death penalty to premeditated murder, and Fred acted in an unthinking rage.

But let's assume that we're in a state in which Fred can be charged with a capital crime. The judge has instructed us, as jurors, to look at aggravating and mitigating circumstances. These may vary from state to state, but for our purposes let's take the ones often mentioned in statutes. The first aggravating circumstance is the fact that Fred's crime involved a risk to many persons, since a shotgun blast in a crowded barroom could kill or injure more than just the intended victim. Second, Fred has two prior convictions for assault. Mitigating circumstances are Fred's youth, and the fact that he was drunk at the time and didn't know what he was doing.

In addition to listing mitigating and aggravating circumstances, some statutes allow additional factors to be brought before the jury. Possibly you would be told of Fred's remorse for his crime. What else? How about the fact that he goes to church every Sunday, or is the sole support of his mother? The prosecution might bring in evidence of additional aggravating factors; Fred, for example, might be a drunkard and have been warned not to drink too much.

What about Jill? Some states make the "cruel" or "atrocious" nature of the crime an aggravating circumstance. Does what she did come within this category? She coldly took her time about it, inflicting great pain, and showed no remorse afterward. Moreover, it was her husband she killed, leaving her child without a father. But perhaps this is nullified by his brutal treatment of her. As to mitigating circumstances, let's say she has no previous criminal history. If the statute allows

additional circumstances to be considered, the jurors might be reminded of how her husband beat her, and of how her child begged for
her return. Is the fact she's a woman and a mother a mitigating circumstance? But wait a minute — isn't deciding her punishment on the
basis of her sex just as bad as deciding a black defendant's on the basis
of his race?

Are you now clear how you would decide Fred's case, or Jill's? You
don't have any choice about John — he can't be executed, at least not
under the present Supreme Court standard — but it's up to you
whether the other two live or die. You've been supplied with aggravating and mitigating circumstances; but as you can see, they don't necessarily lead to an obvious conclusion about whether to impose the
penalty. This balancing process, however, is important: It gets you
thinking about considerations that at least are arguably relevant, and
away from other factors — race, politics, or social status — that should
have no part in your, or any juror's, determination. Moreover, in
virtually every state any verdict for death would be reviewed by a
higher court to be sure that it doesn't show signs of having been based
on considerations other than those deemed relevant by the Supreme
Court.

* * *

For the present, the Supreme Court has determined that capital punishment is not unconstitutional. Perhaps at some time in the future it
will change its mind and conclude that it constitutes the kind of cruel
and unusual punishment prohibited by the Eighth Amendment. If it
does so, it probably will reflect not so much a change in attitude on
the part of the nine justices, but rather their perception of a change
in what you — and the rest of the community at large — think of the
appropriateness and usefulness of this sanction. For the answer to the
question "What is cruel and unusual punishment?" turns ultimately on
public attitudes; confining oneself to pure legal reasoning leads into
a dark blind alley.

As long as the death penalty may be imposed, however, judges and
juries must see that it is done fairly, and in accordance with the purposes for which it is employed. If nothing else, this will ensure that its
use is minimized. And this is as it should be. The death penalty is
unlike any other punishment and its use must be scrutinized more
closely than any other sanction. Error or prejudice is intolerable in this
context, for once implemented, there is no appeal, no pardon, no
possible correction of its misapplication.

POINT OF LAW:

Not Guilty by Reason of Insanity

One September morning, Cora Patterson was reading the Scriptures when she saw the angel of death. In obedience to the angel's wishes, Cora went to a kitchen drawer and took out a butcher knife. She then summoned her seven-year-old daughter, and stabbed her twenty-one times.

Cora told police afterward that she was Abraham and the child was the sacrificial lamb. With that, the police did some research into Cora's background. They found her past dotted with a history of mental illness and a series of hospital stays. Each time she was committed, she "recovered" under treatment with psychotropic drugs. She then would be discharged and urged to continue taking her medicine. But sooner or later she would stop and relapse. The last time, she was sent off to a mental hospital after she had threatened a total stranger who happened by her house. With her imaginary angel beside her, Cora tried to stab the stranger. Unlike her daughter, he escaped.

Cora's murdering her daughter certainly is a crime, but she's no ordinary criminal. She didn't really know what she was doing, so it's difficult to say she had the "intent" required to make her guilty of a criminal act. Nor does sending her to jail seem to serve any purpose. The threat of a prison stay can't deter someone who is incapable of thinking about the consequences of her deed, much less of knowing exactly what she has done. Retribution — society's expression of outrage at the crime — makes no sense when the object doesn't know she's done anything wrong. And if rehabilitation is the goal of criminal punishment, putting Cora behind bars won't do any good. She needs a psychiatrist, not a jail warden. She'll never improve if she's simply locked up in a cell. Yet Cora is just as dangerous to the public as the killer with all his wits about him — perhaps even more so. And someone did die because of Cora's act. What's the criminal justice system going to do about that?

First of all, the police will charge Cora with murder. It's not up to them to decide if she's insane or not. Then there will be a hearing in court to determine whether she is legally competent to stand trial. To be "competent," Cora must be able to understand the proceedings against her and to participate in her own defense. A minimal level of mental capacity is necessary in order for her to get the fair trial to which she is constitutionally entitled. If Cora can't even tell her lawyer what happened, he can't very well decide how best to represent her.

And if she doesn't even know she's in a courtroom, it's hard to say that Cora is able to confront the witnesses against her — as the Constitution guarantees. If Cora is found to be legally incompetent, she will be sent to a mental institution to see if she can recover enough to stand trial. With today's drugs, which often can put mental illness into remission, Cora most likely will be back in court within the year.

Once the question of competency is settled, Cora's lawyer will have to decide whether she should plead not guilty by reason of insanity. It seems clear that she was crazy when she stabbed her daughter, but there may be strategic reasons why a lawyer would not want to raise the insanity defense. The defense necessarily means that the defendant must admit she committed the crime; if the evidence against the accused is weak, the lawyer may decide there is a much better chance of getting an acquittal by poking holes in the prosecution's case. Also, the defense bears the often insurmountable burden of proving the accused's insanity; when the trial begins, even the looniest-acting defendant is presumed sane. A lot of expensive psychiatrists will have to testify, and the jury, confronted with the grizzly details of the crime and pictures of the innocent victim, may be reluctant to buy the insanity plea. Finally, the defendant herself may balk. Some defendants would rather risk jail than be labeled maniacs. And a fixed term in prison may seem preferable to an indefinite stay in a mental institution. Of course, from our Olympian perspective, we hope the lawyer *does* choose the insanity defense. An outright acquittal would put Cora back on the streets again with the angel of death not far behind. A conviction and prison term would mean Cora will not get the treatment she needs.

What will the lawyer have to show if Cora is to be found not guilty by reason of insanity? States vary as to the precise legal test. The oldest one — still used by more than twenty states — is called M'Naghten's Rule. It was named after Glasgow workman Daniel M'Naghten, who killed the British prime minister's secretary (mistakenly believing the secretary to be the prime minister) in the mid-1800s because he thought that the prime minister, among others, was conspiring against him. M'Naghten's Rule says that a defendant is not criminally responsible for an act if he didn't know what he was doing or didn't know his acts were wrong. Some states have tacked on an additional test: A defendant who commits a crime because of some "irresistible impulse" cannot be said to be responsible. Cora seems to pass both insanity tests with flying colors. She thought her daughter was a sacrificial lamb; she knew as little about what she was doing as the man who strangled his wife thinking he was squeezing an orange. Even if she realized she was killing, she thought she was doing God's work. She certainly wasn't in control of herself; the angel told her to do it.

So if the jury finds Cora insane, we at last can rest easy knowing that Cora will get treated and society will stay safe with her in a mental institution. The problem's solved, right? Wrong. It's just beginning.

In most states, Cora will go through a civil commitment proceeding following her murder trial. She may have been adjudged insane when she killed her daughter, but to be institutionalized, she must be shown to be insane *now,* and years may have passed. To be committed, Cora must pose a present danger to herself or others and/or be in need of psychiatric care. It's very possible that, by this time, she is neither. Mental illness is often cyclical in nature, with periods in which the patient is near normal. Also, the drug treatment that Cora received to restore her competency for trial may have put her in remission to the extent that it may be difficult to show that commitment is currently necessary. It may well be that the judge will have no choice but to discharge her. But how long will her present mental health last? Cora's been down this road before, if you remember — she's treated, released, and then sooner or later relapses. How long before the angel of death appears and she gets out her butcher knife?

States have responded to this problem in two ways. First, well over a dozen now have automatic commitment of those found not guilty by reason of insanity; they are institutionalized for a limited period of time and then, after the required stay, a civil commitment hearing is held. Second, a few states couple a patient's discharge with out-patient treatment. Close supervision may assure that Cora keeps taking her medicine. The notion is that if she is constantly monitored, any deterioration in her condition can be caught before someone else is killed.

But let's say Cora is in fact committed. How long would she stay in a mental institution? How do we get her off the merry-go-round of recovery and relapse and at the same time protect the public from the angel of death? Once upon a time, the criminally insane were institutionalized for life. Society certainly could feel safe; the public essentially had gotten rid of the problem of the mentally ill by banishing them forever from everyday life. They were locked up and forgotten, and the treatment they received, if any, was very crude. In the last few decades, however, two developments have occurred that make automatic lifelong commitment out of the question. First, medicine has progressed to such a stage that it now is possible for the mentally ill to become contributing members of the community. Second, there has been a corresponding trend on the legal side toward recognition of an individual patient's rights. Institutionalization is a deprivation of liberty; liberty should be taken away only with good reason and only to the extent necessary. We can't keep someone in a mental hospital just because he's a little "weird."

But Cora is more than weird. She's downright dangerous, or so the judge decided when he committed her. She can't be kept in the mental institution, however, once she ceases being dangerous and no longer is in need of treatment. Who decides when that point is reached? Basically, it's up to the psychiatrists who treat her; certainly they're in the best position to decide. But are they? Medical people may have more on their minds than just an individual patient's health. Particularly in state institutions, there often is a shortage of beds. As soon as Cora reaches some minimum level of sanity, they may be anxious to push her out the door so as to make room for the more desperately ill. Conversely, hospital personnel may be more reluctant than they should be in releasing her. In some states, they can be sued if they prematurely release a patient who then goes out and hurts someone shortly thereafter. Of course, even if the hospital staff does guess right and Cora is in full remission because she is taking psychotropic drugs, we still have no assurance that she won't stop taking her medicine, just as she did in the past.

In order to deal with these problems, more than half the states now subject the hospital decision to release a patient who has been through the criminal justice system to review by a court. The judge is not susceptible to the same economic pressures hospital personnel may feel and can focus on the question of public safety. And since he often is the same judge who presided at the patient's criminal trial, he is fully aware of the patient's past capacity for violence and the danger that would be posed by a premature release. In an attempt to slow down the merry-go-round of recovery and relapse, a few states will treat the patient who eventually is discharged much like a prison parolee. The patient may have to check in regularly with someone to make sure that his mental condition remains stable. It is this out-patient treatment that could best assure that Cora's future will not simply repeat her past.

There's no perfect solution to the problems of the criminally insane. We can't treat them like ordinary criminals and lock them up, or banish them to mental institutions for the rest of their lives, but neither should we forget about them once they're discharged. Until we find a "cure" for mental illness, the vicious cycle of recovery and relapse most likely will continue. We only can hope that there's someone there with a helping hand before a person like Cora goes beyond help.

Agreements
and Relationships

8

JOB CONTRACTS:

Are They Worth the Paper They're Printed On?

WE ALL SHOULD HAVE some familiarity with employment contracts, if for no other reason than most of us who work have one. There may not be a written document with all sorts of legal clauses, but if you work for someone else, whether an individual or an organization, you have a contract, even if it's only an oral understanding. And if you belong to a union, there's a collective bargaining agreement between it and your employer covering you.

Employment contracts generally call for the employee to perform services for the employer in return for a salary and possibly other benefits, such as hospitalization or a pension. But how binding are they? If you decide to walk out on your boss in violation of a contract, what can he do about it? If he fires you, can you go to court and get help? The answers to these questions can turn as much on questions of enforcement — on the practical limits on the law's power to coerce human action — as they do on what the contract actually says. As you will see, despite its claims to promote justice in every instance, the law does not like to bite off more than it can chew.

Enforcement of Personal Service Contracts

Let's consider the rights of employers first by looking at actual examples in which an especially valuable employee has attempted to walk off a job he had promised to perform.

Perhaps no single employee is any more valuable to his employer than Johnny Carson, the host of *The Tonight Show,* is to NBC. His presence on the show is almost a guarantee of high ratings, and the advertising revenue it generates is a major source of network profits. So what happened in 1979 when Carson threatened to leave the show even though he had two years yet to go on his contract? Did NBC haul its star to court and have the judge order him to appear on the tube through 1981? No, they tore up the old contract and offered him a new one for much more money, which Carson magnanimously accepted.

Another valuable employee was Chuck Fairbanks, the coach of the New England Patriots professional football team. Before coming to the Patriots, he had been the highly successful coach of the University of Oklahoma football team, a perennial college power, which won fifty-two games and lost only sixteen under his tutelage. That's why Billy Sullivan, the owner of the then hapless Patriots, hired him away from Oklahoma on a multiyear contract at $150,000 a year to build his team into a winner.

After three years, and steady improvement in the team, Fairbanks decided right before the Patriots entered the play-offs that he'd rather coach college football at the University of Colorado than finish out the years left on his contract with the Patriots. Did Sullivan wipe a tear from his eye as his coach packed and left? Not exactly. Sullivan went to a Massachusetts court and had the judge order Fairbanks not to coach at Colorado. Thus while Fairbanks refused to coach for his old employer, he was not allowed to work for his new one. This impasse led to a negotiated settlement, in which certain Colorado football fans with lots of money paid off Sullivan to let Fairbanks go. (Thus far, those fans have not gotten much for their money — their team has had nothing but losing seasons since he arrived; but things may be beginning to look up.)

Both these incidents raise the same question: Why couldn't the employer just force the employee to honor his contract? Why did NBC cave in to Carson's demands? Why was Sullivan unable to get more than a compromise, one that left him without what he really wanted — Fairbanks as the Patriots coach at a critical time?

Remember that in both instances the contract unquestionably was legally valid and binding. Certainly they were binding on NBC and Sullivan. For example, if it had been the other way around and NBC had decided to replace Carson, he could have gone to court and had the judge order NBC to pay him through the remainder of his contract, and the same is true if Sullivan had fired Fairbanks before the agreement came to an end. The typical contract in the fields of athletics and entertainment calls for the person performing services to be bound to the job for a certain period in return for payments during that time; the employer is free not to use the services, but he must continue to pay as long as the employee stands ready to perform.

If the employee can sue the employer for the money he contracted for, why can't the employer sue the employee to obtain his services? A contract is supposed to bind both sides. Besides, weren't we brought up to honor our promises? Shouldn't the law step in to see that people fulfill their moral obligations? So why is it so easy for the employee to walk off the job?

The answer lies in the limitations on the law's ability to control people's behavior. More specifically, it turns on the range and effectiveness of the "tools" or "remedies" available to the law to deal with people who disregard their contracts. Keep in mind that breaking a contract is not a crime; thus someone who doesn't honor a contract can't be sentenced to prison for what he did. Instead, the court is left with civil — or noncriminal — remedies. These are (1) rescission, (2) damages, and (3) specific performance. To understand the inherent limitations of these remedies, let's examine each and see how much good it would be in the Johnny Carson and Chuck Fairbanks situations.

RESCISSION

Rescission simply means that when one party to a contract breaches it, the other party can call it off. Let's say that you get a craving for pizza. You call up Sam's Pizzeria and order a large pepperoni and onion pizza and specify that you want it right away, and Sam agrees to get it to you pronto. You and Sam have made a contract: He'll deliver the pizza reasonably quickly and you'll pay the delivery boy for it.

Now suppose the pizza doesn't arrive for several hours; by then your pizza craving has long since been satiated by a pepperoni and onion pizza ordered from Al's Pizza Palace. Are you obligated to pay for the one that Sam finally gets around to delivering? The answer is no, because you made it clear that you wanted it right away, and its delivery hours later constitutes a breach of contract by Sam. Your remedy is rescission: Just don't pay Sam's delivery boy. You don't even need a court! When you rescind a contract, you treat it as if it never existed. Of course, this assumes that you refuse to accept the pizza. If you relent and take it, you'll have to pay for it. But if Sam had delivered the pizza on time, you would have been obligated to pay whether you accepted it or not. But his delay allows you to slam the door on the delivery boy and make believe you never ordered it.

Now consider whether rescission would be a useful tool in our two examples. Suppose Carson refuses to appear on *The Tonight Show*.

Since he has breached his contract, NBC can treat it as rescinded; they can cease any further payments on his contract and find another host for the show.

But that doesn't really solve NBC's problem. Getting another host for *The Tonight Show* is not as easy as switching pizzerias. Experience with substitute hosts has shown that Carson is the man for the job — ratings are higher when he appears, and the show seems funnier and livelier. NBC wants Carson, not a substitute, because whomever they got probably wouldn't be as good. In legal terms, Carson's services are not "fungible" and easily replaced; rather they are of unique value. So just calling off the contract — rescinding it — isn't a satisfactory remedy as far as NBC is concerned.

Rescission isn't much good to the New England Patriots either. The unique value of Fairbanks' services may not be as obvious as in Carson's case, yet it's there. Fairbanks was the coach Sullivan had selected to take his football team to the Super Bowl, and the team was making progress toward that goal. Perhaps more important, the players had become accustomed to his system of play, and any change of coach was bound to disrupt their concentration. So again, just calling off the contract would not have been an adequate remedy for the Patriots.

In each case, the personal services that were contracted for had a special value, so the employer could not be satisfied just to rescind the contract. Rescission works in the pizza contract because one pizza is pretty much like another; but the personal services of a Johnny Carson or a Chuck Fairbanks are unique, and employers who contract for them don't want a substitute.

DAMAGES

Damages mean money. The victim of the contract breach goes to court and presents his case; if the victim wins, the person who didn't perform the contract will be ordered to pay him a sum of money as compensation for any financial loss he may have suffered. For example, suppose that after ordering your pizza you had suddenly lost your craving and had refused to accept or pay for it, even though it was delivered on time. You would have violated your contract, and Sam could sue you. The damages — the amount Sam was injured — would be the value of the pizza, since presumably he could have sold it to someone else if you hadn't ordered it. Sounds simple, and it often is, which is why damages are the usual remedy a court awards in a breach of contract case.

But there's a complication: The person suing has to prove the amount of his financial loss. This can be a real problem, since not all cases involve as easy a calculation of damages as our pizza example. Sometimes it's hard to come up with an exact amount, and all you can do is speculate as to what your losses are. But unless you can come up with a fairly definite figure, you might not recover any damages at all. The law will not award "speculative" damages; they must be reasonably certain and not guessed at or open-ended. This is because the purpose of awarding damages is not to punish the person who breached the contract, but to "make whole" the person who was financially injured by the nonperformance.

Now let's see how this works when applied to our two examples. Could the Patriots recover damages for Chuck Fairbanks's running off to Colorado? They would have to prove they had been financially injured, and prove the amount of the damages. But that could turn out to be a very difficult task. Fairbanks himself was not the magnet that sold tickets or brought in television money. The team is the attraction, and probably the only generalization that can be made is that a winner does better at the box office than a loser. But even this rule is sometimes broken, since fan loyalty, style of play, and the particular locality can affect how many people go to the stadium or watch the games on television. Consider, for example, the hapless New York Giants, whose loyal fans support them through thin and thinner.

More important, even if it were possible to tag a financial loss to the team's losing games, the Patriots would have to prove that they would have won more games if Fairbanks had stayed on as coach. But football games are decided by a multitude of factors besides coaching. Nor would it be sufficient for the Patriots to plot a graph showing year-by-year improvement under Fairbanks's direction, since reversals of football fortunes happen so often that no team is assured of steady improvement. In summary, it looks as if the Patriots would have a tough time proving damages with any precision.

What if Carson walked off *The Tonight Show*? Often it's hard to show damages when a star leaves a show, since any fall in box-office receipts might be attributable to other causes, and since even a star can be replaced. For example, Farrah Fawcett-Majors walked off *Charlie's Angels* in a dispute with the show's producers over how much she was to be paid and her wanting the opportunity to act in movies. Although she was one of the biggest attractions on television, the producers, after a great deal of hand wringing, hired Cheryl Ladd as her replacement, and the show continued with great success for a number of years.

In Carson's case, NBC might have a chance to prove damages. They could do their best to replace him, wait until the end of the term of his contract, and then sue for damages based on any decline in advertising revenues resulting from lowered Nielsen or Arbitron ratings for the show. Revenues are tied closely to ratings, so once any decline can be attributed to Carson's defection, NBC should have a good shot at proving damages.

Well, it's not quite that simple! Carson might argue that NBC can't prove that his leaving was responsible for lower ratings. He could say that they would have fallen anyway (especially if the competition got better — ABC's *Nightline* is now catching *The Tonight Show*) or that the network had failed to make a suitable effort to find an adequate replacement or to get another show to fill that time slot. (Under contract law, the injured party is required to "mitigate" his damages, that is, to make an effort to minimize any financial loss.) Carson would be in the odd position of arguing that he isn't the big star his employer thinks he is. "It was all a joke, I was never any good," he might say. But NBC would overcome these arguments by proving that Carson was a unique attraction and was personally responsible for the success of the show. In this endeavor they would be helped by the clear evidence of how guest hosts had failed to get the same ratings as Carson.

Assuming that a court is satisfied that NBC has proved its damages, is the network home free? Not necessarily. There's another rule about damages that's not so much a legal rule as a fact of life — you can't get blood from a stone, or damages from someone who hasn't got the money. We know that Carson is far from broke, but he may have nowhere near the resources to cover the huge advertising losses that even a few lost points in the ratings would create. So after all its efforts NBC might end up recovering only a fraction of its damages.

Of course, the threat of NBC's suing and collecting all he's worth might deter Carson from breaking his contract. But given the uncertainties that always surround litigation, and the possibility that a court would find damages speculative and not allow recovery, he might be willing to take the chance. Thus, on balance, it seems that damages are far from a perfect remedy.

SPECIFIC PERFORMANCE

By now you may be wondering why employers don't skip all that rescission and damages stuff and just get a court to order Carson and Fairbanks to get back to work or else. What you're asking for is called specific performance — the court's ordering the person who breaches the contract to do what he promised to do.

Historically, specific performance was the last of our contract remedies to develop. For centuries in England the victim of a contract breach had to go to the courts of law (called King's Bench — or Queen's Bench in Elizabeth's reign), where he generally was limited to collecting damages. Also, the law courts would handle a dispute only if it fell into certain established categories called causes of action, and they were bound by strict rules and procedures that could defeat even a just claim. In the late Middle Ages, people who could not get help from the law courts began to appeal to the "king's conscience" in the person of the chancellor, the king's chief minister. The chancellor, who was free to decide a case as he thought best, weighed all the "equities" of the dispute and then issued an order or decree designed to achieve a fair resolution. The order could involve more than the payment of money; it might tell someone to do, or not to do, something — for example, to stop cutting down trees on someone else's property, or to stop polluting a common stream.

Gradually, the equity courts (called the court of chancery) developed out of this practice. Their decrees were called injunctions, since someone was enjoined — ordered — to do or refrain from doing a particular act, and were enforced by means of the court's contempt powers, which allowed the judge to fine or imprison a party who disobeyed the injunction. Specific performance, which is really functionally equivalent to an injunction ordering the contract violator to perform his obligations, became the equitable remedy for breach of contract in England and then the United States. The two court systems have long since been merged in both countries, but many of the old rules still govern what relief is available to a litigant and under what circumstances.

One of these rules is that a court will grant specific performance only if the goods or services to be supplied are unique or of some special value. The idea is that you really have to need help before equity will get involved. Thus if Sam had reneged on his promise to deliver you a pizza, you could not have gotten a court to order him to make one and deliver it to you. As we noted earlier, pizzas are pretty fungible, and you can get a substitute. Another principle — based on the historical origins of the equity courts — is that there must not be an "adequate remedy at law," which means that damages or rescission must not be sufficient to make the nonbreaching party whole.

Well, don't our cases fit that description? We've seen that rescission and damages are not too likely to give our employers what they want. Certainly the services we've been considering are unique — there's only one Johnny Carson, one Chuck Fairbanks. It's the specialness of these people that makes their services so valuable. Thus it seems that if either of them tried to walk off the job, a court would grant specific performance and order him back to work. Right?

Sorry, that's wrong. The court probably will do no such thing, since, according to another limiting principle, the law traditionally has refused to grant specific performance of personal service contracts. There are a number of reasons for this refusal.

The first is that forcing someone to work at a job he doesn't want to perform smacks of slavery. Unless there are strong countervailing policy considerations (such as national security justifying the draft, or the public interest justifying laws prohibiting strikes by public employees — although the air traffic controllers were fired, not made to work), specific performance of a job contract might raise a challenge under the Thirteenth Amendment, which prohibits slavery. Another reason is that it might violate the employee's freedom of association. This somewhat nebulous right, which the Supreme Court has concluded is protected by the First Amendment, includes our freedom to associate with whomever we please without undue interference. And forcing Carson to work with Ed McMahon and the rest of the NBC staff against his will might well pose a violation of this right. In balancing the interests of employer and employee, both these considerations weigh heavily against ordering specific performance of a job contract.

A third reason for denying specific performance is purely practical: It's just too difficult for a court to check out whether a personal services decree has been obeyed. Suppose, for example, a court had ordered Fairbanks to coach the Patriots. What if they lost the first game of the season? Could Billy Sullivan have gone to court and demanded that the judge punish Fairbanks for doing a bad job? Ought the judge be asked to decide that on a particular play Fairbanks should have instructed his quarterback to hand off instead of passing? Or that the team should have tried for a field goal in a key situation instead of punting? For a judge to try to second-guess the coach really would be Monday morning quarterbacking. Obviously a judge (who, presumably, has more important issues to handle) is not equipped to answer these questions, and shouldn't be asked to try; nor should Fairbanks risk being fined and imprisoned just because his players foul up on the playing field.

Similarly, a court is in no position to play critic regarding Carson's performance on *The Tonight Show*. What if NBC decides Carson is letting down in delivering his monologue and sketches and asks the judge to order him to be funnier? What if Carson gets on the witness stand and insists he's being as funny as he can? Doc Severinsen might swear Carson was mistiming his jokes, while Ed McMahon could swear his boss is funnier than ever. The court proceeding itself would turn into a comedy routine and the judge become a glorified laugh meter.

All in all, the policy reasons for not enforcing contracts for personal services outweigh any reasons for enforcing them. So where does that leave the deserted employer? We've already seen that rescission won't give him what he wants, and that damages may be impossible to prove, or to collect. Can Carson and Fairbanks get clean away?

The answer is that they can't. The court can use its equitable powers obliquely and place limitations on their taking other jobs. Perhaps the first use of this approach was in a famous nineteenth-century case in which an opera singer tried to break her contract to perform at one theater so she could sing at a competing theater for more money. Although the court conceded that it could not order her to sing at the first theater, it nevertheless ordered her not to perform at the second, noting that the decree might encourage her to fulfill her original obligation voluntarily — a sort of judicial attempt to do indirectly what it couldn't do directly.

In this classic case, the singer had specifically agreed not to perform elsewhere during the term of the engagement with the first theater. But what if there is no such provision in the contract? Does that mean the employer must suffer the additional injury of his erstwhile employee helping his competitor? Many cases say no. The courts reason that certain employment contracts contain what are called implied covenants not to work for competitors. Implying a term in the contract means that the court will assume that the parties meant to include it, only it was so obvious that they didn't bother to express it. The truth is that there's a bit of make-believe to all this — it's called a fiction. The law just doesn't think it's fair to let the breaching employee work for a competitor! In a sense, the court is imagining there is a covenant in the interests of justice.

The implied covenant not to compete is narrowly construed — in general, it will be applied only to prevent the employee from performing the services for direct competitors, and often only those in the same geographic area, and at most for only the term of the original contract. Indeed, equity will hesitate to enforce even an express covenant that goes too far beyond these limitations. But it will do so only when the employee's services are special or unique — performers, athletes, and executives, not factory workers, clerks, or waiters. In a sense the law is saying the employers don't need special help with the latter groups because those workers are easily replaced, like getting a pizza from Al's when Sam's doesn't arrive.

The if-he-won't-work-for-me-he-won't-work-for-my-competitors approach was used almost a century after the opera singer case when the great American actress Bette Davis, who was under a contract to make movies exclusively with Warner Bros., "jumped" to England to do films there. Warner Bros., however, was able to get an injunction from an English court against her performing for the British company, since any picture she made in England would compete against those made by Warner Bros. In this instance, geographical limitations on the injunction didn't apply, because films compete for audiences on a worldwide market. But the court refused to extend the injunction to the full term of the contract, since it thought a shorter period of restraint on Davis would suffice to protect Warner Bros.

Cases of valued employees jumping to competitors are rife in professional sports. For example, Rick Barry, who was once the star of the San Francisco Warriors of the National Basketball Association, was enjoined from jumping to the rival American Basketball Association during the term of his NBA contract. Here the geographic limitations had special significance, since the ABA team that Barry was to play for was in Oakland, just across the bay from San Francisco. More recently, John Matuzak, a monstrous defensive lineman currently playing for the Oakland Raiders of the National Football League, was prevented by a court order from jumping from his original NFL team, the Houston Oilers, to the now-defunct World Football League.

Notice that this negative approach eliminates many of the problems raised by the affirmative technique of granting specific performance. First, the restrictions on the employee's freedom are not as severe. True, he or she is prevented from working for direct competitors of the original employer, but the employee may work for anyone else and is not forced to associate with anyone. Second, the decree is not as difficult to enforce as specific performance, since all the court considers in judging compliance is whether the employee did or did not work for the employer's competitors; the quality of that performance is not an issue.

Let's see how this approach would apply to our two examples. Suppose Carson walks out on NBC to do a talk show for CBS. A court simply could enjoin him not to appear on the other network. The decree involves only a limited restriction on Carson's freedom, and it's easy to enforce, since Carson can't very well appear on national television and not be noticed. But what if he leaves NBC to work in a Las Vegas club? His appearance there doesn't compete with *The Tonight Show*, so there is less reason to grant the decree. Still, the court might decide to enjoin his appearance as a means of encouraging him to go back to NBC. Now what if Carson drops his

Las Vegas deal and decides instead to go on a tour of college campuses? Should the court extend its decree to forbid his appearance at any college? — at high schools? — all educational institutions? — every Middlesex village and farm?

As you can see, as the scope of the decree's prohibition expands, our old problems with specific performance reappear: The employee's freedom begins to disappear, and the decree becomes more difficult to enforce as the court is required to follow the employee around to see that he isn't working in any forbidden job. So the old rule that equity usually will limit the decree to competitors has a practical basis, because in most instances there won't be that many of them and the decree thus will be workably narrow.

On the other hand, what actually happened in the Fairbanks case illustrates how the decree can be kept narrow and also extend to a noncompeting job. When Fairbanks said he was off to Colorado to coach college football, the Patriots got an order enjoining him from coaching there. (This was only a preliminary injunction, which "freezes" the situation until there can be a full trial; but if the Patriots had won at trial, as they very well might have, the injunction no doubt would have become permanent.)

Although college and professional football generally don't compete for the same audience, the court was willing to extend the decree to a noncompetitor, since it remained very narrow: There was, after all, only one football team in the country — the Colorado Huskies — that Fairbanks was forbidden by the decree to coach. Then, with his new job denied him, Fairbanks decided to go back and negotiate with the Patriots, with the result that a settlement was reached that assuaged Sullivan's hurt feelings and let Fairbanks escape to Colorado. (It should be noted that the Massachusetts decree never was reviewed by a higher court, nor was it tested on a practical level by Fairbanks's refusing to obey it.)

*   *   *

A quick reminder: Restricting an employee from working for another employer is a remedy available only when the services are unique. Thus most of the cases have involved entertainers or sports figures, in which the uniqueness of the services is obvious. We might ask ourselves what other services are sufficiently valuable and exceptional to merit equity's intervention. What about a heart transplant surgeon, or a research scientist on the verge of a breakthrough, or a salesman with an exclusive clientele? What about you? If you tried to break a contract with your employer, could he get you enjoined from working for a competitor?

Termination Without Cause

We've been looking at life from the employer's standpoint. Let's turn it around and look at it from the employee's angle. And let's forget about superstar entertainers and big-time football coaches; instead we'll consider what the law can do for the down-to-earth employee faced with a common but unpleasant situation — getting fired.

* * *

Suppose, for a moment, you're a manager — a junior executive — in a small manufacturing company. You've worked there for five years, ever since you graduated from college. You have an oral contract with the president of the company: You're paid $19,000 a year for a thirty-five-hour week, with three weeks' vacation. You've risen steadily in the company, you've taken on increasing responsibility and handle your work well, and you have every reason to believe you'll be made a vice president as soon as one of the incumbents retires.

But that's not how it works out. One day you come to work and you're told you're being let go. Why? Because the president's son has just graduated from business school and he's going to be the new vice president. That leaves you out in the cold, so you're to clean out your office and be gone as soon as you can.

Let's try another version of the story. You're a reporter who has worked on the same newspaper for twenty years. Your contract — again, an oral understanding — gives you a salary of $24,000. One day, without any warning, you're fired. Why? Because there are hundreds of students — all fired up from watching *Lou Grant* on television — pouring out of journalism schools, and the paper can get someone to do your job for half the pay.

* * *

Both not entirely imaginary cases involve what the law calls "termination without cause," and what nonlawyers call getting a really raw deal. Of course, there's always a cause or reason for the firing; "without cause" just means that you weren't fired for any fault on your part, such as incompetence or absenteeism. In both cases you were doing a good job, and in both cases that wasn't enough to keep you from being fired, nor was there a union to protect you.

Can our manager or reporter go to court and get relief? After all, it isn't just — is it? — for people who do a good job to be fired to make room for the boss's relatives, or to cut costs by hiring hungry college grads at coolie wages.

If either does go to court, the first thing the judge will want to know is whether the contract said *anything* about the reasons for which the employee could be fired. Let's suppose in each case the employer, as part of the oral agreement, said in front of witnesses (so it can be proved in court), "You've got a future with us. Do a good job, and you'll have it as long as you want it." Assuming there's no dispute about the employee's being discharged for reasons having nothing to do with job performance, we've got a clear case of breach of contract.

But what relief would the court grant? If you were the judge, would you order specific performance and force the employer to take the employee back on the job? Isn't that just like forcing an employee (Carson or Fairbanks) to honor a job contract? In each case the freedom of the person subject to the decree is impinged upon, and each could involve enforcement problems. You might respond by saying that it's less of an imposition on the employer to let someone work for him than it is to be forced to do the work. You also point out that the law often forces employers to take back improperly discharged employees, as in the context of union disputes, or in cases of discrimination on the basis of sex or race.

But wait a minute. Often a union job involves little personal contact between the employer and employee, and what constitutes an adequate day's work is set by a quota or the nature of the work, which obviates the need for supervision. The employer hardly knows — or cares — who works on his assembly line. And the discrimination cases are special because they involve goals of national importance.

Suppose, however, that in our company the executives work closely with the president, and that a team atmosphere is promoted. Is it fair to impose an unwanted player upon the team? Also, part of your attitude is based on a belief that it's unfair to fire someone to make room for the boss's son. But the boss may have labored long and hard to build up his company, just so his son would have a break in life. Is it fair to deny him the satisfactions of parental devotion? Similarly, the editor on the newspaper may work closely with his staff of reporters, and the publisher may have good reasons for trying to cut costs. There is nothing un-American in keeping costs down. If the paper couldn't, it might go out of business or have to charge more!

Also, the enforcement problems aren't that simple. Suppose a month after you force the president of the company to rehire the manager, he fires him again, only this time he announces it's for doing a bad job, or for being a disruptive influence? How do you, as the judge, determine whether he was doing a good job and wasn't disturbing anyone? What if after you order the reporter rehired by his newspaper, he is fired again because the editor says he has younger reporters who do a better job than he does? How do you gauge when a reporter isn't doing well enough? Isn't the editor the best judge of that? Aren't you back to being a Monday morning quarterback? The only alternative is to recognize that the manager and the reporter have lifetime jobs and a license to goof off.

Even if the employee is kept on the job, there may still be problems in determining if the employer is disobeying the spirit, if not the letter, of the decree. What if the manager is assigned to the least important tasks, or the reporter is sent to cover sewer bond hearings and tugboat launchings? Remember that the difficulties in enforcing a decree requiring an employee to perform personal services were a key reason for not issuing it in the first place. Similarly, these difficulties weigh heavily against ordering an employer to take back an employee, at least when the job involves significant personal contact between the two, and more than routine duties.

Also keep in mind that to get specific performance, the employee presumably would have to show that the job was unique in some way. It could be argued that both jobs meet this qualification, since each involves an investment in time and effort that is irretrievable. This is especially true of the reporter, who may be too old to find another job on a newspaper; for him it really is one of a kind, since he'll probably never get another like it. But there is an argument to the contrary, namely that one job is pretty much like another, and that the young executive could find a comparable job or go into another line of work, and that the reporter probably could find a nonnewspaper job. In any event, the court may well hesitate to say that either job is unique, if only to avoid the enforcement problems. As we noted at the outset, the law doesn't like to bite off more than it can chew.

All right, suppose our employees say they don't want specific performance of their job contracts; they say that the last thing in the world they'd do at this point is go back to work for their miserable old bosses. They want money damages. Very well, how much? The executive wants damages to cover lost wages and the moving expenses he incurred after taking a job in another city. Since these damages can be quantified and proved fairly easily, and since they resulted from the firing, he has a good chance to recover.

Our reporter, however, presents the court with a sadder story. He claims that to support himself he has taken a job as a night watchman. As damages, he wants to be paid the difference between his old salary and his somewhat meager new salary for as long as it takes him to get another newspaper job. Can he recover? The answer is that if his contract was for a specific period, such as a year, then he can. The court simply would award him his salary over that period, less his earnings on the new job, since that would put him back in the position he would have been in if the newspaper hadn't violated the contract. But if the contract was open-ended, he might have trouble getting damages, since there would be no limit on how long and how much he could recover. After all, who knows when he'd get another job as a reporter, or if he'd really try to find one. In effect, damages would be speculative, and as we have seen, they must be reasonably certain in order to be recoverable. The chances are he would get something, but it might be a bit of a crap shoot if the case went to trial.

* * *

Thus far we've assumed that the employer breached a provision in the contract by firing the employee. But what if the contract is silent, or ambiguous, on the question of when and under what circumstances the employee can be discharged? Keep in mind that this often is the case. People tend to be careless about these things and the oral arrangement may well not have covered termination without cause. So what is the court to do if the employee comes before it seeking damages? In deciding a dispute arising out of a contract, the judge is supposed to read it, and then be guided by the parties' intention as expressed in the document. But in our situation the parties never agreed on what would happen in the situation that eventually came up. So how does the court rule?

The answer is that if no provision of the contract specifically prevents him from doing so, the court assumes the employer can fire the employee whenever he wants, with or without cause. This is based on the view that the employer has the basic right to decide who will work for him, and so, absent a promise otherwise (and subject to the laws against discrimination), can hire and fire at his sole discretion. If the employee does not want to risk being fired without cause, then he or she must bargain with the employer before taking the job to get some assurance that it won't happen. Should the employer refuse to give that assurance, the employee is free to go find another job.

If this analysis, with its emphasis on the freedom of the parties to contract and of employers to choose their own work force, seems reasonable to you, consider the following two situations:

You've worked as a valve washer in a factory for more than twenty-nine years. You're not a unionized employee; instead you have a contract that prescribes your wages and grants you a pension of two-thirds pay after thirty years' service, and that's all it says. Let's say that six months before you've earned the pension you're fired. Why? No reason given. Just clean out your locker and be off the premises by the end of the day.

Or you're a salesman for a computer company. Your contract calls for a base salary and a commission on sales. For the past eight months you've been negotiating with a Wall Street brokerage house to sell them a new computer system to handle their expanding data-processing needs. It will be a huge sale, the largest in your company's history, and will earn you a correspondingly large commission. Two weeks before the sale is to be formally closed, the sales manager tells you you're fired. So long job; also, so long commission.

In both cases, the employee stands to lose more than a job; he will also lose a benefit — a pension in one case, a commission in the other — that he already has substantially earned. Once again, we are dealing with termination without cause, except we can guess easily enough that the reason for the firing was to avoid paying the employee his benefit.

Can a court do anything? Both contracts are silent on the question of termination. Will the law take its traditional position and say that absent a provision prohibiting this sort of thing, the employer can get away with it? Until recently, the answer was yes, he could, and the employee would be out of luck. But the basic unfairness of the result has led some people to doubt its validity. At the very least, it has been suggested that we re-examine the old rule that assumes the employer can fire without cause.

Before looking at how the law might be revised in this area, let's consider a very important aspect of these two cases: In each there is a simple remedy — just award the employee the money value of the benefit. The commission could be paid in a lump sum, and the pension could be paid out over its original period under the court's direction, much as a court enforces alimony payments. There is no need for any significant court supervision, nor is there any impairment of the freedom of association of the employers. Thus any legal theory that can be advanced to help the employee is greatly strengthened by the court's ability to provide an effective remedy.

Three approaches might be used to protect the employee. The first is to imply a covenant of good faith in the employment contract. Remember how courts imply a covenant by an employee not to work for a competitor? Well, here they go again. The covenant of good faith says in effect: "We each agree to deal with each other in good faith — or with basic fairness and honesty — in interpreting and acting under the terms of this agreement." So when the employer fires the employee just to do him out of a benefit he's really earned, he violates the covenant of good faith. Having violated the contract, he is liable to the employee for damages, and so must pay him the value of the benefit.

A second approach is for the court to say that the firing violates a public policy — an important principle designed to protect the public good. The problem is finding a public policy that might apply to our examples (a mere injustice won't do; there must be a definite policy involved, usually one expressed in a statute). There have been a number of cases in which an employer has been held liable, either for breach of contract or in tort, for firing an employee for refusing to do something illegal, such as filing false reports or committing perjury. But our examples don't involve anything like that. A recent case, however, said there could be a violation of public policy if an employer systematically fired employees before their pensions vested. The court noted that federal and state laws regulating pensions reflected a significant public policy that they vest properly. So our valve washer might be in good shape if he could bring his case in a court that agrees with this decision. It doesn't help our salesman, however, since there is no comparable regulation of salesmen's commissions.

A third, and very theoretical, approach is to assume that the parties didn't fully negotiate the employment contract, either because there wasn't time or because they didn't stop to consider the more unpleasant circumstances that might arise. For example, suppose that twenty-nine years ago the factory owner had said to the valve washer: "By the way, when you've put in twenty-eight or twenty-nine years' service, there's a good chance we'll fire you to prevent your collecting on your pension. I'm not saying for sure that we'll do it; we'll have to consider our profit picture and see if we really need you, but keep in mind that it's a real possibility." Upon hearing this, our young valve washer might well either have gotten some assurance against this happening, or looked for another job.

Of course, this dialogue never actually took place. But perhaps it should have as part of a complete bargaining process in which both sides had the time to think everything through. So why not let the court supply the terms that the employer and employee left out? Common sense tells us that no one would agree to be gypped out of his pension, or that a prospective employer would expect him to. Since it's reasonable to suppose that the employee would have asked for a provision in the contract against its happening, the law should assume he did and give it to him in the name of fairness. Once we do that, we can say that the employer violated that term of the contract and is liable in damages.

* * *

Question: Can the public-policy, the good-faith, or the fill-in-the-blanks-in-the-contract approach be used in termination situations other than when the employee is being cheated out of a benefit like a pension or commission? How about our earlier examples of the executive and the newspaper reporter? They were just fired — the injustice lay in their losing jobs they had done well. Suppose their contracts had been silent on the issue of termination without cause, and so they had to rely on these new-fangled approaches to get relief from the court?

The answer is that these approaches don't work so well when there's no single benefit that the employee is being done out of. It's harder to find a definite public policy than it was in the pension situation. (One cause suggests there is a public policy in people not being fired in bad faith, but subsequent cases have declined to go that far.) As to good faith, even if we imply this covenant, we'd have a hard time saying that it necessarily extended to not firing the employee to make room for a relative, or for a younger and lower-paid replacement. Similarly, we can't be as sure as we were in the pension or commission situation that the employee would not have accepted the job with these risks attached. Remember, the court has to be guided by the intention of the parties. And when the situation becomes more ambiguous, it is more difficult for the court to figure out what they intended. If the court goes ahead to force the result it thinks is fair, it may be rewriting the contract, and once this can be done, the freedom of people to make their own agreements will be impaired.

Against the risk of impinging upon this freedom, the law would have to balance the amount of good that would be accomplished. As we have seen, even if the court finds a breach of the contract, it may be unable to supply much of a remedy. Specific performance would present difficulties, and damages could be limited to interim expenses and lost wages before the employee found another job. Although it's difficult to predict how the law will develop in this area, it would not be surprising if these new approaches were used sparingly, basically to remedy the truly egregious situation in which the employee is being cheated out of something he already has all but earned.

*　*　*

The law's reluctance to grant specific performance of job contracts reflects a common-sense notion of its own limitations. The law is a blunt instrument for controlling the actions of people in the employment situation, particularly when the services involve the special talents or skills of the worker. One reason for the creation of the courts of equity was the unwillingness or inability of the traditional law courts to do more than award damages. But even equity will not order Johnny Carson to be funny or Chuck Fairbanks to win football games —

that's just too much to expect a court to enforce. Nor, as a rule, will it tell employers to take back discharged employees — again the enforcement problems are too great.

Robert Browning wrote in *Andrea del Sarto,* "Ah, but a man's reach should exceed his grasp,/Or what's a heaven for?" But the law is a bit less adventuresome. Rather, courts think they'd better not reach for more than they can get a hold of and hang on to.

POINT OF LAW:
Judicial Activism versus Judicial Restraint

"Judicial tyranny!"
"The judges are running the country!"
"Impeach Earl Warren!"

How often in the last twenty years have you heard or read angry comments like these? Ever since the early years of the Warren Supreme Court, the judiciary has been increasingly sensitive to the rights of individuals and been willing to expand the constitutional guarantees of due process and equal protection. In many quarters this has been greeted by loud complaints about judicial activism.

The concern is hardly an abstract one. It reflects a fear and a distaste for the direction taken by the Supreme Court during these years in deciding a series of cases that profoundly affect how we all live. As the Court recognized the rights of blacks and other minorities to equality and first-class citizenship, gave meaning to the procedural rights of those accused of crime, announced that every person's vote should be weighted the same, and expanded a host of other civil liberties, various individuals and organizations felt threatened by what they perceived as judicial intrusions on their own rights and prerogatives. The Court was accused of "coddling criminals" and losing the war against crime by handcuffing the police. Whites in various parts of the country fought desegregation, especially school busing, and blamed judges for destroying quality education and the neighborhood-school concept. Legislators and powerful interest groups tried to torpedo court-ordered reapportionment by dragging their feet and taking half measures.

Throughout this period, the opponents of judicial activism charged that the courts had bitten off more than they could chew and, worse yet, had invaded the province of other organs of government — the legislature, the executive and administrative agencies. Some even

voiced fears about the ability of our system of checks and balances to
survive these continued judicial intrusions.

You might well ask why judges who are afraid to order Johnny
Carson to be funny for NBC or to make Chuck Fairbanks coach the
Patriots would be so cavalier about directing the busing of thousands
of schoolchildren in a big city, running a statewide prison system, or
supervising mental health institutions. After all, who selected them to
do these things? Most judges aren't elected, and very little in most of
their backgrounds suggests they have the competence to handle these
jobs!

In part the answer lies in the fact that the very bigness of the stakes
obliges the courts to "try harder" — to expend their energies to arrive
at a just result. The importance of the social issues brought before
them led the nation's judges to reach deep into their equity pockets
and draw upon centuries of experience in framing and enforcing judicial decrees. And let's face it, one major reason for this activism has
been the reluctance or refusal of other branches of government to do
these difficult and unpopular jobs. Legislatures are unwilling to reap-
portion themselves; school boards find it difficult to achieve desegregation; and governors and prison officials find subjects such as prison
reform distasteful and politically unprofitable. Feeling duty-bound to
give meaning to the Constitution, judges have filled the vacuum
created by the inability or unwillingness of other governmental entities
to do their jobs. By and large the judiciary has gotten precious little
thanks for its efforts.

But there's no doubt that the judicial activism of the 1960s and early
1970s has created a reaction against the courts roughly comparable to
the one we are witnessing in the political arena. With the advent of the
Nixon Supreme Court (Chief Justice Burger and Justices Blackmun,
Powell, and Rehnquist were all appointed by him), the pendulum
began to swing away from activism toward restraint, a trend that is
bound to continue during the Reagan years. This trend is confirmed
by examining the work product of the Supreme Court during its most
recent — the 1980–1981 — term. The Court's increased willingness to
defer to society's other institutions and its growing restraint are illustrated by a number of its decisions: It upheld the deal struck by Presi-
dents Carter and Reagan with Iran for exchanging that country's fro-
zen assets for American hostages; it honored Congress's decision to
treat men and women differently for draft registration purposes; it
went along with Minnesota's decision to ban plastic milk containers;
it refused to second-guess prison officials who responded to over-
crowding by putting two inmates in cells initially built for one; and it

validated the State Department's decision to revoke the passport of someone deemed a threat to the nation's security — CIA antagonist Philip Agee.

But beware — judicial restraint raises its own set of problems. Even those who cried out against the incursions of the Warren Court may yearn for the judicial activism of the past if they personally find themselves ignored or oppressed by the other institutions of society. To a certain extent, what constitutes an unwarranted intrusion by the courts turns on whose ox is being gored.

9

PRODUCTS LIABILITY:

Must the Buyer Beware?

FIRESTONE TIRES, Ford Pintos, asbestos hair dryers, Rely tampons. What do these products bring to mind? Highway blowouts, fiery crashes, cancer, and toxic shock syndrome perhaps? They share the dubious distinction of having made the news as things that are claimed to be dangerous to consumers.

Products liability is the term used to describe the field of law concerned with determining whether people who are injured by defective products should be compensated. Of course, the law also is concerned with *preventing* product-related accidents; there are federal, state, and local laws that regulate everything from the quality of food and drugs to the flame resistance of fabrics. But elaborate as this network of safety requirements is, some unreasonably — and often unforeseeably — hazardous products inevitably fall through the regulatory gaps and end up in the marketplace, where they injure unwitting consumers. Let's explore the law's response to these injury-causing products; but first, a little history.

* * *

The term *products liability* is relatively new to the law. Before last century's Industrial Revolution, the Latin maxim *caveat emptor,* "Let the buyer beware," summarized the attitude of the law regarding product-related injuries. Unless he could prove that the seller had acted fraudulently (as by intentionally concealing a large crack in a buggy axle with grease) or that the seller had falsely warranted the soundness of the goods (as by stating that a flimsy ladder is "made from the strongest hickory"), the buyer of defective or dangerous goods generally had no recourse against the immediate seller. His own eyes were his best protection and the law expected him to use them.

The law's indifference to the injured purchaser's plight perhaps was justified in the days when life was lived close to the soil and people did not have to rely on others in order to meet their basic needs. Of course, people did turn to traders and peddlers for items they couldn't grow or make themselves, but these dealings were done on a face-to-face basis, giving the buyer ample opportunity to inspect the goods and satisfy himself as to their soundness before the purchase. And since the item purchased was likely to be no more complicated than a bolt of fabric or a handsaw, it made sense to charge the buyer with the burden of inspecting his bargain before the purchase. Anyone who bought a three-legged horse had only himself to blame.

But as the pace of technology quickened, and products became more complex and specialized, the old rule began to seem a little harsh. Today's consumer, faced with a bewildering array of alluringly packaged and aggressively advertised merchandise, can hardly be expected to find the defects in a product or to understand the possible harmful qualities of what he is buying. Sure, you can test-drive a car before you buy it, kick the tires, and poke around under the hood all you like, but if you're like most people, you still won't be able to tell if you're buying a lemon or, worse, a dangerous vehicle. And in many modern commercial transactions, you don't even have a *chance* to examine what you're getting. For example, when you purchase an airplane ticket, the reservation agent doesn't ask you if you'd like to inspect the plane before taking off, and even if he did, the opportunity would be useless unless you happen to be an expert in a dozen or more technologies.

The law held fast to the caveat emptor principle for some time, even though its major premise (that the buyer could adequately protect himself by examining the goods) no longer held water. Part of the reason for the perseverance of the rules was the traditional Anglo-American reliance on "precedent," which simply means adherence to the existing legal doctrines announced by the courts to give them stability and predictability. (You might recall that Chapter 1, School Prayer, provided an illustration of the effects of precedent.) But part of the reason was also that the rule was a convenient fiction that had the result of encouraging and protecting fledgling industries and promoting free enterprise. Even the judges of the United States Supreme Court were not above using the caveat emptor principle to further these objectives, for they said in an 1870 case that the rule "requiring the purchaser to take care of his own interests, has been found best adapted to the wants of trade in the business transactions of life."

However, when it finally became clear that the profusion of new and complex products on the market had the unfortunate consequence of increasing the accident toll, the policy of promoting industrial expansion had to give way to the policy of protecting human life and limb.

The law responded by slowly chipping away at the old precedents; more and more exceptions were carved out from the basic rule, and an increasing number of cases were found to fall within the exceptions. The result has been a shift in the law 180 degrees away from caveat emptor: The *seller* now has a duty to watch out for and guard against potential hazards associated with the use of his product. And sometimes the seller will be held liable to a person injured by his product, *even though the seller's behavior was entirely reasonable.* But that's getting ahead of ourselves. Let's use a real case to trace the development of products-liability law.

*   *   *

Picture yourself as a lawyer. You practice in a small city with two other lawyers who were your law-school classmates. One morning after you've just settled down at your desk with a cup of coffee, two new clients walk through your door. They introduce themselves as the McCormacks and proceed to tell you their story.

About a year ago, they bought an electric steam vaporizer from a neighborhood druggist for use in the bedroom of their two children, Andrea, three years old, and Alison, almost two. They had used the vaporizer for several months without mishap until one night, Andrea knocked it over on her way to the bathroom. Scalding water spilled out, severely burning her. Since the accident, Andrea has undergone three skin-graft operations and has been hospitalized for eighty-seven days. Her head movements are restricted and will be for the rest of her life. Her face is permanently scarred.

The McCormacks then ask you whether they can recover from the manufacturer of the vaporizer for Andrea's medical expenses and for the injuries she suffered. They don't want to sue the druggist, who is an old family friend with limited resources.

*   *   *

If this were 1915, it would be easy to answer the McCormacks with a categorical no. In those days, the law said that an injured buyer could only recover from the one who had sold him the goods. Or, to put it in legal jargon, the parties to the suit had to be in "privity of contract." The privity requirement represented a policy determination that the manufacturer's liability should be limited somehow; it was thought that if manufacturers could be held liable to *anyone* who was injured by their products, this threat of liability would hinder the growth of industry and commerce because manufacturers wouldn't risk innovation in design or experimentation with new product lines.

All of this changed, however, in 1916 when New York's highest court considered a case involving a man who was thrown from his car when one of its wheels collapsed because of a defect. The injured driver sued the manufacturer of the car, the Buick Motor Company. But there was a dealer between the car purchaser and Buick, and that was what the controversy was about. The privity rule said that except in cases involving "inherently dangerous" products such as poisons, drugs, explosives, and guns, an intervening resale by a retailer "insulated" the manufacturer from direct liability. The only way a "remote purchaser," like the Buick owner, could circumvent the privity requirement was by suing the dealer, who in turn could sue *his* seller, but this was of no use to the injured buyer if the dealer didn't have enough money to pay the judgment or was a good friend, like the McCormack's neighborhood druggist.

At the time of the Buick case, the privity requirement had come under increasing attack by forward-looking legal scholars. They argued that in a world of mass-produced and nationally marketed goods that passed from manufacturer to distributor to retailer before finally reaching the consumer, the rule just didn't make sense anymore. When Buick, for example, sells cars to a dealer, it certainly knows that the dealer is not going to use them itself. The Buick Company *expects* and *intends* that the cars will be resold to consumers. Why should Buick be liable if it sold the car directly to the injured driver, and not liable if it sold the car to a dealer, knowing that the dealer will resell it? they asked. In either case, Buick has sold a defective car. Moreover, these visionary writers argued, by placing its cars on the market and advertising them for sale, Buick assumes a responsibility to ensure that these machines are reasonably safe. And finally, however desirable it may be to encourage industrial expansion and experimentation, it cannot be good social policy to do so in a way that encourages disregard for human safety.

These arguments fell on receptive ears in the Buick case. The court, in an opinion by a very famous judge, Benjamin Cardozo, who later sat on the United States Supreme Court, allowed the injured driver to recover from Buick, even though he was not in privity of contract with Buick. With this precedent on the books, other judges were quick to follow suit, and today the privity requirement is a thing of the past. The field is wide open now; not only is the class of defendants not limited to immediate sellers, but the class of people who may sue is not limited to actual buyers of the product. Any ultimate consumer of the product who is injured during its use may recover. Innocent by-standers may sue as well. Thus, the pedestrian who gets creamed when a car suddenly veers off the road because of a defective steering mechanism can sue anyone in the manufacturing and distribution chain whose negligence caused the accident.

* * *

But the McCormacks aren't interested in all this ancient history. What do you tell them? Like most questions clients ask their lawyers, their inquiry has only one correct answer: "It depends." The story they've just told you is certainly a sad one and you feel very sympathetic, but you know that the law does not provide redress based upon sympathy alone. The law needs a *theory,* and in order to build a theory, you need more facts. But knowing that the McCormacks will not be happy with an "it depends" answer, you explain that there are basically three ways to win a products-liability case.

One is to prove that the defendant was negligent, or that it failed to use reasonable care at some stage in the design, manufacture, or sale of the product. Another possibility is to sue for breach of warranty, which requires proof that the defendant made some statements about the product that turned out to be false. The third theory, called strict liability, requires proof that the product was "defective" and "unreasonably dangerous." To succeed under any one of these theories, you explain, will require a lot of digging into the facts. The vaporizer company's manufacturing and advertising methods will have to be looked into, a comparison of the McCormack's vaporizer with the ones made by other companies should be undertaken, and testimony from product-design engineers may be required.

Your clients seem a bit daunted by the news that what they thought was a simple case of a dangerous vaporizer that had injured their daughter severely is much more complicated than that, but they decide they want to continue to explore legal action anyway.

After weeks of investigation and questioning of the various parties involved, the following facts come to light:

The vaporizer consists of three parts: an aluminum base, a one-gallon glass jar (or water reservoir) that is inserted into the base, and a plastic cap to which is attached a tube containing the heating element. To operate the device, the glass jar is filled with water and the plastic top rests on the neck of the jar with the heating tube extending down into the jar. Water from the jar enters the heating unit through a small hole in its lower section. There it is heated until it boils and escapes through a hole in the top.

Within one hour of operation, the water in the heating chamber reaches 212° and the water in the glass jar reaches temperatures upwards of 172°. Water of 140° will burn a small child. However, a user of the vaporizer could not determine by sight that the water in the reservoir reached scalding temperatures, and no warning of that fact was included in the instruction booklet that came with the device. In fact, from the explanation in the instruction booklet, a user reasonably might conclude that, since steam was generated only in the heating core, the water in the reserve bowl remained at room temperature.

To guard against the possibility of an explosion from the build-up of steam, the cap and heating unit could not be fastened securely to the jar in a manner that would prevent the water from spilling out instantaneously when the vaporizer was overturned. Although this design was not necessary to accomplish the purpose of preventing an explosion, many other brands of vaporizers on the market at the time were designed in basically the same way.

The spill hazard could have been eliminated by the adoption of a simple, practical design that would have fastened the plastic top securely to the jar.

The vaporizer was advertised as "tip-proof." The instruction booklet stated that it was "safe" and "practically foolproof."

The vaporizer could be upset by a force of about two pounds.

Prior to Andrea's accident, at least ten to twelve children had been burned in the same manner as she was. The manufacturer was aware of these accidents.

Now what? Where do you go from here? Being a very careful and conscientious lawyer, you decide to try to build a case for Andrea under all three theories of liability: negligence, breach of warranty, and strict liability. As one of your law professors explained it, each theory is like an arrow that you shoot at your opponent. One arrow is sufficient to win the suit, but in case it doesn't fly, or your opponent dodges it, it's always better to have some other arrows in your quiver.

You select your first arrow — negligent design. It seems to you that a device for boiling water that's intended to be used around children but has no safety feature to guard against spills is downright dangerous. And you think that a reasonable manufacturer should have known of that danger. That, basically, is the definition of negligence: conduct that a reasonable person should recognize creates an unreasonable risk of harm to others.

Your problem is to convince the jury that you're right. What will you say to them? It *might* go something like this:

"Ladies and gentlemen of the jury, the law says that a manufacturer must design a product that is reasonably safe for its intended or foreseeable uses. Now, you don't have to be an engineer or know anything about product design in order to find that this vaporizer was not reasonably safe for its intended use. The facts speak for themselves. A vaporizer boils water to generate steam. Its primary intended use is in the treatment of children's colds. It is meant to be left unattended in children's rooms. Ladies and gentlemen, I ask you, did this manufacturer exercise reasonable care when it designed this device in a way that the boiling water spills out instantaneously when the unit is tipped over?

"And remember, ladies and gentlemen, this manufacturer didn't have to stretch its imagination very far to foresee how an accident might happen. It *knew* that at least a dozen children already had been burned before Andrea's accident.

"And what's more, these tragic accidents could have been avoided had the defendant adopted one of the inexpensive alternative designs that would have secured the top to the jar and prevented the water from escaping.

"Ladies and gentlemen, it's your job to evaluate this evidence, but I suggest that when you consider the foreseeability of an accident and the feasibility of an alternative design that would minimize the harm from that accident, the conclusion is inescapable that this vaporizer was negligently designed."

So ends your brilliant summation in front of your bathroom mirror. But histrionics aside, is your analysis correct? Your statement that a product must be reasonably safe for its foreseeable uses is accurate, but troublesome. For assuming that "reasonably safe" does not mean "accident-proof," just what does it mean? How safe does a product have to be to avoid being branded negligently made or designed? For example, is a bulldozer that is intended to move backward negligently designed if it's impossible for the operator to see a person standing anywhere from one to forty-eight feet behind him in the direct path of the machine? Suppose the danger could be reduced substantially by the installation of rearview mirrors and blinking back-up lights or a warning noise?

Courts confronted with questions like these have not found answers easy to come by. They often resolve the case by balancing the likelihood of harm from a product and the magnitude of the loss that may result against the cost of the precautions necessary to avoid the risk. Thus, applying this risk-benefit analysis to a bulldozer that ran over the man standing in the blind spot behind it, the Supreme Court of California decided that the manufacturer had violated its duty to design a reasonably safe product. The court was persuaded that the accident could have been prevented by the simple and relatively inexpensive expedient of installing mirrors or flashing lights.

It appears, then, that the rough risk-benefit calculations that you performed in your practice argument to the jury were on the right track. But is there anything you left out? What about the fact that your client's vaporizer was no more dangerous than many other vaporizers on the market at the time? Since your opponent almost certainly will draw this to the jurors' attention, you should be prepared to remind them that it is their duty to decide what is reasonable and that compliance with industry standards is relevant on this issue, but it is not dispositive. A whole industry may have dragged its feet in the adoption of new and available safety devices. You should point out that if they allow the defendant to get off the hook merely by proving it was acting in accordance with industry custom, the members of the industry could set their own standards and those standards might be dangerously low.

This principle was announced in a famous negligence case in which a cargo-laden barge that was being pulled by a tugboat sank during a storm off the New Jersey coast. The cargo owner sued the tug owner on the ground that, had the tug been equipped with a radio, the crew would have known about the impending storm and would have averted the disaster by seeking shelter. The court agreed and held the tug owner liable despite the fact that at the time — 1932 — radios were still rather new-fangled devices and not yet commonly carried by coastal vessels. No doubt the court was influenced in its decision by a desire to encourage the industry to adopt the latest safety devices available.

Anticipating that the defendant will try to establish that the real cause of the accident was the McCormacks' failure to place the vaporizer in a safe spot, you have questioned the couple extensively about their handling of the device. In the course of one of these conversations, you learn that they always used the same procedure to replenish the water in the vaporizer: They removed the plastic cover with a potholder-type glove as a protection against the steam, poured water into the jar, and replaced the cap. They understood from the explanation in the instruction booklet that the water was heated only after it passed into the cap and heating-chamber assembly, and since they always wore a protective glove while changing the water, neither of them ever discovered that the water in the reserve jar also became very hot.

After hearing this explanation, it suddenly occurs to you that had the instruction booklet warned that *all* of the water in the device reached scalding temperatures, perhaps they wouldn't have bought it in the first place or would have taken other precautions. And it seems that the manufacturer should have known that some people might be misled by the absence of a warning and that this would increase the risk of a mishap. Is this a good case for charging the manufacturer with negligent failure to warn?

In failure-to-warn cases courts typically engage in the same kind of risk-benefit calculations as in negligent-design cases. However, because it's so easy and inexpensive to increase the safety of a product by including instructions and warnings about using it carefully, as long as the harm is only slightly foreseeable, the calculus almost always comes out in favor of giving the warning. Thus, even though a manufacturer is not negligent in using a certain design, it may be held negligent for failing to warn of the product's hazards.

Consider the case of Mrs. Boyl. She bought a can of weed killer, a major ingredient of which was arsenic, a compound that is very long lasting and can enter the blood stream by absorption through the skin, inhalation, or ingestion. The container bore a skull and crossbones on the front and back, as well as directions for the prevention of personal injury while using the weed killer. It described an antidote for internal ingestion, but gave no warning about the long-lasting quality of the poison. There were no instructions about how to dispose of the product safely after use, save for directions to wash the container thoroughly and destroy it when empty. After reading the labels, Mrs. Boyl donned protective clothing — a scarf, gloves, and a long-sleeved shirt — and proceeded to spray the cracks in her driveway. When finished, she rinsed out the container and dumped the residue on a rough grass area in her back yard. Five days later, dressed in a bathing suit, Mrs. Boyl lay stomach down for a sun-bathing session on the grassy area where she had poured out the rinse water. Shortly thereafter, she became critically ill from skin absorption and inhalation of the weed killer. In the lawsuit that followed, the court held the manufacturer of the weed killer liable for failure to warn of the lingering risk from contact with earth that had been contaminated with the weed killer.

In the *Boyl* case, the court came down very hard on the foreseeability-of-harm factor in holding the manufacturer liable for failure to warn. But notice that it did not say that the manufacturer was negligent in selling such a dangerous product: The only negligence was selling it without sufficient notice of the danger. Is requiring manufacturers to warn of the latent hazards of their products the perfect solution to the product-safety problem, then? It decreases the risk of injury to consumers without putting manufacturers out of business. Right? Not so fast. There are other factors to consider.

One is that even when some harm is foreseeable, it doesn't necessarily follow that a warning always must be given. What about this case?

Research by the Consumer Product Safety Commission has shown that adults who slide headfirst down swimming-pool slides into shallow water face a one in ten million risk of hitting the bottom of the pool and becoming paralyzed. Taking into account that the risk of being killed by lightning is greater than this, is it negligent not to warn? The probability of injury is very slight, but this perhaps is counterbalanced by the severity of the harm (paralysis) that may result. What about the burden of precautions necessary to prevent the harm? A warning sign is cheap, but there may be costs associated with it other than the cost of making it. That is, if the duty to warn is imposed too indiscriminately, and we are surrounded by signs, the warnings will be ignored as overly alarmist. How effective, for example, is the warning on cigarette packages that the surgeon general has determined that smoking is dangerous to your health? And, more important, manufacturers may think their duty to supply a reasonably safe product is discharged by tacking on a warning label rather than producing a more careful design.

* * *

You have to take a break one afternoon from your research on the vaporizer case to go to a pretrial settlement conference for another client, Joe Johnson. Joe's case is a rather strange one. He stormed into your office one day waving a newspaper clipping that he thrust in front of you, saying, "I want to sue these bastards." The clipping was a full-page illustrated ad for "Fatted Fowl Boned Chicken." It featured a picture of a package of Fatted Fowl's chicken and the description:

> Fatted Fowl Boned Chicken. All luscious white and dark meat. No bones. No waste. Fatted Fowl's — finest chicken in the land. Chosen by poultry experts. Specially bred and fed. Fatted Fowl cooked to juicy perfection!

It seems that this advertisement had prompted Joe to go out and buy a package of the chicken. And while enjoying his "Fatted Fowl Boned Chicken" in front of the TV set one night, a bone suddenly lodged in his throat, necessitating a trip to the hospital and substantial medical expenses.

You arrive at the conference and find the other attorneys waiting — one from the Fatted Fowl Company and one from the supermarket that sold Joe the chicken. You open the meeting with an offer to settle for $10,000. Shaking his head, the lawyer for Fatted Fowl says: "The Fatted Fowl Company is very sorry about the bone that almost choked Mr. Johnson, but we think we've done all we can reasonably be expected to do in order to ensure that our chickens are bone free. We

use the most modern equipment and techniques available for debon-
ing our chickens and inspecting the packages before they leave the
plant. The Fatted Fowl Company was not negligent; the bone in Johnson's chicken was just a fluke, and we are confident that the jury will
agree."

The lawyer for the supermarket also refuses to settle, citing cases
that say that a supplier of goods made by a third party is not liable for
the injuries caused by the product, unless it knew or had reason to
know the product was dangerous.

Now it's your turn to speak. "What about breach of warranty?" you
ask.

The Fatted Fowl lawyer's eyebrows arch. "What warranty? We never
guaranteed to anybody that our chickens were bone free."

You open your briefcase and remove the newspaper ad and point to
the part that says "No bones." You take out a package of Fatted Fowl
and point to the label "Fatted Fowl Boned Chicken."

The Fatted Fowl lawyer begins to sputter. "But those aren't warranties. You only have a warranty when there is some sort of promise
about the quality of the goods — like the Midas muffler lifetime guarantee. We didn't promise anything."

"Look," you respond, "you represented, both in your advertisements and in the name of your product, that your chickens were bone-
less. My client relied on that; he read your ads and they induced him
to try your product. And he almost choked to death because of them.
I think we have an open and shut case. If you're not prepared to settle
at $10,000, perhaps we'll get more from the jury."

The Fatted Fowl lawyer doesn't capitulate immediately, but asks for
an adjournment of the meeting until the following week. By that time,
he apparently has done his homework, because you shake hands on a
settlement for pretty close to what you asked for.

* * *

Nice work. Can you pull the same move in the vaporizer case? After
all, it was advertised as "tip-proof," and the instruction booklet said
it was "safe" and "practically foolproof." Do those statements amount
to a warranty?

A buyer suing for breach of warranty doesn't have to show that the
seller acted unreasonably, but merely that the seller made statements
— representations — about the goods, which the buyer relied on, and
that those statements turned out to be false. In other words, the buyer
need only show that the goods were not all they were cracked up to
be, regardless of any fault on the seller's part.

The seller's statement may arise from an assertion of fact or a promise about the goods (for example, a tag attached to a garment announcing that it is "shrinkproof"). Or, the statement may be a description of the goods ("boned chicken"), or a sample or model (for example, a store's use of a stereo as a floor model would be a warranty that other stereos of the same model are as good as the sample).

Does this mean that a warranty is created every time a seller says anything at all about the goods to the buyer? Not quite. The law allows sellers some leeway in touting their products. A statement that purports merely to be the vendor's opinion about the goods is considered a "sales puff" or "seller's talk," and does not create a warranty. But it's often hard to draw the line between opinions and statements of fact. For instance, when Sam Sleaze, the used-car dealer, says, "I've got a great little car for you," and you buy the car based on his recommendation and drive yourself into a ditch because the brakes are bad, you may not be able to recover from Sam for breach of warranty. His statement sounds like a sales pitch, but on the other hand, since the defect was hidden and you were relying on Sam's superior knowledge about cars, a court *might* find that his words created a warranty.

Sometimes a warranty arises when the seller hasn't said anything at all; it may be implied from the mere fact that the manufacturer placed the goods on the market. Recall from Chapter 8, Job Contracts, that "implying" is what the law does when it supplies a provision to a contract that the parties meant to include but left out or that should be included as a matter of fairness. For example, when you part with some of your hard-earned money to buy a new car, at a minimum you expect that it will have four wheels, brakes, and a steering wheel. If it doesn't, it's not much good to you, or in the lingo of the law, it's not "merchantable." The warranty of merchantability is not a promise that the goods will be perfect; rather, it is a guarantee that they will be of passable quality or fit for the ordinary purpose for which they are used. Thus, a bag of apples that are slightly bruised is merchantable, but one filled with apples that have been contaminated by insecticide is not. The law implies a warranty of merchantability into every sale of goods by one who is in the business of selling such goods. In other words, this warranty does not apply when you sell a lamp that you made in your home workshop, assuming you're not in the lamp business.

But suppose the seller knows that the buyer has a particular purpose in mind and is relying on the seller's superior skill or judgment to furnish goods suitable for this purpose. In this situation, the law imposes another implied warranty — that the goods will be fit for that *particular* purpose. Take, for example, a woman who asks a shoe salesman to outfit her with boots for mountain climbing and the ones he recommends cause her to slip and fall down a mountain; the salesman will be in breach of the implied warranty of fitness for a particular purpose, even though the boots are fit for ordinary walking and thus are merchantable.

Okay, we've got express warranties, which arise from the seller's words or conduct, and implied warranties, which are imposed by the law in order to give effect to the unstated intention of the parties and principles of fairness. Does any of this apply to Andrea's case? You'd have to stretch a little to make the argument for breach of the implied warranty of fitness for a particular purpose because the McCormacks didn't buy the vaporizer for any particular purpose that was different from its ordinary purpose of humidifying children's rooms. What about the implied warranty of merchantability? Remember, merchantable means suitable for its ordinary purposes. This one is a closer question. The vaporizer was perfectly serviceable for its ordinary purpose of generating steam, but a product cannot be considered merchantable if it can't carry out its purpose safely. On the other hand, this vaporizer isn't as clearly unmerchantable as the bag of contaminated apples was; after all, the McCormacks had used it many times without incident before Andrea tipped it over.

Although the warranty of merchantability is more plausible than the other implied warranty, fitness for a particular purpose, your best lawyering bet is probably an express warranty claim — like the one you used in the bone-in-the-boneless-chicken case. The seller made untrue statements about the product ("safe," "practically foolproof," "tip-proof"), which the buyers relied on. Is that all there is to it? Not quite. One thing every good lawyer would do at this stage is anticipate the arguments that the vaporizer company will make against your breach-of-warranty theory.

One possibility is that the manufacturer "disclaimed" the warranty. A warranty may be disclaimed by an express clause in the sales contract ("seller's liability limited solely to replacement of the product or refund of the purchase price" — watch for that next time you send your vacation pictures in for processing), or by selling the product "as is," or by any other language that is commonly understood to mean that the buyer bears the risk as to the quality of the goods. For example, suppose Carla Consumer buys a cast-iron frying pan that is marked "Factory Second." The first time she uses it, the handle breaks off as she picks it up from the stove. The pan and the sizzling bacon in it fall to the floor and hot grease spatters on her legs, causing third-degree burns.

Let's analyze Carla's case. Is there an express warranty? No, the seller didn't promise that the handle wouldn't break off or describe it as "unbreakable." What about the implied warranty of merchantability? Lifting the pan while it contains hot food is an ordinary purpose for a frying pan and this pan clearly wasn't fit for it. But there's a catch: The "Factory Second" label operates as a disclaimer of liability, so our friend Carla probably will not be able to recover.

But to return to your vaporizer case, it doesn't look like the disclaimer defense will present a problem. The instruction booklet that came with the McCormack's vaporizer didn't say anything about disclaiming liability, and the box wasn't marked "as is." Are you in the clear, then? Not yet. Another requirement of warranty law is that the purchaser give the defendant notice of the breach of warranty within a reasonable time after he discovers or should have discovered the breach. The notice-of-the-breach requirement is a technicality that traps many unwary would-be claimants who don't know about the rule until it's too late. Suppose, for example, that Carl Consumer purchases a power tool that is a combination saw, drill, and wood lathe. While using the tool as a lathe, a piece of the wood he is working on suddenly flies out and hits him in the head, inflicting severe injuries. Carl does not notify the manufacturer or retailer until he files suit almost ten months later. Carl probably will lose his case because he didn't notify the defendant within a reasonable time.

Your clients the McCormacks may run afoul of the timely-notice-of-the-breach rule also. It never occurred to them to notify the vaporizer company until after they hired you, and that was almost a year after the accident. Does this mean that your warranty theory doesn't stand a chance of success? Not necessarily. The limitations on the breach-of-warranty theory grew up in the context of contracts between commercial buyers and sellers. The timely-notice requirement, in particular, was designed to prevent the buyer from delaying notification of the seller until it was too late to remedy the defect or minimize the damages. Since the reason for an injured consumer's delay in notification usually is ignorance of the law, not a desire to prejudice the defendant, courts usually are more lenient when a consumer fails to give timely notice. So although the strict letter of the law may be against you on this one, its growing consumerist spirit is on your side.

* * *

But there is still another arrow you can aim at your opponent — strict liability. This theory developed because the technical requirements of warranty law and the difficulty of proving negligence left many injured people without redress. The liability is called "strict" because the injured party does not have to prove that the defendant acted unreasonably. Nor does he have to worry about technicalities like timely notice and disclaimers of liability.

What is the justification for imposing liability on a manufacturer who has acted entirely reasonably, but whose product proves to have a defect that causes injury? The reason most often advanced is that the loss should fall on the party who is in the best position to prevent it. Lacking the specialized knowledge to assess the risk of being harmed by a product, the average consumer can't protect himself, and relies on the manufacturer to provide a reasonably safe product. Indeed, most manufacturers encourage this reliance in their advertising and marketing techniques. Moreover, manufacturers as a class are in a better position than individual consumers to absorb the costs of accidents or distribute them to the public by taking out insurance and adding that cost to their product's price. If a business finds that it *can't* absorb the costs of accidents caused by its products, or that adding that cost to the price of the product would make the product uncompetitive, then the business is not "paying its way" and society will not be worse off if it folds up. Finally, even if the manufacturer is entirely free from fault, it at least is responsible for the article being on the market, so as between it and the innocent purchaser, the manufacturer should bear the loss.

With all the burdensome problems of proof eliminated, does strict liability mean that all a plaintiff has to do is limp into court and announce that he's hurt in order to recover? It's not quite that easy. The accident victim has to show that he was hurt by a *defective* product that was *unreasonably dangerous.* He can't rely simply on proving that his car crashed; it may have crashed because he fell asleep at the wheel or because he was driving recklessly or because he swerved to avoid a child who ran into the road chasing a ball. He has to prove that something was wrong with the car that made it unreasonably dangerous to operate.

Defective condition, unreasonably dangerous — that sounds easy enough to understand. If you think so, test yourself on these cases. Are strawberries that may cause an allergic reaction in some people defective and unreasonably dangerous? What about a bottle of whiskey, which may cause delirium tremens in an alcoholic who drinks too much of it? All the courts and legal scholars agree that a manufacturer will not be liable in these cases because there is nothing defective about strawberries or whiskey, even though they in fact are dangerous to a number of people. Ironically, it's the allergic person or the alcoholic who is defective; there's nothing wrong with the product.

In practice, two tests have evolved for deciding whether a product is defective and unreasonably dangerous. One asks whether the product is more dangerous than an ordinary consumer who purchases it would expect. Under this test, a bowl of clam chowder that contains a bit of a clamshell probably will not support a strict liability claim, while a Coke bottle with a dead mouse in it will. Few consumers expect to find dead mice in their soda bottles, but a piece of shell in clam chowder does not seem quite so startling.

Another test that courts use to decide whether a product is defective and unreasonably dangerous asks whether the sale of the product created an unreasonable risk of harm to consumers. This test is similar to the one described earlier in connection with the negligence discussion. The two tests overlap but are not exactly the same. In the negligence context, we said that a defendant may be liable if he knew or should have known that he was selling an article that created an unreasonable risk of harm to others. Under strict liability, however, we don't care what the defendant knew or ought to have known. All we care about is whether he actually created an unreasonable risk of injury. The strict liability test is a more objective evaluation of the costs and benefits of the product because the seller's knowledge is irrelevant.

But strict liability does not mean that a manufacturer will be held liable *every time* its product causes harm. The risk still has to be unreasonable. This is when cost-benefit analysis comes into play. The risk of a mishap may exist but be so negligible that it's reasonable to sell the product. For instance, someone who slips and falls and is stabbed in the heart by a pencil he is carrying in a shirt pocket will not be able to recover against the pencil manufacturer. The risk of being stabbed by a pencil point is one we are willing to accept because the chances of its occurring are so slight and because the utility of the pencil is so great.

That last element is an important one. Liability may be avoided if the product, though dangerous, is of significant social utility. Rabies vaccine is an example of a product that falls into the latter category. The vaccine is known to cause very bad side effects in some people who are injected with it, but since the alternative is almost certain death, strict liability is not imposed on the vaccine manufacturer. Or, the change in design necessary to make the product safer may unduly impair its utility. For example, it may not be unreasonable to sell a power saw without a blade guard if the guard would make it impossible to perform common woodworking operations.

* * *

Having completed your research, you've filed a complaint against the vaporizer company alleging negligent design, negligent failure to warn, breach of express warranties, breach of the implied warranty of merchantability, and strict liability. A few weeks later, you receive the defendant's answer. It contains a whole list of defenses, some of which you're not too worried about — like compliance with industry standards and failure to give timely notice — and some of which will require some more thought.

Stripped of all its legal jargon, one of the worrisome defenses says: "Plaintiff is barred from recovery because any defect caused by defendant's failure to secure the top to the jar was obvious." What about that? The rule used to be that the manufacturer had no duty to guard or warn against "patent" dangers or ones known to the user. Although the manufacturer was answerable for latent defects in its products, it was free to make dangerous articles as long as the danger was obvious. For example, a glass-breaking machine with exposed moving parts that crushed a man's hand when he reached in to free a piece of glass was held not to be negligently designed, even though the machine had no safety guards or emergency cutoff switches. The court also held that the manufacturer was not negligent for failure to warn of the danger, saying: "We hardly think it necessary to tell an experienced factory worker that he should not put his hand into a machine that is at that moment breaking glass than it would be necessary to tell a zoo keeper to keep his head out of a hippopotamus's mouth." In another case, it was held that there was no duty to warn that slingshots can be lethal. "Ever since David slew Goliath, young and old alike have known that slingshots can be dangerous and deadly," said the court.

The rule precluding recovery for injury by a blatantly hazardous product basically is a historical artifact from the days of caveat emptor when the injured person had to prove that the defendant had misled him. That was pretty hard to do when the hazardous quality of the item was in plain view. But in this age of consumer protection, many courts have adopted the view that the obviousness of the danger does not automatically preclude recovery; it's just one of the factors to be considered. So even if the court finds that the vaporizer was openly dangerous and that Andrea's parents were negligent not to have realized it, that shouldn't be dispositive of the lawsuit. You might argue that even if the danger should have been obvious to the parents, it certainly couldn't have been obvious to a three-year-old child.

Before we dismiss the patent-danger doctrine as an unwelcome holdover from the Dark Ages when the law didn't give a hoot about injured consumers, it's important to realize that the rule is still worth preserving in some situations. After all, we don't want to require a manufacturer to warn of every conceivable mishap that may occur from using his product. What would you think of a law that decreed that the handles of all new hammers must bear the legend: "WARNING! This hammer may mash your thumb if misdirected"? Nor do we want to impose a duty on manufacturers to design absolutely accident-proof products. If we required that kitchen knives be blunt enough so as not to cut when dropped on a foot, they would be pretty useless.

In other words, we don't want the law to go overboard in its zeal for safety. Considerations of cost and utility must be given some weight. At the same time, we want to be sure that the maker of an electric saw accompanies its sale with warnings and instructions, and that it provides some type of safety guard. The hard cases are the ones that fall in between the kitchen knife and the power saw. In which category would you place a plastic champagne cork that flew out of a bottle when the restraining wire was partially loosened and hit the person opening the bottle in the eye, causing permanent loss of vision in that eye? Is it so commonly known that a champagne cork may pop suddenly in the process of opening the bottle that a bottler need not warn of that possibility? Or must it unaesthetically adorn the label?

* * *

"Plaintiff is barred from recovery because the vaporizer was unforeseeably misused by virtue of its placement in a spot where a child could tip it over." Thus reads the vaporizer company's next defense. The rule is that a manufacturer is not liable if its product is perfectly safe for its intended purposes, but the damage results from the consumer's use of it in a way that was not reasonably foreseeable. The law does not require the manufacturer to anticipate and warn or guard against *un*foreseeable misuses of its product. Thus, the maker of a chair should expect that someone may stand on it to reach a high shelf, but a shoemaker is entitled to assume that a customer will not wear shoes a size too small for her feet. And a butcher would not be liable to someone who bought a fresh steak from him and became ill after letting it sit out in the hot sun all day before barbecuing it. Nor would a soft-drink seller be liable to a consumer who knocked the bottle against a radiator to remove the cap and cut his hand.

Let's try some harder cases now:

Case 1: A four-year-old boy who wanted to see what was cooking on top of the stove opened the oven door and stood on it. His weight tipped over the stove, spilling simmering spaghetti sauce over him.

Case 2: A teen-age girl poured cologne on a lighted candle in order to make it scented. The candle burst into flames and burned her friend who was watching.

Is it stretching the limits of "reasonable foreseeability" to say that the stove maker should be held liable for designing a range that would fall over when the oven door was stood upon, or that the perfume company should have expected this use of its product and warned against it? In both cases, the *particular* misuse that occurred was easily imaginable. In Case 1, the stove manufacturer certainly should have contemplated that the oven door might be used as a shelf on which to baste a heavy turkey, for instance.

What about Case 2? Shouldn't the perfume maker have thought of the possibility that its cologne might be used in the proximity of an open flame, say from a match being used to light a cigarette, and warned against the danger?

In general, a manufacturer can be held liable even if it doesn't anticipate the precise details of a freak accident. It's enough that the general type of harm or manner of its occurrence is reasonably unforeseeable. Thus, in Case 1, the Rhode Island Supreme Court held the stove company liable because it should have foreseen the door's use as a shelf, a use that was very similar to the one that actually occurred. Likewise, in the flammable-perfume case, a Maryland court held Fabergé liable because it could have foreseen that in its normal home environment the cologne might come close enough to a flame to cause an explosion.

What about the vaporizer? It's hard to see how leaving it unattended in a child's room constitutes a misuse of the device, since that was precisely its intended use. The only way it could have been an unforeseeable misuse would be if it was set up on a spot that was so dangerous it just invited tipping over. You'll have to do some more investigating to make sure this wasn't so in the McCormacks' case.

* * *

"Plaintiff is barred from recovery because the injury was caused by the intervening conduct of plaintiff's mother in setting up the vaporizer in an unsafe spot, not by defendant's negligence or breach of warranty or by the defectiveness of its product." The defendant is right; it is not liable under any theory unless it was the *cause* of Andrea's injury. The point is so obvious, it's easy to overlook.

What does it mean to say that a manufacturer's behavior "caused" an event to happen? In legal terms, a defendant's behavior is a cause of an event if it wouldn't have occurred "but for" the defendant's behavior. The but-for test is easily satisfied in most cases. For example, is there any doubt about the cause of a person's becoming ill immediately after consuming a bottle of Coke with a dead mouse at the bottom? In many other cases, though, the causation requirement proves to be the stickler: A malfunctioning fire extinguisher is not the but-for cause of a blaze that already was too big when discovered for an extinguisher to be of any use. But if the fire had been detected shortly after it was started by a cigarette stub in a wastebasket and the extinguisher failed to work, the product's defect would be a but-for cause of the house burning down.

Another situation in which the but-for test will present a barrier to recovery is when the injury is the product of two independent causes, either one of which would have been sufficient to cause the injury. To illustrate, go back to that teen-age girl who tries to scent a burning candle by pouring perfume on it. She splashes some cologne on the candle, flames spring out, and her blouse and the nearby curtains catch fire. At the same time, her four-year-old brother is downstairs in the kitchen wondering what his mother is cooking for dinner. He opens the oven door, stands on it, the range tips over, and the flame from the gas ignites his toys on the floor. Both fires spread and together they destroy the entire house and everyone in the family. The truth is, either of the blazes would have done the same damage.

Both the perfume company and the stove maker will argue that although its product may have been defective in terms of a failure to warn or in its design, it should not be liable because the defect was not the but-for cause of the damage. Rather than let these two defendants who are both at fault escape liability on account of the fortuity that their respective products happened to prove defective at the same time, the law says that the causation requirement is satisfied if either one was a "substantial factor" in bringing about the harm.

Although there are cases that the but-for test does not reach — like the concurrent-cause cases — there are also cases that it does cover and shouldn't. Remember our mountain climber who relied on the shoe salesman's representation that the boots she bought were fit for mountain climbing? Suppose that while she was hiking with the new boots on, the climber's feet began to hurt, and she had to cut short her ascent. On the way back down the mountain, she was hit by a meteorite. Under the but-for causation test, the salesman's warranty that the shoes were fit for mountain climbing "caused" the climber's injury by the meteorite since she would not have been in that place at the time when the meteorite struck but for the salesman's breach of warranty.

Even the most ardent consumer advocates would stop short of imposing liability for this freakish result of the shoe salesman's breach. Even though the boots fail to satisfy the warranty of fitness for a particular purpose, it just doesn't seem fair to hold the shoe store responsible for *every* consequence of the breach, no matter how remote. For the most part, the courts have agreed with this reasoning and have limited the defendant's liability to results that are reasonably foreseeable or "within the risk" created by the defendant. A sprained ankle or even a broken leg is within the risk of selling boots unfit for hiking, but being struck by a meteorite is not. The "risk rule" represents a policy judgment by the courts that a manufacturer or seller should not be liable for *all* the consequences of its conduct. Thus, a car manufacturer whose "sin" lies in selling a bad car will not be liable when the car breaks down and the buyer is mugged while waiting for a tow truck. The risk associated with selling a rotten car is that the car will malfunction and someone will be hurt in a collision, not that someone will be mugged.

To get back to our vaporizer case, the burns Andrea suffered were "caused" by the fact that the top of the vaporizer was unsecured to the jar, since the accident would not have occurred but for that fact. Was it within the risk created by the manufacturer? It seems so. The risk was that someone would be burned and that is exactly what happened. Again, unless Andrea's mother positioned the device in a very dangerous spot, like on a chair in the doorway, her conduct probably will not be seen as an intervening or superseding cause that exonerates the manufacturer from liability.

* * *

In the actual case, the court held the vaporizer manufacturer liable for negligent failure to warn, negligent design, breach of warranty, and strict liability. Since then, the manufacturer has redesigned its vaporizer with an "exclusive cover lock safety feature" and a "double wall tube safety feature" that "reduces water temperature in the reservoir." The new instructions caution that the vaporizer should be placed only on the floor, "so that no one will be below the unit if it is accidentally tipped over."

* * *

In the centuries-old battle between consumers and manufacturers over who should bear the risk of injuries from defective products, the consumers are gaining on the manufacturers. The law of products liability has moved steadily away from the old "let the buyer beware" principle toward holding manufacturers responsible for the damage caused by dangerous defects in their products. And by imposing liability, the law has created incentives for developing and marketing safer products.

This movement reflects the law's ability to adjust to changing circumstances. Now that industry is no longer in its infancy — indeed, it has grown into a mighty giant — the law has reacted by shifting its protection from the producers to the consumers. Alert to the evolving needs of the marketplace, the law has created a new maxim: "Let the producer be careful."

POINT OF LAW:

The Pinto Case — Can Corporate Carelessness Be Criminal?

The movement in products-liability law from caveat emptor toward imposing greater responsibility on sellers has been achieved through civil actions brought by consumers. The objective of these suits has been to compensate the victims — to make them whole — but they also have had the effect of hitting the manufacturers where it hurts, in the pocketbook, and thus encouraging safer products.

But sometimes economics work in the opposite direction; a manufacturer may discover that it's cheaper to defend lawsuits and pay judgments than to make the product safer in the first place. This has led some to conclude that when the manufacturer has made a conscious decision to sacrifice safety for dollars, it may be appropriate to punish it under the criminal law.

The state of Indiana tried to do just that in a highly publicized case in 1980 arising out of the deaths of three Indiana teen-agers. One August evening in 1978, the three were on their way to high-school basketball practice when the 1973 Pinto they were riding in suddenly was rammed from behind. The force of the collision ruptured the Pinto's gas tank and the car exploded into flames, killing the three girls.

Indiana charged the Ford Motor Company with three counts of reckless homicide under a 1977 statute that said corporations could be tried as individuals in criminal proceedings. Ford's maximum fine in the case was limited by the statute to $10,000 for each death, but Ford engaged one of the nation's most skilled trial attorneys — former Watergate prosecutor James F. Neal — and a veritable battalion of New York lawyers to defend it, at a total estimated cost to the company of $1 million. The reason for pulling out the big guns was obvious: A conviction in this case could spawn more criminal prosecutions, as well as traditional civil suits by other victims, and the damages could climb well beyond the cost of defending the Indiana prosecution. No doubt Ford also feared the impact a guilty verdict would have on its sagging reputation.

The Elkhart, Indiana, county prosecutor, working from a no-frills budget of $20,000, and assisted by eight student volunteers from nearby law schools, sought to prove that the Pinto gas tank system was unusually prone to rupture when the car was rear-ended, and that Ford officials knew this and failed to correct the problem or warn owners of the danger. A former high-ranking Ford engineer testified for the prosecution that it would have cost Ford only $6.65 per car to reduce the likelihood of gas tank fires from rear-end collisions.

Ford denied the charges, arguing essentially that the 1973 Pinto was no more dangerous than its competitors. Ford's accident-reconstruction experts crash-tested American Motors' Gremlin, GM's Vega, the Dodge Colt, and the Toyota Corolla, and showed the results to the jury. All the cars were heavily damaged and the gas tanks ruptured.

The trial lasted eight weeks. The testimony included a statement by a Ford engineer who had helped design the Pinto that he considered the car so safe that he had bought one for his eighteen-year-old daughter, and an emotional closing argument by the prosecutor urging the jury to "send a message that will be heard in boardrooms across the country." The jury deliberated for twenty-five hours and returned a verdict of not guilty.

Many observers claim that Ford would have been convicted if the judge hadn't excluded from the jury's consideration several controversial documents about Pintos from years other than 1973 and hundreds of internal Ford memoranda in which the Pinto gas tank system was discussed. The judge felt the documents were not relevant to the Pinto involved in the accident and might cause prejudice if shown to the jury.

There were other anomalies about the case, such as a surprise witness Ford produced after six people testified for the prosecution that the Pinto was moving at the time of the impact. Ford's witness was a hospital orderly who testified that the driver of the car had told him before she died that the Pinto was not moving when the crash occurred. The significance of whether the Pinto was moving is that few, if any, gas tank systems could be expected to hold up if the car is struck in the rear-end at high speed while it is at a dead standstill.

Because there were so many peculiarities about the Pinto case, the fact that Ford was exonerated doesn't diminish the importance of the precedent set by the trial. The prosecution marked the first time an American corporation has been tried on criminal charges for injuries caused by its defective products. The case easily could have come out the other way. And *that* message is one manufacturers will not soon forget.

The Pinto case makes us think about how far we are willing to go in holding manufacturers responsible for the damages done by their products. The threat of being branded a criminal for what seemed like a rational business decision may encourage manufacturers to give more weight to the safety factor when evaluating the costs and benefits of marketing a particular product. But we should recognize that increased safety will not be cost free. There may have to be an aesthetic sacrifice, or a higher price tag. For example, auto makers could build a vehicle that would be almost impregnable in accidents, but it probably would look like a Sherman tank and the purchase price would be more than most of us could afford.

Another problem with using the threat of criminal sanction as the stick to scare companies into greater safety consciousness is that it may scare them *too* much and inhibit creativity and innovation. The experience with swine flu vaccine in the 1970s shows that this is a real risk. Because of several cases holding polio vaccine manufacturers liable for unexpected side effects, the drug companies were hesitant to supply swine flu vaccine without insurance against liability for any side effects that vaccine might cause. But the insurance companies had read the polio cases too, and were unwilling to provide insurance until the vaccine was more thoroughly tested. Congress finally ended the impasse in 1976 by passing a statute that shielded the manufacturers from liability for injuries resulting from the vaccine that were not attributable to negligence by the manufacturer; the statute made the United States liable instead.

The swine flu situation arose before the Pinto case, at a time when the only foreseeable liability was civil. If it occurred today, with the specter of *criminal* punishment haunting every manufacturer, you can bet those drug companies would be even more cautious. Are we willing to coerce greater care out of American industry with the threat of using the criminal law when the effect might be to delay the marketing of socially useful products, let alone potentially life-saving medical technology or drugs?

10

LIVING TOGETHER:

Should the Law Promote Virtue?

IS THE LAW too moralistic? Does it retain too many Victorian attitudes for this day and age? Or is the problem just the opposite — the law, reflecting a permissive society, is becoming too tolerant of immoral behavior?

The legal system generally is viewed as a highly conservative institution and resistant to change; yet the law does not exist in a vacuum and it cannot avoid being influenced by the changing mores of the world around it. In this chapter we'll examine how moral considerations can affect the content of the law and how it's applied. We'll look at what has become a common arrangement, a couple living together without being married, and then focus on custody battles between them over their child.

* * *

More and more couples are living together in relationships that the law traditionally has termed *meretricious,* a word the dictionary defines as "characteristic of a prostitute." What the law means is that the couples are cohabitating without being married. The living arrangement may be in anticipation of marriage, it may be for economic reasons, it may reflect a rejection of traditional morality, or it simply may result from a desire for an informal, unstructured way of life. In any event, it has become a common practice, regardless of how much the law and the more conservative elements of society may disapprove.

Most people involved in these relationships probably view themselves as outside the framework of laws that govern the affairs of married couples, and may well prefer it that way. Yet when the relationship goes on the rocks, and it's time to divide up property and, in some cases, decide who gets the kids, one or both of the parties may want the protection the law accords spouses. But the lack of traditional legal — and moral — sanction for the living arrangement affects the way a judge will treat the participants, and may lead to harsh results in disputes between them. Consider, as an illustration, the following possible history of one of these relationships:

Tina and Harry are in love. She's a budding interior decorator working on a free-lance basis; he's an aspiring journalist. They decide to live together, but they don't plan on getting married, at least not yet. "People who are really in love don't need marriage," says Harry. They also want to have a child; again, they don't feel it's necessary to be married to be good parents. "The important thing is that the child is loved," Tina says.

So they set up their happy home in a garden apartment. Things go smoothly at first. Tina is busy developing her interior decorating business, and Harry works hard at being an investigative reporter. Their combined incomes let them live well — well enough to afford a sports car, a Porsche no less (bought secondhand, of course). Just as a matter of convenience, Harry takes title to it.

When Tina becomes pregnant, both she and Harry are very pleased. After a while, however, she finds that her condition interferes with her work, which often is physically strenuous, and eventually she has to give it up and stay home, even though it means a serious setback in getting her career established. "You can always start up again," Harry tells her, but Tina isn't so sure.

Meanwhile, Harry has written a six-part exposé of the city sewer commission and has gotten a lot of publicity out of it, and he's now hard at work on a book about his exploits as a reporter. With the advance from his publisher, he is able to support both of them.

In due course Tina has a baby girl, whom they name Melody. Tina finds that caring for the baby is a lot of work, but Harry helps out, although not as much as she'd like. Harry is very busy, since his book has been published and he's traveling around the country making promotional appearances on television and giving speeches at college campuses on government malfeasance and the need for everyone to read books exposing it. There's no financial strain on the couple, since the book has reached the best-seller lists.

Gradually Tina settles into what becomes her new routine: She stays at home and cares for Melody while Harry gives lectures and attends conferences devoted to controlling government irresponsibility. Two years go by; then one day Harry informs Tina that he's moving out, since he has fallen in love with Joyce, his high-powered agent, who has just sold his book to Hollywood for a million dollars. (The film is to star Robert Redford as the intrepid reporter, and Jack Palance and Mickey Rooney as corrupt sewer inspectors.) As he walks out the door following a lengthy shouting match, Harry tells Tina that over the years he's outgrown her, that she's become little more than a boring housewife.

* * *

Thus ends the story of Tina and Harry. Or does it? Not really, because two weeks later both of them are in court. Tina is demanding that Harry pay her a settlement, including child support, as part of their "divorce"; Harry is insisting that the court grant him visitation rights to Melody. If Tina and Harry had been married, the law would step in and settle matters such as alimony, child support, division of property, child custody, and visitation rights. But they weren't, so what will the court do?

Let's take Tina's claims first. She wants child support for Melody plus half of Harry's now considerable assets as a property settlement. (We'll assume that Harry and Tina live in a state with community property laws or one whose courts typically divide property acquired during a marriage equally, so that if they had been married her demand would be granted.) If she can't get half his property, she wants to be paid alimony, since she feels that for all intents and purposes she acted as Harry's wife.

As to child support, the answer is clear. The law in every state now imposes upon the unmarried father ("unmarried" refers here to someone like Harry, who was not married to the mother of his child) a duty to support his child. This duty is similar to a divorced father's obligation, and will be enforced by a court in much the same way, with Harry subject to various sanctions if he refuses to pay.

That's fair enough, isn't it? After all, Harry wanted a child, so why shouldn't he assume at least part of the burden of supporting Melody? Even if he didn't want a child, he went ahead and had one, and so must bear the responsibility.

But suppose Harry has no objection to supporting Melody. He objects, however, to Tina's demand that she be given half the property accumulated while they lived together. This would include the proceeds from the sale of his book to Hollywood, since the deal was closed while he was still living with Tina. Harry, of course, says that alimony and community property laws should apply only to marriages, not to people who were just living together.

Can Tina collect one half of the property Harry acquired during their relationship? Alternatively, can she get the court to grant her alimony? The answer is that she probably can't. Harry is right about community property and alimony laws not applying, since they are directed specifically to the marriage relationship. Tina and Harry weren't married, so it's unlikely a court would extend these very special remedies to help her.

But Tina argues that she should be paid a settlement on the basis of an "agreement" she had with Harry that they would share any property that came into the household. She claims that there was an understanding between them when they moved in together. The idea was that she would devote herself to taking care of any child they might have and to keeping house in return for half of any earnings or other property that he acquired. She says that she fulfilled her side of the bargain, and now Harry must pay up.

To this, Harry indignantly replies, "Show me a copy of the agreement." Tina has to admit that they never wrote anything down; nor can she remember a specific instance in which Harry orally agreed to the plan. "It was just understood that that was how it was to be," she says. Does the absence of an express contract, written or oral, mean Tina can't recover on her contract theory?

The answer is: Not necessarily. Tina can try to recover on the basis of a contract "implied in fact," a theme we first encountered in the discussion of job contracts in Chapter 8. An implied contract is one that can be inferred from the circumstances and from the acts and conduct of the parties who entered into it. To prove its existence, Tina might point to such evidence as their sharing incomes before she gave up her work, a joint checking account, or any other "pooling" arrangement between them. She also could argue that it made no sense for her to give up a growing career and devote herself completely to taking care of Harry and raising his child unless she had a financial guarantee that he would take care of her, especially since she couldn't count on the protection the law accords a wife.

Alternatively, Tina could try to recover at least for the value of her services in *quantum meruit,* which is Latin for "as much as he deserves." This doctrine is based on fairness notions and applies in cases in which one person supplies services to another without any agreement between them on payment. If the person receiving the services benefits from them and is aware that they are being provided with an expectation of payment, the law will "imply" a promise on his part to pay a reasonable amount for them. For example, a carpenter might mistakenly make repairs on someone's property (believing it to be the property of the person who actually hired him) in full view of the owner, and then recover against him for the value of the repairs, even though the owner never formally agreed to pay for them.

Notice that quantum meruit is different from the implied contract that we've been discussing. With quantum meruit, there's no real agreement, oral or written; rather, the court "imagines" that one exists in order to come to a fair result. A contract implied in fact, on the other hand, involves an actual agreement, but one that hasn't been written down or otherwise formally expressed. Another way of putting it is that in quantum meruit the agreement is implied "in law," that is, the law makes it up and imposes it upon the parties in order to do justice.

Quantum meruit also is more limited than an implied contract, since it allows relief only for the value of the services, and then only to the extent that the person who received them benefited without paying. But Harry can argue that he did pay for them, that he provided Tina with food and shelter in compensation. Thus Tina would have to show that her services were worth more than the support she received from Harry, which will be difficult unless the court is willing to place a high value on them. But perhaps the court would view them as being worth a good deal. After all, she had Harry's baby and cared for her; arguably, "mothering" is an extremely valuable service all by itself.

But Harry claims that neither theory applies. He says there was no agreement, implied or otherwise, that she would get half his property. He says that when they moved in together they were in love, and that neither of them was thinking about property settlements. Her domestic services, he maintains, were a gift, given without any intention by either of them that she be compensated with a financial guarantee from him. He points to the marriage relationship, in which wives keep house and raise children without any expectation of financial reward, and says that his dealings with Tina should be construed in that light. Moreover, he points out that if they had wanted to put up with all this legalistic mumbo jumbo, they would have gotten married, and that the whole idea was to keep things simple!

The fact is that Harry has a good chance of winning. The law generally has presumed that services provided in a domestic situation are given as a gift. This assumption makes it difficult for Tina to prove an implied contract, since it negates the inference that both she and Harry intended that Tina be compensated for her contribution to the relationship. Moreover, it keeps Tina from recovering in quantum meruit for the value of her services, since the doctrine requires that the person performing the services expected to be paid. Notice how Tina gets it in the neck both ways: She isn't married, so she doesn't get the rights of a wife to a property settlement; but her relation to Harry resembled that of a wife, so she's assumed to have taken care of him and Melody for free, as if there had been a marriage.

Stop for a moment. What if Tina had looked ahead when her relationship with Harry began and considered what could happen if they broke up? Suppose she had done what most people find impossible — namely, overcome the romanticism of the situation and sat the then love-struck Harry down and persuaded him to sign an agreement under which he would divide his property with her if they broke up. Now Tina has an express, written contract, so there's no need to imply anything — it's all set out in black and white. Is she home free?

The answer is that she still might lose. Courts in some states have taken the position that they won't enforce a contract that is made in connection with the so-called meretricious relationship. This refusal is based on the doctrine that the law will not enforce an illegal contract or one contrary to public policy, such as a contract to pay gambling debts (where gambling is illegal) or a contract to kill someone. To these courts, Tina's agreement with Harry is unenforceable because it can be interpreted as a contract to share Harry's property in exchange for illicit sexual services. It's not much different, they say, from a prostitute suing for damages for breach of a contract to pay for her services. Moreover, in states in which fornication or adultery are crimes, these courts may have another ground for invoking the doctrine of illegality and refusing to enforce the agreement.

A recent example of this rather moralistic approach is a New York case in which rock star Peter Frampton was sued by a woman who had lived with him for five years. Penelope McCall told the court that she had left her husband, who managed the band that Frampton was then with, to live with him and to devote herself to furthering his career. She claimed she had helped support him and had performed promotional work. In return, Frampton was alleged to have promised to make her a partner in his earnings and property. When the two later broke up, she took him to court seeking to recover on the contract.

The trial court, however, decided that even assuming the contract existed, it was unenforceable. The judge pointed out that adultery is a crime in New York, and that McCall had never been divorced from her husband. (Frampton divorced his wife sometime during his relationship with the plaintiff.) Thus, the court said, the contract was "clearly opposed to sound morality," as it was based on the "illicit association of the parties." On appeal, however, it was decided that she did not lose her right to sue Frampton simply because of the existence of the adultery statute, and the case was sent back for trial — an indication that moralism may be on the decline in the New York courts.

A number of courts have been willing to enforce contracts between people who are living together when the agreement can be separated from the meretricious relationship. For example, it sometimes happens that one of the parties will supply money to acquire property, or will provide services in connection with a jointly run business, pursuant to a contract under which he or she is to share in the property or the profits of the business — indeed, Penelope McCall's promotional work fell into this category. In these cases, courts often have enforced the contract, treating it as severable from the illicit relationship and as existing independently of it. (This type of contract also is easier to imply than one involving purely domestic services, since there's less of an assumption that "business" services were given as a gift. Indeed, courts sometimes imply a partnership or joint venture in these cases.) But even in those courts that have enforced these separable contracts, Tina still could lose, since her services were of a domestic rather than a business nature.

Do you think that Tina and Harry were engaged in a meretricious relationship — that she was like a prostitute and that he was her customer? They lived together in a domestic arrangement for several years; indeed, their relationship lasted as long as many marriages do nowadays. So should the mere fact that they weren't legally married brand their arrangement meretricious?

Consider some variations on our basic story. Suppose Tina and Harry had stayed together for only a few days before they broke up. Would it be easier to term the relationship meretricious? How about a couple of months — are we moving away from meretriciousness? What if they had stayed together for thirty years, had raised Melody along with two other children, and in general had established a household indistinguishable from a long-term marriage — indeed, one that led all their neighbors and friends to assume they were married? A relationship that lasts this long arguably is more of a marriage than most of the legal ones that end in divorce.

Does the motive for not being married affect the "morality" of the relationship? The law itself may create economic incentives for couples not to marry. For example, imagine Tina and Harry as elderly people, both living on social security, and both widowed. They're in love with each other and have moved in together, but without getting married, since under the law they might lose a portion of their benefits if they remarried. As it is, they're barely getting by, so they literally can't afford to get married — or live apart! Surely this isn't the meretricious relationship that the courts have so scorned in the past.

But despite the many different unmarried arrangements that are seen in today's society, from short-term flings to lifelong domestic devotion, *meretricious,* as a legal term, is broad enough to apply to all unmarried couples, regardless of circumstances. (About the only exception that has been recognized generally is when one or both of the parties believe themselves to be legally married.) And despite a liberalizing trend in the courtrooms on this issue, which we'll discuss later, it is possible that in some parts of the country Tina still would find her contract with Harry to be unenforceable, especially if she had violated a statute against fornication or adultery. Have we carried our quest for morality too far by having the law reject these agreements no matter what the circumstances?

Let's say Tina gives up on her contract theories and tries a different tack. She claims that regardless of the existence or enforceability of a contract, she should recover from Harry on principles of fairness and equity. Remember our discussion in the chapter on job contracts of how the English equity courts provided justice in cases in which the traditional law courts were unable or unwilling to act? The key was that an equity judge would intervene to help those who really needed and deserved help.

So Tina says that fairness and good conscience require that she receive a settlement from Harry, especially since she sacrificed her budding career to provide him with a happy home. She'd like half his property, but she's willing to settle for less. In addition, she claims half interest in the Porsche, since she helped pay for it.

At long last can Tina get something in settlement? Certainly the relief she requests is within the court's equitable powers. Even without an agreement between the parties, equity can divide up property or make an award when considerations of fundamental fairness compel that result. Equity also has some very effective remedies for situations in which one person has title to property that someone else helped purchase. If fairness dictates, the court will require the title holder to transfer part interest to the other person. That helps her with the Porsche.

Ah, but there's one more snag in Tina's plans. Equity always has had the rule that anyone who comes before the court must have "clean hands." The idea is that if you want the special treatment and remedies equity provides, you must deserve them. This doesn't mean that you necessarily have to be a great person or have led a blameless life, but it does require that you not have done anything wrong or unfair in connection with the transaction that brings you into court.

Under this rule, some judges have said that no equitable relief is available to one party to a meretricious relationship in a suit against the other; the result is that each is left to his or her own devices in settling any disputes arising out of the relationship. A few courts even have gone so far as to deny equitable relief to someone who has paid for property that another took title to. So if Tina finds herself in a court that takes a harsh view toward unmarried couples, she may not have much of a chance of getting a settlement from Harry on the basis of fairness. And it's even possible — although not likely — that she wouldn't be able to recover on her half interest in the sports car.

* * *

What do you think of denying Tina relief on these moralistic theories of "unclean hands" and illegality? The whole purpose of equity is to arrive at a fair result, yet is it fair to refuse Tina any settlement just because she wasn't married to Harry? Keep in mind that Harry is equally guilty of any wrongdoing, yet under the policy of leaving the parties to their own devices, it seems that he benefits unjustly from the relationship.

What about the law's refusal to enforce the contract? How can judges take the position that a couple's living together takes away either partner's right to have contracts enforced? Tina is a citizen, she pays taxes; why shouldn't she have the same recourse to the courts as everyone else?

You might respond by saying that marriage is one of the cornerstones upon which our society is built, and that it is perfectly legitimate for the law to promote it by discouraging unmarried couples from living together. It's not unusual for laws to encourage or discourage certain favored or disfavored forms of behavior. That's one basic purpose of both the clean hands and the illegality doctrines. Other examples are tax laws that encourage people to give to charity by granting them deductions for charitable contributions; special taxes on cigarettes that try to discourage smoking by making it more expensive; and the strict, often cumbersome regulation of liquor sales in most states, which reflects to some extent an official disapproval of drinking alcoholic beverages.

You also might point out that the law is not coercing Tina and Harry and couples like them to get married; all the court is saying is that it will not grant equitable remedies or enforce an agreement that is connected with an illicit sexual arrangement. Moreover, the law is perfectly evenhanded about its policy: It will not help Harry against Tina either, to the extent that he has claims arising out of their meretricious relationship.

Wait a minute. Aren't these courts being a little Victorian about all this? As noted at the beginning of this chapter, people increasingly are choosing to live together without benefit of marriage, a condition that reflects the changing mores and attitudes of society, as well as the desire of many to experiment with different lifestyles. Whatever may have been true in the past, we are much more tolerant and liberal toward different living arrangements than we used to be. Few would seriously try to enact a statute making it a crime for unmarried couples to cohabit (even in states in which "fornication" is a crime, the law is rarely, if ever, enforced), so doesn't it smack of an outdated moralism to apply the law selectively to deprive people of their rights because of their lifestyle? Moreover, since the trend toward living together continues, isn't it clear that this attempt to "discourage" it isn't all that effective in pushing people into marriage?

A number of courts, in fact, are tending toward a more tolerant attitude. Take, for example, *Marvin* v. *Marvin,* the famous "palimony" case in California involving movie actor Lee Marvin and Michelle Triola Marvin. Michelle charged that they had lived together for five and a half years pursuant to an express oral contract under which she gave up her singing career to take care of him, and he agreed to support her for the rest of her life and to share with her equally any property that they might acquire. When he broke off the relationship and stopped supporting her, she went to court to collect. The lower court, however, dismissed her claim without a trial, apparently because it viewed Lee Marvin's promises to her, assuming they had been made, as unenforceable because they were based on an illicit relationship.

But on appeal, the Supreme Court of California reversed, holding that Michelle Triola Marvin had stated a claim that the law would recognize — if she could prove the facts — and that she had a right to proceed to trial to try to establish it. The court said that the old rule about not enforcing contracts connected with a nonmarital relationship could be stated narrowly as follows: Such an agreement is unenforceable only to the extent it is "explicitly and inseparably based upon services as a paramour." In effect, the court limited *meretricious* to its dictionary meaning, and made all contracts enforceable, except those that truly are "characteristic of a prostitute." Since Michelle had performed a whole range of services for Lee, including keeping his house and acting as his companion, it was concluded that his promises to her were not based solely on her supplying sexual services.

The California court could have stopped there, since the issue before it was whether an express agreement between the two was enforceable. But it went further: It said that in the absence of an express contract, the law should be willing to examine the conduct of the parties to determine if an implied contract exists between them. It also said that equitable remedies, including quantum meruit, could be applied to arrive at a just result. Finally, and very significantly, the court rejected the presumption that services performed as part of living together are contributed as a gift; rather, it said that it should be presumed that the parties intended to "deal fairly with each other."

When the case went back to the lower court for trial, Michelle lost on her claim for half of Marvin's property, since it was determined that neither an express nor an implied contract existed. On the other hand, the court, relying on principles of equity, awarded her $104,000 for "rehabilitation" purposes so that she could learn new skills or polish her old ones to become employable again. The amount equalled $1000 a week — the most she had ever earned as a singer — over a two-year period. But the saga has not ended, because the case has been appealed again, this time by Marvin. The first appellate court has reversed the award, terming it unprecedented. It seems headed for the California Supreme Court once more.

*   *   *

Consider how the *Marvin* approach would apply to Harry and Tina. First, agreements between unmarried couples are enforceable as long as sexual services aren't the sole basis for the contract. In our case Tina provided Harry with companionship, helped support the household until she stopped working, kept house, and raised Melody. Clearly there was a lot more involved on Tina's part than just sexual services, so any contract between them is enforceable.

Even if the contract isn't written down, or even expressed orally, Tina still can recover on the basis of an implied contract. Under the *Marvin* approach, the court doesn't assume that domestic services are contributed as a gift. Thus Tina would have a "fighting chance" to prove that both she and Harry meant to divide the property in return for her housekeeping and child-raising services. There's no guarantee that she'd win on this theory, since any understanding between them may have been amorphous at best — after all, they were in love with each other, not in business together. As noted in Chapter 6, Sports Violence, the person suing, the plaintiff, has the burden of proof, and in the absence of a clear showing that there was an agreement and what its terms were, Tina may well lose.

But remember that the *Marvin* case did say that it should be presumed that the parties meant to "deal fairly with each other." How this presumption is to be applied is not clear, but perhaps a court would take the position that when two people live together, especially in a relationship that closely resembles a traditional marriage, they must have intended to treat each other as spouses with regard to a property division. In effect, this approach would shift the burden of proof to the defendant to show there wasn't any such intention, a difficult task in situations in which there is little evidence of what the parties really were planning. As we shall see in a moment, however, treating "pals" as de facto spouses raises numerous questions.

In addition to contract remedies, *Marvin* opens the door to equitable remedies. Again, if her domestic services aren't presumed to be a gift, Tina might recover in quantum meruit for their value, less any support Harry provided her. Certainly she would get her half interest in the sports car; after all, that's plain fairness. What if Tina asks for compensation for giving up her decorating career? She maintains that she should be paid for her sacrifice, since Harry benefited from it, in that he got Melody and built-in child-care services. Perhaps, like Michelle Triola, she would be awarded something to make up for her lost or possibly stalled career. Damages could be difficult to evaluate, and as we saw in the job contracts chapter, damages are not recoverable to the extent they are uncertain or speculative. But a jury might settle upon some amount to compensate Tina, or at least to tide her over while she tries to get her career going again. We may have a better sense of what's possible when the *Marvin* epic ends.

What if Tina pushes on one step further? Conceding that Harry never agreed to divide his property with her, she says that as a matter of equity and fairness she should get half of it anyway. She argues that she lived with Harry and performed all the services of a wife, including having and raising his child. Tina cites the *Marvin* court for the proposition that Harry should be presumed to have intended to treat her fairly. Therefore, she says, he should treat her now as he would a divorced wife, which in a community property state, and many others, means he should give her half of what he acquired during their "marriage."

Are you on her side? Do you think a wedding ceremony should make so much difference in defining the legal rights of the parties? Remember, we're not talking about a weekend fling; for all intents and purposes Tina *was* Harry's wife, so why not treat her as such? But it may be that you have moral objections to this approach. There's a difference, you say, between granting contract enforcement and equity to unmarried couples, and going so far as to bring them under the legal principles designed solely for people who are married. No matter how liberal and tolerant we are, perhaps we ought to restrict the protections and rights that the law grants spouses to those who formally have assumed the full responsibilities of marriage.

Ironically, it's quite possible that the *Marvin* approach, carried all the way to treating pals as if they were spouses, would encourage marriage. If Lee Marvin had known he was going to assume all the obligations of a husband toward Michelle Triola, maybe he would have decided to marry her, since he stood to gain little by keeping things informal; alternatively, he might have called the whole thing off rather than risk the possibility of being forced to divide his estate or pay palimony later on. In either event, traditional morality would have been served.

As you can see, trying to resolve the question by attempting to promote morality tends to promote confusion instead. We can't even be sure whether the effect of the *Marvin* decision is to encourage or discourage marriage. Perhaps the best approach is not to use the law to try to push people into marriage, either directly or indirectly, but rather to let the institution stand on its own merits; in the long run it's probably better if those who marry do so simply because they want to, without any nudging from the courts.

Are there other reasons, besides moral considerations, for not treating Tina as a wife? Consider this: Tina is seeking to recover on equitable principles, that is, on the idea that basic fairness requires her to be allowed to share the property. But does it? Remember that Tina and Harry chose not to get married, and one reason for that decision was their desire not to be tied down, or to have to assume the obligations and responsibilities that go with marriage. Indeed, it might be said that the facts surrounding the arrangement indicate an implied contract between them not to invoke the legal protections normally accorded spouses. So is it fair for Tina to turn around now and say that she wants to change the terms of the deal, that regardless of what both of them may have intended, she wants the law to intervene to grant her rights against Harry that he never meant her to have? How can you call that equity?

Tina does. She says that fairness turns on more than what Harry intended her to have. Anyway, she claims that their relationship was not based on either side's having well-defined intentions, and that the court must look to what took place during the relationship and to where the parties now stand. She says that Harry's earnings as a writer and lecturer were accumulated through their mutual efforts, in that her taking care of the apartment and Melody freed him to go about his business, and therefore she is entitled to share in those earnings.

As we can see, opinions differ on what's fair. Yet equity is supposed to supply remedies whose fairness is manifest. At least that's how courts of equity got started in the first place. When those English chancellors originally began granting relief to people who couldn't get help from the law courts, they weren't dealing with cases in which there was a lot of confusion about what the fair result was; rather, they were stepping into a situation in which the right result was reasonably clear, albeit unattainable from the law courts. Given this historical background, maybe a modern court should hesitate to grant Tina half Harry's property unless she can show truly compelling reasons for so drastic a remedy.

Perhaps our real problem is that the law governing these arrangements is in flux — as is true of our attitudes — and so the parties can't predict with any certainty what the legal consequences of their relationship will be. (Indeed, even married couples can't always be sure nowadays how property will be divided upon divorce, since women increasingly are breadwinners themselves.) Under these circumstances, there can be a great deal of dispute about what their intentions were when they moved in together, and what's fair now that one of them is moving out. But if the courts regularly begin to treat unmarried couples as spouses when it comes to support, alimony, and division of property, then both parties would have a better idea of what they were getting into when they started the relationship. That at least would eliminate the possible unfairness of having the settlement come as a complete surprise to one — or even both — of them.

But wait! If the law treats all living arrangements as marriages, aren't we cutting down on the freedom of the parties to elect how they are going to live? If we're so tolerant, shouldn't we let people elect alternative lifestyles that won't be treated as marriages? To the extent that one of our goals is to maximize personal freedom, then we seem to be going in the wrong direction by making every relationship a de facto marriage. Now people aren't just being pushed into marriage, they're starting off there whether they like it or not. Is certitude as to the legal effect of people's living together worth the possible loss of freedom that uniform treatment entails?

* * *

How the law will resolve all these questions remains to be seen. The *Marvin* case suggests that some courts may be willing to assume a great deal of power in making settlements when unmarried couples break up. They can do so either by imposing their view of the fair result through their equitable powers, or by being receptive to implying a contract from the actions of the parties.

What should you do if you're a couple contemplating an unmarried living arrangement but want to minimize the chances of ending up in court haggling over how the judge should divide things up? First, you should keep in mind that the willingness of the court to treat the arrangement as a de facto marriage may turn on how much the relationship resembles a traditional marriage. After all, if it looks like a marriage and everyone has acted as if it's a marriage, it's easy for the court to treat it legally as if it were a marriage. Thus a relatively long-term domestic arrangement will be more apt to be treated as a marriage than a short-term affair. Moreover, such things as having children, acquiring property jointly, maintaining a joint checking account, or holding yourselves out as husband and wife could lead a judge to treat you as spouses. So you may be able to protect yourselves, at least to some extent, by structuring your relationship so that it doesn't exhibit these or other attributes of marriage.

Probably a more effective way to make sure your intentions govern the dissolution of the relationship is to enter into a written agreement at the start, setting forth what you want to happen. If this seems unpractical ("How," you ask, "can we anticipate now all the contingencies that might come up in the future?"), another approach would be to enter into a separate agreement each time you acquire a substantial piece of property, or each time one party to the relationship provides significant services or gives up some personal opportunity to benefit the other. Another possibility would be a mutual release, which is an agreement that absolves each party of any legal or equitable claim that might arise by virtue of the living arrangement. If you use this last device, be sure you want whoever currently has title to the property to keep it, since the release will prevent a court from making any adjustment in ownership, even though the result of doing nothing may be unfair.

* * *

We've been looking at Tina's rights. Now let's consider Harry's. Suppose he wants to be allowed to visit Melody every Saturday and to have her stay with him for the weekend once a month. That's not unreasonable, is it? She's his daughter, and he is a good father to her. Indeed, he is now paying child support, so how is he any different from a divorced father, who usually will be granted visitation rights, unless there is a very good reason for denying him access to his children?

But Tina says no. She says she never wants to see Harry again, and she doesn't want her daughter exposed to his influence. What would happen if Harry went to court and asked the judge to grant him visitation privileges so that he can see Melody?

The answer is that until recently Harry wouldn't have had much of a chance to win. Before 1972 only six states allowed an unmarried father visitation rights over the opposition of a mother who had custody. This was in keeping with the general legal attitude that an unmarried father had very limited rights in such matters as visitation, custody, or adoption regarding his children. The attitude persisted even after the law imposed a duty on him to help support his offspring. Thus an unmarried mother had greater rights, as against the father, than did a woman who had been married and then divorced.

Does that seem fair? Here's the poor father who can't even get to see his child, and here's the mother with a power to exclude him that she wouldn't have had if they had been married. Once again, we might ask, Why should a marriage ceremony make so much difference? No doubt one reason for this approach was society's moral disapproval of the unmarried father — he was viewed as a bad guy, a seducer, an irresponsible womanizer. After all, an honorable man would marry the woman! By refusing to grant him the rights of a married father, the law attempted to encourage him to marry the mother, or at least to legitimize the child. (That's a legal process by which the unmarried father officially recognizes the child as his and assumes all the normal rights and obligations of fatherhood, with or without marrying the mother.) In theory, this approach also discouraged having children out of wedlock in the first place. A more practical reason for the law's attitude was that the unmarried father often was hard to locate; indeed, instead of being anxious, like Harry, to see his child, he might well be only too happy to sever all connection with his "family." Thus it made sense to give the mother control over the child, since she often was the only parent around.

But how does all that apply to Harry? He's not running off to escape his responsibilities; rather, he's helping to support Melody and wants to continue his relationship with her. It's Tina, not Melody, that Harry walked out on. You might say Harry doesn't deserve to see Melody, since he didn't see fit to marry her mother. But before you decide the issue on moral grounds, consider Melody's interests for a moment. Isn't she entitled to have the benefits, psychological and otherwise, of continued contact with a loving father? We can punish Harry by taking Melody away from him, but aren't we also punishing her? Keep in mind that one of the guiding rules for a judge in a family dispute is that the best interests of the child are paramount. So perhaps the law shouldn't stick with its position that the unmarried father is odd man out as far as his children are concerned.

Fortunately for Harry, in 1972 some changes were made in the law. In *Stanley* v. *Illinois,* the United States Supreme Court extended constitutional protection to the unmarried father's relationship with his child. The case involved a man who had lived with a woman off and on for eighteen years and had assumed parental responsibility for their illegitimate children. When she died, the state took the children from the father's custody and declared them wards of the state, all without giving him a hearing on his fitness as a parent or any showing that he had neglected them.

The Supreme Court held this procedure to be unconstitutional on two grounds. First, it denied the unmarried father due process of law, since it gave him no opportunity to show he was a fit parent; rather, it just presumed he wasn't. Second, it discriminated improperly between the unmarried father and other parents, since it failed to grant him the hearing on parental suitability that it granted to them; in constitutional terms, the unmarried father was denied equal protection of the laws. Both equal protection and due process are guaranteed by the Fourteenth Amendment to the Constitution.

How far this constitutional protection extends to the unmarried father, and to what extent the law can still draw distinctions between unmarried fathers and other parents, remain to be seen. However, in two subsequent cases, both dealing with whether an unmarried father could prevent the adoption of his child by the mother's husband, the Court drew a line between responsible unmarried fathers who have maintained a relationship with and helped support the child, and irresponsible unmarried fathers who have done neither. The cases indicate that it is constitutional to exclude the latter group from many of the rights of married and responsible unmarried fathers; conversely, the former must be treated more like married parents.

Well, Harry's responsible, isn't he? So it seems he should have at least some rights to visit Melody. As a matter of fact, most states that have dealt with this issue since *Stanley* v. *Illinois* probably would grant Harry visitation rights, particularly if it were determined that a continuing relationship with Melody was in her best interests. Indeed, in a recent New York case, that state's highest court went so far as to refuse to allow a divorced mother to take a child to Las Vegas, where she wanted to start a singing career, because the move would jeopardize the child's continuing relationship with the father.

Fair enough? At least it's in keeping with the trend not to stigmatize partners to an unmarried relationship. Just as the law is becoming less inclined to leave the parties to their own devices to sort out who owns the property accumulated during the relationship, so too is it less inclined to leave unmarried fathers out in the cold when it comes to their children. Overall, it reflects the law's slow, and perhaps grudging, realization that these arrangements result in "families" and, at least to some extent, these units will have to be treated as such, if only to avoid punishing the children because we disapprove of their parents' conduct.

* * *

Let's move a bit forward in time in the saga of Tina and Harry. Three years have passed; Melody is now in kindergarten; Harry has married his agent, Joyce, and they have a two-year-old son. If anything, Harry has toned down his lifestyle; he has become an editor of a newspaper; he and his wife live in a quiet suburb, both belong to the country club, and Joyce is the leader of a Girl Scout troop.

Tina, on the other hand, has taken up with Jack, an unemployed jazz musician, who has moved in with her and Melody. Jack spends most of the day watching television, while Tina supports all three of them with her new job as a waitress in a local hamburger joint. She seems to have given up her interior decorating career.

Harry is somewhat upset with this arrangement. Now that he has become a pillar of the community, he can't help but disapprove of Tina's having a live-in boyfriend. So he goes to court and asks that custody of Melody be taken from Tina and given to him and Joyce. He argues that they can provide a healthier and more stable environment than Tina can. In particular, Harry cites the doctrine that custody disputes must be resolved with a view to the best interests of the child.

Tina hires a lawyer and fights back. First, she reminds the court of the "tender years doctrine," which presumes that a very young child, especially a girl, is better off with her mother. Second, she argues that there is nothing wrong with her living with Jack, and that even if the relationship could be construed by some people as immoral, it has no bearing on her fitness as a mother. She also points out that Harry is in no position to complain about the arrangement, since it's the same as the one she had with him.

So who wins? Actually, it's difficult to say how a court would decide. Courts in custody disputes have a great deal of latitude to weigh any element they think pertinent in determining what's in the child's best interests. Thus a large number of factors, including the judge's subjective views, can affect the decision, which makes prediction difficult.

One recent case, however, suggests that Tina's living arrangement could count heavily against her keeping custody of Melody, at least if she lives in Illinois. That state's Supreme Court decided that custody over three children should be taken from a divorced mother and given to the father, because she was cohabiting with a man to whom she was not married. The court was influenced by the fact that in Illinois "open and notorious" fornication is a crime, and determined that the mother was setting a bad example for the children by violating the state's public policy. The dissenting judges, however, claimed that in effect the court was creating a conclusive presumption that the mother's lifestyle harmed the best interests of the children, since all the other evidence indicated that they were being well cared for. They noted that in *Stanley* a statutory presumption that an unwed father was an unfit custodian was held unconstitutional. Since the United States Supreme Court has declined to review the Illinois Supreme Court decision, the issue raised by the dissenters remains unresolved.

How would the Illinois Supreme Court decide our case? It's different because Harry and Tina weren't married in the first place, so Harry himself was once a violator of the fornication statute. Perhaps the court would be favorably impressed by Harry's having gotten married — gone straight, if you like. Then again, perhaps it wouldn't. Since moral judgments often are highly subjective, elements such as these can make the outcome especially unpredictable.

Let's try another variation on the theme. Suppose Tina has taken Melody and moved into an apartment with Julie, her lesbian lover. Although neither Tina nor Julie is particularly flamboyant about their relationship, neither makes an effort to hide it. As in the last case, Tina has never gotten back into the decorating business; she's content to clean the apartment, cook, and care for Melody, while Julie supports them all.

Once again, Harry goes to court and asks that custody of Melody be taken from Tina and given to him and Joyce. He says that Tina can live any way she wants to, but that her new lifestyle could well be psychologically damaging to Melody. Tina argues that she and Julie are providing Melody with a loving and stable homelife, and that there is nothing intrinsically unhealthy about choosing one sexual preference over another. Finally, she says it's a denial of her due-process and equal-protection rights to deprive her of her child just because of her sexual preference.

Again, it's difficult to predict who will win. Nonetheless, it's safe to say that the courts have shown a reluctance to give custody of children to a lesbian mother, and have tended to favor the father in these circumstances. Sometimes, when the father for one reason or another is not viewed as a fit parent either, the court will award custody to the grandparents. One court that refused to give the mother custody noted that state law made homosexual acts a crime, and said that even if these laws were rarely enforced, they still reflected society's disapproval of this type of activity. Another court granted the mother custody, but ordered her to end her lesbian relationship.

But courts have granted custody to a lesbian mother in some instances. In one case in which the mother was allowed to retain custody, the children had lived with her for five years, and there was psychiatric testimony that they were well adjusted. Furthermore, there was evidence that the mother had tried to minimize any negative impact that her sexual preference might have on the children. Finally, the father in that particular case was viewed as a less than ideal custodian.

Another court went so far as to award custody to the deceased lesbian mother's lover, in preference to the child's maternal aunt. Apparently the lover had been a "secondary parent" to the child for years. An expert testified that continuation of the relationship was important to the child's mental health and development. Moreover, the court found that the woman had no intention of forcing her preferences on the child, and in fact preferred that she grow up to be heterosexual. The determining factor was that the woman offered the child a more stable environment than did the aunt, who had marital and psychological difficulties.

As these cases suggest, the fact that Melody is being raised in a lesbian household could count against Tina's maintaining custody. One especially moralistic court refused to allow custody to a lesbian mother, noting that she had "boldly and brazenly" practiced lesbianism; so, at least in a court that thinks the same way, it could make a difference how "open" Tina was about the relationship, especially with Melody. The cases described above also indicate that it would help Tina if she testified that she would not encourage Melody to adopt lesbianism. Finally, the court will look to Harry to see if he offers anything better. Possibly a judge would be favorably impressed with the home environment Harry and Joyce would provide. On the other hand, perhaps he would hold it against Harry that he was an unmarried father to Melody, or that he was the one who walked out on Tina in the first place. As noted before, many factors can be weighed in a custody battle, and subjective considerations can play a part in how much weight each is accorded — after all, the judge is human, and in the main, flexibility is essential if the law is going to try to do the best it can in paticular circumstances.

What about Tina's claim that her constitutional rights will be violated if Melody is taken from her because of her sexual preference? She probably would have a good case if she could show that was the *sole* reason. One court has said that homosexuality does not in itself render a mother an unfit parent, and it is likely that the Supreme Court would agree if the issue came before it, just as it held in *Stanley* that an unmarried father couldn't be conclusively presumed to be an unfit parent. But so far no court has said that the sexual preference of the mother — or father — can't be considered as a factor in determining what's in the child's best interests. In a sense, the rights of the parent, whether or not protected by the Constitution, must give way to those of the child in determining who gets custody.

Is the law's tendency to treat homosexuality as a negative factor in custody battles simply another example of its moralistic posture? Or is it a justified position, one that should not be put aside prematurely until more is known about the effect of the parent's sexual orientation on the child's development? It's a difficult question to answer, since it turns in part on feelings that run very deep, and that aren't easy to sort out with any great precision. Indeed, that's one difficulty with moral issues in the courtroom — they can't always be disposed of with reason and logic, the two tools with which the law historically has felt the most comfortable.

* * *

A cynic once defined morality as the fixed prejudice of the community. One problem the courts face nowadays is that the morals or prejudices of the community aren't as fixed as they used to be. Ours is a pluralistic society, in which a significant number of people distrust many of the traditional norms of behavior, or at least are willing to experiment with other possibilities; unmarried couples living together is a prime example. The question then arises: To what extent should disapproval of the relationship color the resolution of legal disputes involving the couple? Another way to put it is to ask to what extent justice is, or should be, influenced by the morality or, if you will, the "fixed prejudices" of the court.

POINT OF LAW:
Galimony

Recently a young woman named Marilyn Barnett brought a well-publicized lawsuit against tennis great Billie Jean King. Alleging that they had been involved in a lesbian affair, Barnett claimed King had promised to give her a house she owned (and in which Barnett, who was partially paralyzed from a fall, was living) and to support her for life. The media, with their usual bent for phrase making, immediately labeled the dispute "galimony." As yet the case has not gone to trial, and many factual details may still come to light.

Once again the variousness of contemporary lifestyles and the law meet. Actually, from a legal standpoint, galimony isn't much different from palimony. Each involves a lawsuit based on an alleged express or implied contract between the parties or a request for the application of equitable principles. In both contexts the love affair provides the factual background from which the existence of the contract or what is fair can be established in the absence of a formal written agreement.

Could a court that strongly disapproves of homosexuality refuse to enforce the contract on the grounds of its being illegal or against public policy? Prediction is difficult. As we have seen, the law is tending away from that sort of moralism. The rule stated by the Supreme Court of California (the state in which Barnett's lawsuit will be heard if it is not settled) in *Marvin* v. *Marvin* is that the contract is enforceable unless "explicitly and inseparably based upon services as a paramour." Reportedly, the King-Barnett affair involved companionship and affection in addition to sexual relations, so Barnett may get her chance to prove there really was a contract. In tennis terms, Barnett's first serve is in, and now it's up to Billy Jean to return it as best she can.

But keep in mind the travails of Michelle Triola, whose match with Lee Marvin still isn't over. Perhaps the King-Barnett business also will last several sets.

11

LANDLORD AND TENANT:

How Can We Modernize Ancient Rights?

FINALLY, YOU'VE FOUND IT. Four months of classified ads, Yellow Pages, phone booths, and false starts at last have produced an apartment. It's not perfect, and it's not the chic palace you had imagined, but given the cost and scarcity of rental units, you count yourself lucky to have a home and an end to your housing troubles. But are your troubles really over?

At the ritual lease signing, you are handed a four-page document by Horace Hightower, your landlord to be, filled margin to margin with minuscule typescript setting forth the various obligations of "Lessor" (landlord) and "Lessee" (tenant). Having been brought up to read everything before signing, you discover:

> The Lessor agrees that he will furnish reasonably hot and cold water and reasonable heat during the regular heating season . . .

That's fine with you, but a few paragraphs later you find:

> The Lessor shall be obligated to fulfill all of the Lessor's obligations hereunder to the best of the Lessor's ability, but the Lessee's obligations, covenants, and agreements hereunder shall not be affected, impaired, or excused because the Lessor is unable to supply or is delayed in supplying any service . . .

By now your eyebrows are raised up to your hairline. Is it *possible* that you could be without heat for days or perhaps weeks, and still be obliged to pay full rent? Is it *reasonable* for you to pay for services not rendered or repairs not made? Possible — definitely; reasonable — probably not. Well then, how did we arrive at this state where you don't get what you pay for?

In part the answer is that landlord-and-tenant law has firm roots in history, so much so that many people say it's bogged down in the past. At the very least, it's preserved some pretty antiquated notions of property and possession that won't be obliterated in a day. Indeed, despite many efforts, which we are about to discuss, the law has not been able to obliterate them in decades.

In the meantime an impatient landlord awaits your signed copy of the lease. Reading on, you arrive at the final provision:

> The Lessee agrees upon execution of this lease to pay a security deposit of two months' rent. Said deposit will be returned to the Lessee by the Lessor upon full performance of the terms of this lease.

Here again you are baffled. Isn't this a rather vague statement for a rather large sum of money? Given the cost of borrowing these days, shouldn't there be some provision for paying you the interest earned on your security deposit?

Technically a security deposit belongs to the tenant, although it may be held by a bank or by the landlord during the tenancy. In either case, the deposit earns interest, which fairness suggests *should* be given to the tenant; however, a recent study of form leases in major American cities showed that none specified whether you get the interest on your own money. So, you are not alone in having reason to be upset.

One solution is for you to play lawyer and insert a statement into your lease that you don't have to pay the rent if you don't get heat and hot water, and a clause providing that interest on the deposit will be paid to you. If you're lucky, your landlord will agree. The far more likely possibility is that Horace Hightower will shake his head sadly and impatiently explain that the lease you are signing is a form lease — one of thousands just like it — printed and used by landlords all over the city. It was prepared, he tells you, after long and careful study by a friendly and public-spirited landlord's association in order to standardize lease conditions and save everyone time and aggravation. He's implying, of course, that you're causing him aggravation. The landlord goes on to say that with hundreds of tenants to worry about, he can't be bothered to negotiate every last detail with each eager apartment seeker; besides, he claims that the lease is essentially fair, and that other tenants have lived quite happily with it.

By this time, you may have concluded that Horace's position makes some sense. And even if you still felt inclined to fight for your rights, you understand there are risks. You don't want to antagonize your prospective landlord, since his office is crowded with other apartment seekers who, he cheerfully suggests, would be more than thrilled to sign the lease just as is. Chances are that Hightower is right, and you have just run smack into one of the fundamental realities of many landlord-tenant situations — you need a place to live and apartments are scarce. Your landlord wants to rent and takers are plentiful. Even when the market is in better balance, landlord associations concoct form leases that put you on the defensive by forcing you to swim upstream against a current of legal jargon and technicalities.

Now, having assessed your precarious position, you swallow your pride, shrug your shoulders, and sign on the dotted line. Horace Hightower may prove to be an ogre, but you *have an apartment.*

Let's make a 180-degree turn and see if life looks any rosier from the landlord's perspective. Actually, your new landlord probably is almost as fed up as you are with the details of lease signing, tenant seeking, and "making a buck." Every time a new tenant moves in, Hightower hears the same complaints about provisions in the form lease — especially about security deposits. And every time he wonders why these tenants don't understand that keeping track of a tenant's accrued interest requires separate bank accounts, which requires added bookkeeping, which consumes more time, which eats up additional money, which would mean higher rent if he couldn't keep the interest! Why can't tenants understand that a landlord is in business to make a profit, just like the butcher, the baker, and the candlestick maker?

*   *   *

Our little vignette about the trials and tribulations of lease signing for both sides illustrates three major sources of tension permeating landlord-tenant law. The first and most obvious is the divergent interests of the two parties to the transaction. By now it should be clear that you, as tenant, and your landlord have differing and frequently conflicting aims. You want a nice place to live at as reasonable a price as possible. Your landlord wants a "successful business," which means as much profit on his investment property as he can make. The gap between these respective goals widens when housing is scarce, money is tight, and maintenance is expensive. This raises the second source of tension, illustrated by your landlord's uncompromising attitude on the subject of security deposits — inequality of bargaining power between you and him, with him in the driver's seat and you getting run over by his bulldozer.

The third source of tension may be less obvious than the other two, but it has had an equal impact on the development and current status of landlord-tenant relations. It's the problem of what lawyers call independent covenants, or promises, as exemplified by the provisions in your lease that you may not withhold rent just because the landlord doesn't perform stated duties, such as providing you with heat! What it all means is that breach by one party (that is, the landlord) of a covenant does not justify nonperformance by the other party except when the breach goes to the heart of the lease by depriving the tenant of possession. (Contrast this to the job contracts discussed in Chapter 8, in which one party's breach of a covenant excused the other party from performance.) Independent covenants are a product of the property law of feudal England, which although substantially modified over the years, has not yet been totally discarded. To understand it, let's go back through history to feudal England to unearth the roots of our landlord-tenant war.

* * *

The first important truth is that feudal landlord-tenant law was *possession*-oriented rather than *service*-oriented. This made perfect sense to the medieval farmer, since he was self-sufficient and wanted nothing more than to be left alone to "tend his own garden" and his flock, while the landlord, a feudal lord, was off warring or hunting. Let's face it, in merry olde England there were no complex plumbing or heating systems in the tenant's abode that required maintenance by the owner. If you shed your twentieth-century vision of the urban landscape and look back to the feudal countryside, it should become apparent that the use of land was the hub around which all landlord-tenant law (and much of society) revolved. In many respects this is what the *law* is still about, although urban reality is quite different.

In the traditional feudal landlord-tenant relationship, the landlord conveyed *possession* to the tenant for a specified period. The landlord's only obligation was to yield possession and to refrain from interfering with the tenant's peaceful possession. In other words, upon renting a piece of land to a tenant, the lord of the manor no longer was free to bring his hounds through on a romp, or to entertain neighboring lords and ladies on his tenant-farmer's plot. Once possession was transferred, the tenant became obliged to pay rent. Because land itself was the crucial commodity, the condition of structures affixed to it had no bearing on this duty. Repairs, maintenance, and new construction were all up to the tenant. Roof thatching was entirely his concern, not the landlord's, for the tenant's promise to pay rent was a covenant that was independent of any general obligations the landlord, as owner, may have retained regarding the condition of the land or anything on it.

Notions of possession were central to determining whether either party's covenant had been breached and the remedy therefor. If a tenant failed to pay rent, his lord rode in on horseback and evicted him; there was no suit for back rent. If a landlord evicted a tenant before the rental period ended, the tenant, no longer in possession, was relieved of any obligation to pay rent. If the tenant recovered possession, his rent obligations were revived. Theoretically, the lowly tenant-farmer had the right to go to court and sue his lord to recover possession (although not to recover money damages for loss of crops, and the like), but in reality it generally was impossible for the tattered peasant to challenge the mighty lord.

So far we've been discussing extreme examples — total eviction and complete failure to pay rent. What happened in less-than-extreme cases? Suppose that rather than evict the tenant, the landlord just interfered with his peaceful possession, harassing him daily by exercising his hunting dogs in the tenant's fields? In the twelfth century a tenant would have had no recourse. Technically he still had possession and hence could not abate the rent. If he abandoned the premises, he still was obliged to pay rent for the duration of the lease agreement. By the sixteenth century the tenant might have had a right to sue the landlord for "ejectment" or "trespass." And in the twentieth century one of the remedies the tenant is armed with is the doctrine of constructive eviction, which states that when a landlord's action or inaction is so heinous and disruptive that it amounts to an actual eviction, it will be treated as such, and the tenant's rent obligation will cease. As we will see, even this remedy is inadequate in many situations.

What was once a sensible system in feudal, rural England becomes nonsensical when imposed upon American city life in the latter half of the twentieth century. In the feudal system based on land and possession, the model landlord was one who did the least and interfered with the tenant as infrequently as possible. The model tenant was a self-sufficient worker who paid his rent and tended to all his own needs — housing, food, water, and repairs. Compare this "noble peasant" to the typical urban apartment dweller, who is barely competent to change a fuse. Today's tenant really is not concerned with land at all, but rather with the space enclosed by his walls, ceiling, and floor.

Unfortunately, the old rules have not adapted well to the new setting. Unlike his twelfth-century predecessor, the twentieth-century tenant does not want to be left to his own devices (at least in certain respects), since he isn't self-sufficient. The average apartment dweller occupies one part of a building, but is dependent upon the rest of it for water, light, and heat; he even shares walls, entrances, and exits with the neighbors. Realistically, a tenant in this situation could not be self-sufficient even if he wanted to be. Living on the fifteenth floor of an apartment house, how could you provide your own heat and hot water? Would you even be able to find the "gas-fired hot-water heater" in the bowels of the basement, let alone fix it?

Because you and all other tenants are collectively dependent upon the services provided by the landlord, the law must thwart any individual tenant's actions that threaten the "quiet possession" enjoyed by the others. Imagine that it's 6:30 P.M., you're exhausted from work, and you've just walked into your apartment. When you flip on the lights, nothing happens — there's no electricity. Remembering that your neighbor across the hall is a self-proclaimed handyman, you knock on his door and ask for help. He grabs his toolbox, and within minutes discovers the problem — a faulty outlet has knocked out two fuses. While he tinkers and rewires, you leave to get new fuses from the superintendent. Suddenly the lights in the hall go out, and through closed doors come the sounds of neighbors complaining that their lights have just died. Despite noble intentions, the handyman hit a wrong wire and now the whole building is dark. Your neighbor's supposed self-sufficiency has interfered with everyone else's mealtime.

Clearly, each resident cannot be expected to make his own repairs. The lessor, charged with responsibility for all inhabitants, must provide these services. Thus, most leases contain clauses stating that the landlord agrees to provide heat, water, electricity, and maintenance of elevators and other common areas.

As leases become less like transfers of possession and more like sales or service agreements, property law loses its effectiveness and the particular terms of the contract between the landlord and tenant are increasingly called into play. Unfortunately, recognition of the need for this shift has been slow and tortuous in coming, and obsolete, historical remnants of property law continue to plague landlord-tenant relationships. For example, in this day and age one would expect that if the landlord failed to take care of the property, the tenant would be relieved of his promise to pay rent. Certainly if you order a refrigerator that is not delivered or is defective, you need not pay. But if the lease says nothing about the relationship of the covenants, the traditional rule of their being independent means that the tenant's rent duty continues. The situation is made worse by the fact, as you witnessed on lease-signing day, that most leases provide that the tenant is not so readily relieved of his duty. The lingering tenacity of the independent covenants notion, reinforced by the average tenant's poor bargaining position, is just one example of the failure of property law to adapt to new circumstances.

Another example: Under feudal property law a tenant was permitted to terminate a lease upon destruction of its subject matter. Since the subject matter was the land rather than the structure on it, and since land is rarely destroyed, the tenant continued to be liable for full payment of rent even if the building burned to the ground. Today the courts in many states still refuse to terminate a lease when the dwelling is damaged, unless that destruction is nearly total and the premises really are uninhabitable.

*   *   *

By now you may be wondering whether the law has evolved at all since the sixteenth century. Could it still be stuck in the mud of the English countryside? Isn't there anything you can do if the landlord fails to provide services? After all, if your lease is really supposed to be a fair contract, aren't you paying rent for those services, like making sure that the washing machine and dryer in the basement are in good working order?

If it's any comfort, the law has evolved, albeit slowly. In the early stages of the process, new rights and duties were engrafted onto the old notion of rent as a quid pro quo for possession. These rights and duties were considered incidental to and independent of the rent-possession relationship. Consequently, a two-level landlord-tenant relationship developed. The first embodied rent-possession principles; the second encompassed new contractual-service duties. The two remained completely distinct, which meant that although a tenant could sue his landlord for failing to provide the agreed-upon services, he was not permitted to withhold rent.

This doesn't sound so bad, does it? At least it's some recognition of your legal right to maintenance services. Let's see how it works in practice. Suppose you've got a long and detailed list of services the landlord contracted to do but hasn't yet performed. For six months you've been patient with Hightower's empty promises to fix the cracked living-room window, replace loose floor boards, plug a leak in the bathroom, and repair an erratic thermostat. You haven't wanted to be a pest, and Horace is basically a nice hardworking soul, but you're finally sick and tired of waiting. It's winter and the wind is whistling through that cracked window, and the "drip, drip" in the bathroom is driving you crazy. What fair-minded judge could resist being persuaded by your cause? That's it! You've made up your mind — you'll take him to court.

Hold on a minute. Pull in the reins and think. Do you have any idea how much it might cost to vindicate your rights? How about the time it will take to process your lawsuit? Can you afford to skip work to sit in a courtroom? Even if you have the time, money, and energy to pursue litigation, if the landlord doesn't shape up, you're still going to be living in a cold, unheated apartment. After all, litigation is an extremely unpleasant business and likely to antagonize your landlord. Unless Horace is intimidated by the threat of a lawsuit or unless he is basically a decent, reasonable person — always a possibility, of course — he may not provide the required services until the court orders him to do so and awards you some damages for your discomfort, which could be a long way down the road. He has no particular incentive to modify his behavior or to settle the lawsuit, because in the meantime he's still collecting rent from you. (Remember, you can sue, but you can't withhold rent.)

The tenant who is unaware of the separate treatment of possession and services and who attempts to do the logical thing by withholding rent when the latter are not provided faces additional problems. As long as he has possession, rent is due and a refusal to pay lacks legal justification. The property owner, therefore, can evict the tenant. The landlord is not required or expected to sue for back rent first.

Just how delinquent can a landlord be in maintaining the property before the law will intervene to protect a tenant? Suppose there's a constantly spreading stain on your kitchen ceiling where a pipe is leaking. Does the plaster actually have to come crashing down before anyone pays attention? Your home slowly is becoming infested by cockroaches and you have seen a few rodents. You kill the bugs at a rate of fifteen a day. How many more before the law will help you out?

In its early stages of adaptation to urban realities, the law required that living conditions be almost completely unbearable before it would grant a tenant any real help. The standard now is somewhat relaxed, so that any act (or omission) by a landlord that renders property "substantially unsuitable" for the purpose for which it was leased or that seriously interferes with a tenant's enjoyment of the property is considered a "constructive eviction" from the property and allows a tenant to terminate the lease. The doctrine of constructive eviction is nothing more than a stretching of the old notion that rent was paid for possession. The idea is that deteriorated physical conditions or lack of essential services at some point can be likened to an actual physical eviction from possession. Just as eviction released the feudal tenant from any rent obligation and from the lease itself, so do the deteriorating conditions or lack of services release the modern tenant from any obligations under the lease.

Alas, the constructive eviction remedy is plagued by problems that in many states prevent it from being as effective a remedy as it might seem. The first question that both you and your landlord might ask is: How bad do things have to get before your apartment is "substantially unsuitable," or before your use of it is being "seriously interfered with"? On a grouchy day, you might think that a noisy steam pipe and a burned-out light bulb in the hallway make your apartment house unsuitable for pleasant habitation. On his worst days, fed up with the gripes of fussy tenants, your landlord might think that minimal heat, and hot water during the daytime, are enough to make an apartment "suitable."

The courts haven't found it easy to define the concept. Decisions vary from state to state, with most courts agreeing only that a failure to make major repairs and to furnish heat and hot water (especially if there is an express contractual promise to do so) constitutes substantial interference with a tenant's right to enjoy the leased premises. In addition, in the case of a covenant to repair, most courts require that the property owner be given notice of the breach and a reasonable opportunity to make the repairs before a tenant is entitled to terminate the lease.

But for two months now the heat in your apartment has been extremely erratic. On two occasions this winter you had no heat at all, and for three days, turning your thermostat to 85°F only brought the temperature up to 58°F. You have pestered Hightower daily, calling him almost hourly on particularly bad days, and in fact done everything short of camping out in his living room or picketing his home. Will constructive eviction come to your rescue now? Not quite; you've still got a few hurdles to jump over. For the parallel between actual and constructive eviction to be complete, the tenant must abandon the premises within a "reasonable time" after the landlord has rendered them unsuitable. The perfect Catch-22! When faced with nonperformance or harassment by the landlord, the tenant may either quit his home or stay and continue paying rent for the deficient premises.

During severe housing shortages, the constructive eviction "remedy" tends to become worthless, since abandonment is not a realistic option for most tenants. It certainly isn't realistic for poor tenants. Even if it were, the worth of the remedy would be dubious at best. A tenant must abandon the premises before he can go into court and claim constructive eviction. Thus, he must incur the moving and relocating expenses without any assurance that the court will conclude that the premises are sufficiently substandard to sustain a claim of constructive eviction and release the now displaced tenant from the lease obligations.

Don't forget that "reasonable time" requirement. If you abandon your apartment too quickly, you could be charged with not allowing the landlord sufficient time to rectify the situation, and thus you might end up still liable for rent payments. But if you wait too long, you may be deemed to have waived your right to complain. Courts just don't like people sleeping on their rights when something could be done about it. What constitutes a reasonable time varies with the specific details of each situation, so it's hard to gauge in advance how long you are obligated to wait.

These shortcomings in the doctrine of constructive eviction recently have led to efforts to do away with the requirement of abandonment. Some courts have attempted to equate the landlord's duty to provide services with the tenant's duty to pay rent, which would make legal relief more readily available to the latter, but many prefer to continue to focus on possession as the basis for landlord-tenant obligations.

* * *

Is there any way out of this mess? Well, in many states, legislatures have attempted to rectify the landlord-tenant imbalance by imposing obligations on the landlord through building and health codes. These establish requirements such as minimum room size, window area per dwelling, the number and condition of sinks and toilets, hot water, heat, and electricity. In theory, violations are subject to criminal sanctions, but the value of these codes often is undermined by bureaucratic realities. Enforcement takes time, effort, organization, and money. In most large cities, enforcement proceedings are so numerous they must go through a screening process that only the most extreme cases survive. Inevitably, less serious complaints are sacrificed to expediency.

There are still other obstacles. Once an enforcement action has been prosecuted successfully, the question arises of how to enforce penal sanctions — by fine or imprisonment? Prison sentences are neither politically realistic nor physically feasible (because of prison over-crowding) nor appropriate given the nature of the offense, so a fine usually is imposed on the wayward landlord. But this usually is an ineffective technique. In New York City in the 1970s, for example, the average fine for a code violation was between $14 and $17 — peanuts to the typical landlord. For the knowledgeable property owner, the whole affair may become a cost-benefit and risk analysis. Since the goal of "landlording" is profit, the important questions for the owner are: How likely is it that the tenant will bring a complaint? What are the chances that he'll win? What is the likely size of the fine and how does it compare to the cost of complying with the code regulations?

The tenant can only wonder if it's all worth it. After all, to press a housing code violation, he may have to spend time wandering through a bureaucratic maze from the Buildings Department to the Health Department, from an administrative assistant at the Department of Sanitation to some junior aide at the Housing Authority. Assuming he survives what often is a shuffle, the tenant probably will have won the right to be placed at the bottom of a waiting list. There's a shortage of authorized inspectors, you know. The process takes weeks, if not months.

If this begins to seem like a rat running through a maze, you may be comforted to know that from the landlord's point of view things look just as bleak. Bureaucracy does not discriminate between owners and renters in its ability to confuse, confound, exhaust, and exasperate. Because so many government agencies and regulations are involved with housing codes, the directives of one agency frequently conflict with those of another. For example, one day you may find Horace Hightower muttering angrily and shaking his fist in the air. It could be because last week the Buildings Department told him his boiler system was unsafe and had to be shut down for repair work, and as a result of the shutdown the Health Department is trying to fine him for not providing adequate heat. You're not the only one with troubles.

Another major bar to the tenant's relying on health and building codes is that in many localities their enforcement, like enforcement of any regulatory act, is delegated to a government agency that alone is responsible for policing and eliciting compliance. In other words, a private citizen cannot bring suit but must wait for government watchdogs. Ironically, this means that landlords occasionally first hear of a housing code violation when a fine notice arrives, rather than from the tenant directly.

* * *

Having decided that you're unwilling to abandon your apartment (as constructive eviction requires) and that you're incapable of deciphering the hieroglyphics of housing codes, what other recourse do you have? Why doesn't the law just do something sensible like allow you to withhold rent payments when there are housing code violations? Well, there's good news! The most progressive regulatory statutes do provide you with this more immediate and effective remedy.

It's called rent abatement, and it means that you don't have to pay for what you don't get. So, if your apartment has been like the inside of an icebox for two weeks, you may deduct a reasonable amount from your next rent payment. *Reasonable* obviously is capable of many interpretations. You may feel that two weeks of no heat gave you a terrible cold that dragged on endlessly, which entitles you to abate 90 percent of your rent; perhaps you'll use the money for a trip to Florida to recuperate. Your landlord, on the other hand, may feel that because it was 60°F outside on each of those "heatless" days, your hardship was not so severe and therefore your abatement should be minimal. To avoid abuse of the remedy and to minimize conflict, permissible abatements or deductions usually are prescribed in a statute or by the courts by a case-by-case building of precedents.

Rent withholding is a court-supervised mechanism similar to rent abatement. The only difference is that rent withholding requires you to pay the deducted amount into an escrow account rather than keep it until the defect is remedied.

The rationale behind rent abatement, as well as rent withholding, is to provide an economic incentive for landlords to maintain and repair their properties. It's not intended to allow tenants to live rent-free. Thus, once a required repair is made, the abated portion of the rent (whether held by the tenant or in an escrow account) must be paid.

Forward-looking courts also utilize these remedies for breach of what is called the implied warranty of habitability. This doctrine regards the rental agreement as being like any other consumer contract under which a purchaser of a defective product is entitled to a refund, replacement, repair, or damages. (Chapter 9 contains a discussion of the implied warranty of merchantability used in products liability.) It establishes a minimum standard of housing and allows the tenant to abate or deduct his rent if the premises or services fall below that level.

The warranty of habitability effects a revolution in landlord-tenant law by overturning the ancient tradition of assuming that all covenants in a lease are independent. It recognizes that services, not possession alone, now are critical. It also acknowledges that unlike feudal rural plots, which could be inspected, appraised, and "taken at risk" by tenant-farmers, contemporary apartment buildings with their complicated heating, plumbing, electrical, and structural systems elude the risk-assessing abilities of the average tenant. Common sense tells us they must be the responsibility of the landlord.

The warranty of habitability is designed to achieve the same goals as the doctrine of constructive eviction, but without requiring abandonment of the premises. The law's acceptance of this theory marks a turning point in favor of tenants' rights and remedies just as the legal concept of warranty of merchantability and attendant product liability was a major step in shifting legal power toward consumers and away from manufacturers. Both concepts reflect the realities of contemporary society.

Despite similarities, the implied warranty of habitability is more difficult to implement than the implied warranty of merchantability — perhaps because it involves more variables. When a product is defective it usually doesn't work, or in extreme cases, it causes injury. But when is an apartment defective? Is an unreliable elevator a breach of the warranty? A broken window? The appearance of a few cockroaches or rodents? Usually the courts say the breach must be substantial — one that impairs health or safety — which is similar to the standard used for constructive eviction. Hence a tenant still may be required to pay rent even though certain "insubstantial" services that the landlord promised are not being supplied.

Another and perhaps fatal weakness in the implied warranty is the transient nature of most rentals. Because a tenancy lasts only for a limited period of time, a tenant's leverage against a landlord begins to wane as the term of the lease does. Once the lease ends, the tenant is totally subject to the landlord's arbitrary decision whether or not to renew it. In addition, many tenants aren't protected by a lease at all. They either never had one or it has expired. They are called tenants at will and are subject to eviction at any time — their tenancy literally is at the landlord's will.

Thus the landlord can wield a tremendous amount of extralegal power against a tenant who complains too much or who insists upon withholding rent. He can threaten a tenant who has no lease with large rent increases, and one who is under a lease with nonrenewal or with retaliatory eviction. A tenant then is forced to think carefully before voicing even a valid complaint about substantial defects. Because the landlord-tenant relationship is not momentary, but continuing, the tenant must evaluate and weigh what might be gained or lost by exercising the right to withhold rent and enforce the warranty of habitability.

* * *

Although you may feel that you've heard enough about the shortcomings of building codes, the warranty of habitability, and withholding rent, read on, because these reforms have had some unforeseen and undesirable results you should know about. You've looked at the shortcomings from the lessee's point of view. What about the lessor? Let's suppose that after a year and a half in your apartment you've realized that Horace Hightower's not the ogre he seemed to be the day you signed your lease (or on several occasions afterward). In fact, he's an honest, decent person — albeit with a temper. More than once, you've seen him throw up his hands in exasperation and declare, "This is it! This is final! I'm getting out of the rental business once and for all. How do they expect me to make enough to survive?"

Because you may have heard the same statement dozens of times, you may think Horace is bluffing. But many landlords in his position have not been. The costs of repairs, materials, maintenance staff, heat, and electricity have escalated faster than rent hikes. In addition, faced with the prospect of diminishing profits and increasing problems as tenants begin abating rent payments, many landlords have begun opting out of the rental business altogether, or at least out of low- and middle-income rentals. They're either converting to condominium ownership (discussed in this chapter's Point of Law), upgrading to luxury rentals, or in the case of severely substandard buildings, abandoning the property altogether. The result is that many of those who fought for the right to withhold rent now find it self-defeating.

The problem is most severe in poor and ghetto neighborhoods where landlords often abandon property to circumvent habitability requirements. In this rental environment, landlords assume — probably correctly — that they could never recover the cost of complying with the law because of the limited resources of their tenants. A survey of housing in New York City in the 1970s indicated that in one neighborhood alone more than a thousand buildings had been abandoned, leaving the tenants in complete limbo. For them, enforcing habitability requirements meant that instead of getting better housing, they suffered the consequences of substandard housing's being driven out of existence before replacements were available. At least for middle- and upper-middle-income tenants, there is the expectation that landlords will comply with regulations, that they will raise rents when necessary to recover the cost of doing so, and that tenants will be able to meet the increase.

* * *

Frustrated? Discouraged? At least now you're an "informed" and "experienced" tenant. Let's say it's now three years since lease-signing day, and in those years of tenancy your rent has been raised five times — three annual increases, one to compensate for higher fuel costs, and one to reflect new property-tax assessments. You have had innumerable hassles with your landlord, your apartment looks smaller and dingier than it did three years ago, and you are at the end of your rope. You want someone to pay attention or you want out! What are your options?

You've heard that throughout the city an effort is being mounted to pass a rent-control statute. That sounds promising. In addition, a neighbor tells you of a tenants' meeting during which the possibility of organizing a tenant union and a rent strike will be discussed. That too sounds interesting. Anything is preferable to what you've got, right? Let's look and see.

Rent control first appeared and became widespread after World War I. The return of thousands of veterans coupled with the lifting of wartime voluntary price controls created a severe housing shortage, which in turn led to vastly inflated prices. At the time, rent control was considered an emergency measure — something to be removed when the housing crisis was over. If there hadn't been an emergency, rent control would have been considered unconstitutional as violating the Fifth and Fourteenth amendments to the Constitution (as these amendments were interpreted at the time); the two provisions prohibit the taking of property without due process of law. Although property is not actually and physically confiscated by rent-control statutes, the ability to earn a profit (which is considered property) would be restricted by the regulation. Courts have interpreted the two amendments as protecting the right to earn a reasonable return on investment free from undue government interference. In 1921, the United States Supreme Court upheld the validity of rent-control laws "as a temporary measure to tide over a passing trouble." Three years later the Court made it clear that it would not countenance extension of these measures beyond the emergency period. It has not spoken on the subject since then.

During World War II, Congress instituted nationwide rent control, which continued in some areas until 1954. Although the termination of federal controls should have made it clear that a state of emergency no longer existed, state and local legislatures across the country went ahead and approved rent-control statutes to meet the problem of ongoing housing shortages in those areas. Even though the Supreme Court has declined to make a decisive statement about the constitutionality of rent control, many lower courts have rejected the requirement that there be an emergency and have upheld rent-control measures in the absence of exigent circumstances.

These courts may correctly sense that the Supreme Court has changed its attitude toward rent control since its last pronouncement on the subject more than half a century ago. Several Supreme Court rulings in the somewhat analogous field of wage and price controls offer good evidence of this. Since 1937 the Court generally has upheld price-control legislation regardless of whether an emergency existed, requiring only that the law be reasonably related to a proper legislative purpose and be neither arbitrary nor discriminatory. One proper legislative purpose for a state, of course, is to protect the health and welfare of its citizens. Many states consider that this embraces the power to enact rent-control legislation, or to delegate the authority to do so to county or city governments.

The most common rent-control statutes are local ordinances. These attempt to balance the divergent interests of landlords and tenants. Thus, landlords are prevented from exploiting housing shortages and raising rent levels to a disproportionate extent compared with maintenance and repair costs. At the same time, their opportunity to earn a fair profit is protected — at least theoretically.

Rent-control usually is administered by an appointed rent-control board consisting of community members. Contrary to popular belief, these statutes do not forbid rent increases, but rather limit their size and frequency. Most rent-control enactments establish a base rate first, from which future increases can be calculated and to which they are added. The base rental is established by a "rollback," which means that the rent-control board chooses a rate from a prior year. This rolling back avoids artificial rent hikes by the landlord immediately prior to the statute's passage. Rollbacks usually must be accompanied by adjustment mechanisms to compensate for past inequities. After all, it would defeat the scheme's purpose if a landlord charging artificially inflated rates in the rollback year were permitted to continue reaping the benefits of those rates by having them established as the base rate. In addition, the rollback year and subsequent adjustments must be chosen carefully lest they destroy the landlord's ability to earn a fair return on his investment, which would pose constitutional problems under the Fifth and Fourteenth amendments.

Several different adjustment methods may be used to avoid charges of unconstitutional confiscation. For example, under the return-on-investment formula, the rent-control board first determines fair profit levels for a base year. Then, on a case-by-case basis, it considers such factors as fluctuations in property taxes, major capital improvements, and extraordinary deterioration or destruction of property in deciding whether any given unit yields a fair profit and whether to grant a rent increase. Another method, called the percentage-increase technique, is even easier to administer. It regulates rent increases either by setting a uniform ceiling on the annual allowable percentage increase, or by tying the annual increase to cost-of-living increases (as reflected in the Consumer Price Index). Also, rent-control statutes may make hardship adjustments available in addition to the annual rental increase. Landlords unable to meet mortgage payments or maintenance costs may apply for them. Many rent-control boards also are empowered to *decrease* permissible rent in a controlled dwelling as an adjustment for a decline in necessary services.

Since landlords could evade rent control by evicting tenants who refuse to pay arbitrary rent increases, many laws limit the grounds for eviction and establish procedures for enforcing the statute's terms. These measures are an attempt to take account of the unequal bargaining power that exists when housing is short and money is tight. "Eviction-for-cause" laws usually recognize exceptions — eviction may be permitted for keeping a pet in violation of lease terms or unreasonably interfering with other tenants' enjoyment of the premises — and expressly forbid retaliatory evictions, although establishing that that was the landlord's motive is difficult.

So far, rent control sounds like the answer to a tenant's dreams. It provides him with relief from the pressures of rising rents when housing is scarce and strengthens his bargaining power against the landlord by prohibiting retaliatory evictions.

Why, then, do people in so many places strenuously resist rent control? Not surprisingly, the most vociferous complainers are the landlords who resent having their profit opportunities limited. Even a tenant can sympathize with the landlord's complaint that he alone among business people is so regulated and restricted. The butcher can raise his price when cattle prices rise; indeed, any merchant is free to hike prices as costs escalate, without having Big Brother peering over his shoulder.

The rent-controlled lessor, however, is watched by a host of Big Brothers. Before he even can get an authorized rent hike — to compensate for inflated fuel costs, for example, or to recoup for major capital improvements, or to reflect increased property taxes — he must petition the rent-control board, which then notifies tenants, who are then invited to air their complaints at a public hearing. Whew! This procedure requires time, energy, and money that might better be spent elsewhere. In addition, the process is likely to take so long that by the time a ruling has been issued on the first petition, fuel prices may have risen again, necessitating another application and a second go-round on the bureaucratic paddlewheel.

The real irony is that tenants also have gripes about rent control. Because it gives landlords a reduced expectation of return on their investments, it leads many of them to cut costs and provide only those amenities strictly required by housing codes and by the implied warranty of habitability, with no frills or fringe service benefits for tenants. The result is that controlled dwellings often are less well maintained, their landlords are less responsive to tenant complaints, and their physical plant and services deteriorate faster than uncontrolled dwellings. In addition, many people feel that in the long run rent control exacerbates rental housing shortages, since the limiting of profit margins discourages lending and investment in rental units.

So much for rent control. What about your second option — a tenant union and rent strikes? Tenant unions were first organized in the 1920s and 1930s as a response to worsening slum conditions. But these early efforts failed, largely because the "slum problem" was not a popular political issue and the public was skittish about anything that smacked of "communism" and the ideas espoused by various supposedly subversive "people's" organizations. Not until the appearance of community organizations as part of the civil rights movement in the 1960s was the climate really ripe for tenant-union efforts.

Tenant unions developed for very much the same reasons as labor unions. In part they were a response to anonymous corporate landlords and absentee individual landlords. Renters accustomed to personal dealings with owners of a single dwelling were overwhelmed by the mass of procedures required to get action on a complaint or request for a repair from a corporate landlord concerned with a number of huge, multiunit dwellings. As corporate landlords grew larger, tenants felt their individual bargaining power diminish. The situation was aggravated by continuing housing shortages that made it relatively easy for the landlord to replace a tenant, and almost impossible for a tenant to change his abode. Tenant unions were an attempt to amass and consolidate enough force to cut through the red tape, and in some cases circumvent it by getting the attention of the source of the trouble — the landlord.

Another reason for their development was the failure of legislation to solve tenants' problems. In 1949, the federal government passed the first in a series of housing acts whose stated goal was a decent living environment for every American family. During the 1950s, many states adopted the housing codes discussed earlier in conformity with the goals of this national act. Although these laws were of some help, by the 1960s people were all too familiar with their shortcomings and the difficulty of enforcing them. Failure was particularly glaring with respect to substandard housing where the need was most pressing, because individual tenants lacked the education, money, and know-how to fight the bureaucracy. Thus the time was ripe for tenants to take things into their own hands.

All right! You're ready for a bout of political activism and grassroots community organization. Forget about rent control and the slow-moving cogs and gears of the legislative process — you're going to strike and force the landlord to bargain. Any problems? Well, the first question is, How do you do it? Unless you're a child of the sixties, you've probably never been a petition signer or pamphleteer, nor have you ever picketed or "sat in." If you want to maintain a relatively low profile and conserve some semblance of a good relationship with your landlord, you might want to try less radical possibilities first.

The simplest and mildest form of organization is an ad hoc committee. All you have to do is knock on neighbors' doors and invite them for coffee and conversation at your place. After you've all agreed on the specific and glaring problems, such as the garbage piling up in the halls because of too few trash cans, you arrange for a group "rap" with your landlord or a housing administrator, or circulate a petition requesting relief. Your lessor may well respond by either remedying the problem immediately or making other conciliatory gestures such as having monthly meetings with the tenants or installing a suggestion box in the lobby. The other possibility, of course, is that the union's entreaties fall on deaf ears. The landlord won't budge; in fact, he wants to break the union. Get ready for trench warfare.

Under either scenario, it's likely that by this time an outside tenant union has learned that your building is a hotbed of political activism, and has contacted you and your band of rabble-rousers. Interested in expanding its own power and prestige, the union will have trained organizers begin recruitment drives in your building. Soon there will be more meetings than you ever wanted to attend — information meetings about the union, bull sessions about specific problems in your building, and training sessions for union leadership. In addition, you'll receive and be asked to distribute leaflets to educate tenants on the finer points of "unionism."

Hooking up with an outside organization has the advantage of giving you ready-made power, prestige, and leadership, which otherwise might take time and effort to develop. It does, however, have disadvantages. Some of your neighbors may distrust the union and the notoriety of certain of its past activities. In addition, landlords, and the courts, often are extremely suspicious of "outside agitators" (sometimes rightfully), especially when they have been avid rent strikers.

Other problems? Although all states recognize tenants' rights to unionize, many states still don't accept rent strikes as a legal means of exacting landlord compliance with housing standards. Furthermore, a strike is risky on several fronts. In states or localities without eviction controls, retaliatory eviction is the landlord's best method of dealing with agitators. Even where this type of eviction is forbidden by statute, landlords may overcome tenant activism simply by outlasting a strike. Depending upon the size and resources of the corporate landlord and the scope of the strike, the landlord may be better equipped to survive a month without rent than tenants are to survive a month without heat.

Ironically, there's also a danger that the protests of tenant unions will be heard only too clearly. If the authorities overreact to charges of housing code violations, a building may be condemned and ordered vacated, leaving tenants homeless. And there's always the danger that rent strikes will be misused. In states that forbid retaliatory eviction and look leniently upon tenant activism, tenants have little to lose by not paying rent and thus may be tempted to do so too cavalierly.

* * *

Is it utterly hopeless? Are landlords and tenants destined to be perpetually at each other's throats?

A major defect that all "tenant reforms" — housing codes, warranties of habitability, rent control, and rent strikes — share is that they can't rectify the imperfections of the rental housing market. Most industries respond rapidly to fluctuations in demand by manipulating supply or the unit cost of a product or both. But the landlord only can manipulate cost with any immediacy, since increasing supply by constructing new buildings requires a lot of time, during which there's the risk that demand will drop. Thus, unlike most other entrepreneurs, the landlord cannot increase his net income simply by increasing volume — adding to the units available for rental. Certainly in some cases smaller units may be carved out of larger ones, but this too is regulated by local laws.

Moreover, most merchants can improve their net income by selling more merchandise at a lower unit price, but a landlord with fixed-sum leases or a fixed number of units can only increase earnings by reducing operating costs or raising rent upon lease expiration. In the latter situation, a disgruntled tenant must either pay the increased cost, without getting any apparent increase in benefits, or find a new home. In the former situation, the landlord runs the risk of tenant action (possible rent abatement or rent strikes) and sanctions by local agencies charged with policing housing code violations.

Another problem shared by all the modern reforms is that, from the landlord's point of view, they may go too far. Each represents a shift in bargaining power from landlord to tenant, and each places new burdens on the landlord's shoulders. Much of the shift is not a problem, but rather a desperately needed modification of antiquated property law and a recognition of the unequal bargaining position that generally exists. But to the landlord it's all a big pain in the neck and it's slowly driving him out of the rental market. Landlords, unable or unwilling to meet the obligations imposed by the reforms, are either abandoning uneconomical housing or converting to cooperatives and condominiums. The result is that in recent years fewer rental units have been built than have been lost to the market. Thus, the reforms instituted to secure decent housing for tenants in the long run may be responsible for denying them housing altogether. Sometimes in law, as in life, it seems you just can't win.

POINT OF LAW:

Condominium Conversion

You really can't deny it; the life of a landlord can be fraught with difficulties — from minor tenant complaints to collective tenant legal activism. Is it all worth it? There must be a better way to earn a living.

Faced with rising costs and plummeting profit margins, landlords across the country have found that there is, in fact, an easier way to earn their daily bread — convert rental units to condominiums, sell the condos, and forever wash their hands of tenant gripes and bureaucratic hassles. Sounds like a great idea — for landlords, that is. It's also a boon for those who want to be property owners and live in or near an urban area, but can't find or afford the inflated cost of a single-family home with a yard. The scarcity and exorbitant prices of such homes has created a huge demand for condominiums.

One group notably displeased with today's "condomania," as you might guess, is tenants — both current and prospective. When an apartment house is converted to condominiums, some tenants are displaced because they either don't want or can't afford to purchase. What becomes of them? Does the landlord owe them any obligation? Does the law protect them? And what about all the newcomers to the apartment market — young people, retirees, new arrivers in town? Would-be tenants eagerly pounding the pavement often find themselves greeted at every turn by signs announcing: CONDOMINIUMS AVAILABLE, or CONVERTING TO CONDOS.

Doesn't anybody believe in apartments anymore? What's so wonderful about condominiums, anyway? Although you probably know a condominium when you see one, you may not be familiar with its specific characteristics. It technically is defined as "the common ownership of property jointly with one or more individuals." Each individual is the sole owner of the airspace and "right to enjoyment" within his own portion of the building, and is a co-owner (tenant in common) with the others of the land and public portions of the property. In other words, although each owner has control over his own unit (and can paint murals on the ceiling, knock out a wall, or dye the carpet black), he shares ownership of areas such as the lobby, fire escapes, parking lots, elevators, and central heating units with other condominium residents.

Shared ownership means shared expenses; hence, part of the appeal of condos is the low cost of purchase, maintenance, and repairs, compared to the same costs for a typical suburban home. In addition, for those who react negatively to the gardening and maintenance aspects of home ownership, condominiums are a blessing because the unit owners generally hire an independent contractor to do the upkeep. Finally, as energy, land, and construction costs skyrocket and major American urban centers become more and more crowded so that the space required for detached single-family houses disappears, the "American dream" of home ownership becomes well-nigh unobtainable. Condominiums thus are a compromise, combining the advantages of ownership with those of shared responsibilities and expenses characteristic of renting.

Sounds pretty good. But suppose you've lived in your apartment for seven years. You've fixed it up and it feels like home. It's the perfect spot for you, being close to work as well as all the nightlife of downtown. And it's in a real neighborhood — a rare commodity these days. You have friends and neighbors who look out for you as you do for them, and you've become active in local community organizations. But one day a notice arrives from your landlord: The building is going condo. Since your lease expires in ninety days, you have just that much time to either fork over a down payment or leave. How could your landlord do this to you? More important, what are you going to do?

Never mind how the owner could do this, the fact is that she has. As long as the landlord is not terminating your lease before its designated time, and as long as no local statute forbids condo conversion, she is within her rights as a property owner. So, calm down, pour yourself something cool to drink, and consider the possibilities. You could buy the unit. Let's see, that requires a $14,000 down payment (20 percent of the purchase price). You have $3000 in your savings account and a few shares of stock, but you're already paying off a loan on your car. Okay, so you can't buy. Not only that, you might not want to even if you could. Tying up that much cash in home ownership and mortgaging yourself to the hilt wouldn't leave you much money for other activities.

It looks like you'll be moving, then. It may be a pain in the neck, but it's not the end of the world. After all, a change every once in a while may be a good thing. The real problem is finding a new apartment.

Remember how long it took last time you looked? Now you've got ninety days — and that's it. All that telephoning, running around town, and bargaining with landlords. It's going to be tough, perhaps impossible, to find a place as nice as the one you're in for an equivalent price. If your apartment is rent-controlled, you'll find that prices "outside" have increased dramatically while you've experienced controlled increases for seven years. As if this weren't enough, the quick pace of condominium conversion has made rental housing scarce in many areas and contributed to inflated prices.

What if you don't find someplace else you like in time? Can your landlord throw you out on the street? You know the answer to that. When the lease is over, the landlord isn't required to renew it. But many communities, to protect tenants from this difficulty, have imposed either specific notice of conversion requirements or said that the tenant must be given a "reasonable" time after notice is sent. These periods vary from thirty days to six months, depending upon what is considered reasonable in a given market area. For instance, if you live in a town with a zero-vacancy rate, thirty days might not be reasonable, but six months certainly should be sufficient.

You still may think this is unfair. After all, you have been a quiet, honorable tenant. Now there will be moving expenses you didn't count on, you will have to leave your comfortable neighborhood, and although "reasonable" notice gives you an opportunity to find a new place, it doesn't guarantee you'll find something as nice, or as close to work. Perhaps the law should prevent the landlord from putting you out until you find another apartment that's satisfactory.

But let's not forget the landlord's side of all this. She feels overwhelmed by the risk of tenant abuse and heavy regulation. Moreover, it's her property, and she has a constitutional right to use it to earn a living. What if the building is operating at a loss? Must she keep you as a tenant after your lease expires, and go on losing money until you've found a satisfactory apartment? Certainly that's not the law! Look at it this way: Suppose that your building wasn't going condo, but you had been planning to leave when your lease ended in ninety days. The landlord couldn't make you stay until she found a replacement tenant as nice, as neat, as quiet as you. So how can you expect to stay now that your lease is up and she wants you out?

Nonetheless, there are situations in which termination, even with reasonable notice, seems particularly harsh. What if your widowed grandmother was being evicted to make room for young condominium purchasers? She's seventy-five, living on social security, and, like many of the people in her neighborhood, has been in her apartment for a long time — in her case, for forty years. Aside from all the sentimental and neighborhood attachments she feels, moving is just too big a hassle for her to manage alone. She lacks both the energy to pack up four decades' worth of living, and the money to pay moving expenses. Should the law ban eviction of people over sixty-five? Or give them a year or two to relocate? Perhaps the landlord should be required to pay moving expenses and locate alternative housing for elderly people. What about having the govenment, which means all of us taxpayers, subsidize these costs?

What about handicapped people? Frequently a building has special facilities for handicapped residents or a particular neighborhood may supply them with needed services — shuttle buses, community health clinics, and the like. Moving can impose severe hardship on these people. Should a condo-converting owner be required to compensate tenants or to provide substitute services?

Questions, questions, questions! All part of the big issue: Just how much can the law demand of property owners before it oversteps the constitutional boundaries of the Fifth and Fourteenth Amendments and deprives them of property "without due process of law"?

Since condomania is still a relatively new phenomenon, there are very few answers. Some communities have gone to the extreme of imposing either temporary moratoria or total bans on condo conversion. Although notice requirements and some additional restrictions certainly are constitutional, it is possible that a total ban on conversion will be deemed an unconstitutional "taking" of property. We'll just have to wait to see what the courts do with this issue.

Another technique used by several communities is to permit a landlord to convert a unit only when the existing tenant voluntarily vacates the premises or dies, leaving an open apartment. Eviction problems thus are skirted, and constitutional problems may be avoided as well.

But these measures don't solve several important and controversial dilemmas about the effect of condo conversion on the health and character of a neighborhood or community. For example, banning evictions "locks in" existing tenants and "locks out" prospective buyers. This may discourage newcomers from moving to town, thereby sapping it of new life, vitality, and economic strength. Conversely, what happens to the stability and character of a neighborhood when the present residents are forced to move out? New purchasers (especially those who have acquired the condo as an investment and don't intend to live there) may not have the same sense of community and responsibility as "old-timers," which also can be detrimental to the overall health of the area. Yet (to confuse the picture even more) aren't owners more of a stabilizing influence than renters?

Most parts of the country don't have enough experience with condos to determine their ultimate effect on our social environment. It seems likely, however, that in time they'll be assimilated into the American housing scene and be accepted as part of it. Let's hope that the courts and legislatures prove to be a constructive influence on the course, content, and length of the transition period.

Life and Death

12

THE RIGHT TO DIE:

Does the Law Offer Death with Dignity?

D o y o u h a v e a right to die? This may seem like a peculiar question, since it's difficult to see why you would want to exercise a right like that even if you had it. But think again: Suppose you were seriously ill and in great pain; it's possible you simply wouldn't want to go on living. Under these circumstances, would you have the right to choose death?

Maybe you'd prefer not to think about it. Serious illness and death are not pleasant topics to dwell on. But their existence can't be denied or ignored; indeed, if you have a relative or friend who has been gravely ill, the question of the right to die may well have come up.

Modern medical technology has increased the significance of the question. It is increasingly possible to keep patients alive for long periods in situations in which there is no hope of cure or recovery. Thus the law has had to confront the issue of whether these people should have to linger — often at great cost to themselves in physical pain, and to their families and loved ones in mental anguish and medical expenses — or should be allowed to die a natural and dignified death. The legal problems are especially acute when the patient is too ill or otherwise incapacitated to decide his own fate, since then the question arises of who will decide it for him — his family, the attending physician, the courts, or some combination of the three. As we shall see, the inability of the law to provide clear guidelines on how this decision is to be made has proved a further source of distress in an already painful situation.

* * *

Let's pose an unpleasant dilemma: Imagine that you're suffering from a terminal disease. You're in the hospital, where you're hooked up to a machine that keeps your vital organs functioning; without the ma-

chine you would quickly die of the illness's effects. You're also in
constant pain, which is abated somewhat by injections of painkillers.
The doctors tell you that the progress of the disease is irreversible and
that you'll never recover — at most you have six months to live.
They also inform you that the pain will get worse and worse, as your
system becomes acclimated to the painkillers and as your condition
degenerates.

Sound bad? Well, let's make it even worse. Let's say that the treatment you're receiving is extremely expensive. In addition to the usual
high costs of hospitalization and medical care, there is the huge expense for using the machine that keeps you alive. Up to now your
medical insurance has covered the costs, but soon they will exceed
your coverage, and when that happens the expense is going to fall on
your family. You have a wife and two children, and if you live for even
another three or four months, you're going to leave them with staggering medical bills.

Under these circumstances, you might decide that you would prefer
to have the machine that keeps you going disconnected so that you can
die naturally. But can you elect to do so? Is this a case in which you
have a right to die? The answer is yes.

If you are terminally ill but mentally sound (in legal terms, you're
"competent"), you can refuse a treatment that would prolong your life
yet not offer any possibility of an actual cure. The distinction between
"prolonging" and "curing" is significant. In our example, we've pos-
ited that you are connected to a machine that artificially keeps your
body functioning but won't cure the disease. Thus you would have the
legal right to ask that the machine be "unplugged," so that you could
die naturally.

Note that to have the right to die, you must be "terminally ill." That
means that the prognosis must be a matter of medical certitude
— it clearly isn't enough that the doctors think that you *might* die, or
even that you are *very likely* to die; rather, death must be inevitable.
One might ask if this condition could ever be met, since there always
seems to be a possibility, however remote, that a patient will recover,
or that a cure for the disease will be developed before his time is up.
Still, the possibility of either event occurring in certain cases is so
unlikely that as a practical matter the situation is deemed hopeless, and
the patient is allowed to refuse treatment.

Another requirement is that you not have long to live. In a sense,
we are all terminal, since we will all die someday; what's unique about
the terminal patient is that he is going to die of specified causes, and
relatively soon. There's no exact time span that renders a disease
terminal, but the six-month period in our example probably is short

enough. Note that as the time period gets longer, we can't be sure that a cure won't be found, and so it's more difficult to conclude that recovery is impossible.

The right to die is based on two related legal doctrines. First, there is the centuries-old rule that everyone has a right of bodily self-determination. Simply stated, it's your body and as a general matter you can't be forced to accept medical treatment without your "informed consent." A doctor who violates this right (except in emergencies when there isn't time to get consent) commits a battery and can be sued by the patient. The second doctrine is the emerging constitutional right of bodily privacy, which is discussed in Chapter 13, Abortion. Again, the idea is that you have a right to control what is done to your body and to be protected against unwanted physical intrusions upon it.

Now that you know some law, let's change the situation and test its limits. Suppose that you're terminally ill with cancer, and that at the most you have only two weeks to live. You're confined to a hospital bed, but you aren't being kept alive by any machines or treatment. You're in excruciating pain, which the doctors can do nothing about. Because you know there's no hope of recovery, because there's so little time anyway, and because you want to die a dignified death, you ask one of the doctors to give you a lethal injection that will end your life quickly and painlessly. Does your right to die entitle you to receive the shot?

The answer, as a legal matter, is a definite no. Moreover, anyone who gave you the injection could be put on trial for murder. This is mercy killing, and although juries often refuse to convict someone who does it, especially if the "killer" is a loved one of the patient, it continues to be viewed as criminal behavior.

Suppose that instead of giving you the injection, the doctor simply leaves a cup of poison on your nightstand with instructions for you to drink it "if you don't think you can hang on any longer." Again, this is illegal. Depending on the law of the state you're in, the doctor is subject to prosecution for abetting a suicide, or possibly for homicide; and you might be prosecuted for attempted suicide if you didn't die from the poison. Of course, it's extremely unlikely that any prosecutor would bring charges against you in this situation. As the discussion of prosecutorial discretion in Chapter 5, Self-Defense, indicated, crimes like these don't have a very high priority. But regardless of whether you or your doctor would end up charged with a crime, the law's recognition of your right to die does not extend to getting the shot or being supplied with the poison.

Let's try one more variation. What if instead of being so open about helping you to die, the doctor was more subtle? Suppose he left a bottle of sleeping pills on the nightstand with instructions that you should be careful not to take more than two at a time, since if you took a lot you'd sleep permanently. Literally, all he's done is warn you against the dangers of overdose; arguably, however, he's instructed you on how to commit suicide — if you want to take the hint. Is this illegal? Presumably it is, if it can be shown that the doctor's intention was to help you to die. Realistically, however, it would be difficult to prove this to a jury, especially if they weren't anxious to convict the doctor in the first place.

The difference between the cases involving the injection, the poison, or the pills and our first example, in which you had the right to have treatment discontinued, is that there is an active intervention to bring about your death. The law distinguishes between these situations and one in which a treatment that is artificially *prolonging* a life simply is terminated. Stated another way, you have the right to be left alone to die a natural death, but you have no right to have the process speeded up.

Do you agree with this distinction? Why should we be so concerned with whether death comes naturally or through the intervention of someone who wants to spare the doomed patient further suffering? Isn't the key that the patient is in pain, can never be cured, and wants to die in peace and dignity?

Nevertheless, the law draws this active-passive distinction and insists that nothing be done to hasten the inevitable. The reason is that actively helping the patient to die always has seemed too much like murder to be condoned. It goes against the attitude, strongly rooted in traditional morality, that each life is of value and must be allowed its natural span. On the other hand, this attitude is sorely tested in situations in which the terminal patient is in great pain, as in our cancer case. Indeed, as medical science enables people to live longer and thus increases the likelihood of their contracting diseases such as cancer, the need to do something to alleviate their condition may force the law to re-examine its position. At least one public-opinion poll shows a majority of people are in favor of allowing a doctor to end the life of a terminal patient if the patient and his family request it. But for now the law is clear — mercy killing is a crime, and your right to die is limited to a death by purely natural causes.

* * *

We've been considering situations in which the patient is terminal. What if he will die if he doesn't receive treatment, but will be cured if he gets it? Can he refuse?

If this sounds a little crazy (Why, you ask, would anyone refuse lifesaving treatment?), you should know that there have been actual cases raising this question. A number of them have involved the refusal by Jehovah's Witnesses to accept blood transfusions because the treatment violated their religious principles. Since the patient often will die without the transfusion, the religious position poses the issue of the right to die. The situation usually arises with the patient already in the hospital, where the doctors are obligated to supply all necessary treatment, including blood transfusions, yet also are required to have the patient's consent to the treatment; given this dilemma, the hospital authorities go to court to have the impasse resolved.

Do you think the law should intervene and require — indeed, force — the person to have the transfusion? Keep in mind we're not dealing with a terminal illness or with a life being artificially prolonged by medical science. We're talking about a person who is capable of being cured and living a useful life, but who is going to die unless he receives a blood transfusion — a relatively minor medical procedure.

In this situation, the individual's right to forgo medical treatment (and often his freedom of religion) must be weighed against the interest of the state in preserving life and in protecting third parties who might be affected by the person's death. The interest in preserving life, of course, is much stronger here than it is in the context of the terminal patient, whose life can be maintained for only a limited time and often at the cost of great personal suffering. The third parties whose interests are to be protected usually are the patient's children, who may become wards of the state if treatment is refused and death follows.

The state also has to be concerned with protecting the integrity of the medical profession. The doctors are placed in a difficult position when a patient refuses to consent to a blood transfusion (or any other lifesaving treatment). Once the patient is in the hospital and placed in a doctor's care, isn't he obliged to follow standard medical procedures, which include transfusions when required? If he abides by the patient's wishes, and the patient dies, the doctor may be subject to criminal liability. If, faced with the patient's attitude on transfusions, he refuses to treat him at all, and the patient dies or suffers harm as a result of the doctor's refusal, the doctor again could be subject to criminal liability, as well as to a civil suit by the patient or his survivors.

On the other hand, if the doctor goes ahead and gives the transfusion against the patient's expressed wishes, he conceivably could be sued by the patient for battery. Remember, the historic right to refuse treatment gives the patient a possible lawsuit against a doctor who

violates his bodily integrity. It may be that a jury would hesitate to find
the doctor liable in this type of case, but it's still one more possibility
to worry about.

The doctor's situation is exacerbated by the possibility that the
patient may not be capable of making an informed choice. He may be
so disoriented by illness or injury that he is unable to decide rationally
whether to accept the treatment or not. Yet the doctor, who often must
act quickly, and who is not an expert in deciding what constitutes an
"informed choice" and what doesn't, may find himself embroiled in a
legal controversy if he comes to the wrong conclusion — wrong, because a court, having the benefit of hindsight and more time to think
about it than the doctor had, later decides so!

As you can see, the medical profession has a strong interest in the
legal rules governing these questions. Perhaps the doctors' greatest
need is for clarity and consistency, so that they know what is expected
of them and what they can do without landing in court. But it's also
true that they want legal rules that accord with their own instincts as
healers — rules that will let them cure those who can be cured, and let
them release the incurable from needless suffering.

The cases involving Jehovah's Witnesses are further complicated by
the patient's asserting that the treatment is against·his freedom of
religion, which is guaranteed by the free-exercise clause of the First
Amendment, as we saw in Chapter 1, School Prayer. Although this
right is not absolute, it does weigh in favor of not subjecting the patient
to the treatment.

So what's the result? Can the blood transfusion be refused? The
answer is that the courts have come to different results. For example,
one court concluded that the religious beliefs of the patient permitted
her to refuse the transfusion, since the decision was her own and did
not endanger public health, welfare, or morals. It was significant that
in this case the patient had no dependent children who would be left
destitute because of her death. Similarly, in another case in which the
court concluded that the patient's religious beliefs allowed him to
refuse a blood transfusion, the court was influenced by the fact that the
patient's financial resources were sufficient to provide for his children
if he died.

But a number of courts have imposed the transfusion on the Jehovah's Witness. In one case, the court compelled a woman who was
thirty-two weeks pregnant to have a transfusion, noting that the unborn child was entitled to the law's protection. In another, the transfusion was required in an emergency situation for a woman whose death
would have left her seven-month-old child abandoned. Still another

court likened the refusal to suicide and held that the state's interest in sustaining life overrode the patient's religious convictions.

What if religious beliefs are not involved? A recent case did permit a nonterminal patient to refuse life-sustaining treatment, even though she did not raise religious objections to the operation. The patient was a seventy-seven-year-old woman who had developed gangrene in her leg, which would have had to be amputated to save her life. In balancing her right of privacy against the state's interest in keeping her alive, the court determined that the extremely serious nature of the proposed intrusion upon her bodily integrity entitled her to refuse the operation.

Let's try another case in which religious belief isn't involved. Suppose a great sculptor had an accident that rendered her totally paralyzed and required that she be maintained on a respirator to be kept alive. Unable to practice her art, she no longer wishes to live. Would she have the right to have the respirator discontinued? Keep in mind that she isn't terminal; with the help of the respirator she can live her normal life span.

The answer is that she probably wouldn't. Although the law values artistic creativity (and protects it through copyright), it is not likely to accord it as much weight as religious belief, which is protected by the First Amendment, in balancing the individual's right to control her body against the state's interest in preserving life.

This situation raises the issue of whether quality of life can be the basis for the right to die. The sculptor wants to die, but it isn't pain that creates the desire; rather, it's her belief that her life has become meaningless and so should end.

For a number of reasons, the law has strongly resisted any attempt to allow qualitative considerations to create a right to die. First, there's no objective criterion for evaluating quality of life — what one person finds intolerable might be bearable for another. So the law has no way of determining which subjective desire should be honored and which shouldn't. Also, people who suffer tragedies in time may come to accept what has happened and then wish to continue with their lives, a possibility that's extinguished if the law heeds an initial request for death.

Finally, there's the risk that once we let people make this decision for themselves, they'll begin to make it for others. It's not such a big step from unplugging the sculptor's respirator to unplugging one that keeps alive someone who's retarded, paralyzed, or simply old. If it becomes an accepted practice to allow, or encourage, the extinguishing of lives on qualitative grounds, it may be only another step for those in authority to decide to exterminate whole groups whose lives "lack quality." Admittedly this is a melodramatic scenario, but the mere possibility is enough to make the law wary. The attitude that each life must be preserved may create hardship in some cases, but it's also a safeguard against our becoming a society in which life is insufficiently valued.

As you can see, the determination of whether lifesaving treatment can be administered against a patient's will involves the law in its familiar role of balancing competing rights and principles. Perhaps the most important factor to be weighed is that the choice of death, once granted, is irreversible. It is the removal of this unique element in the case of a terminal patient (he will die soon anyway; the only real question is one of timing) that makes those cases more subject to definite rules. However, as we shall see later, even the terminal case can present special problems not easily reduced to clear legal formulations.

* * *

Let's go back to our sculptor for a moment. Assume that the accident has left her totally paralyzed, but she doesn't need a respirator to stay alive. Again, she finds life meaningless and wishes to die. In fact, this is the situation that was posed in Tom Stoppard's highly successful play *Whose Life Is It, Anyway?*

The difference between this case and our earlier hypothetical one is that now the sculptor is not asking that a life-sustaining treatment be discontinued — something the hospital probably will refuse to do — but that she be allowed to check out of the hospital, go home, and simply pass away as a result of not eating or drinking. She's not asking the authorities to help at all; she'll have two friends come and take her home (remember, she's paralyzed and can't do anything for herself). Once there, she'll tell her friends to lock the door on their way out.

Will the hospital authorities let her go? Let's assume they know what she plans to do, so if they keep her there they can maintain her life by feeding her intravenously. But she wants to go home. In effect, if the hospital is going to keep her from killing herself, it's going to have to hold her against her will.

It seems unlikely that the sculptor legally could be prevented from having her way. It's just too great a restriction on her freedom to imprison her in the hospital simply because of what she says she will do when she leaves. Moreover, since the hospital authorities are not likely to be held responsible for aiding a suicide if they release her, they can't claim that they must hold her to protect themselves from legal liability. And once she gets home, she is protected from prying or interference to some extent by the constitutional right of privacy that extends to the home. So our sculptor may well be able to end her life. She's not so much exercising a right to die as she is committing suicide under circumstances in which others are not legally empowered to intervene and stop her.

*   *   *

We've seen that a terminal patient, in full control of his mental faculties, has the right to discontinue treatment that cannot cure him but can only prolong life. But what happens if the patient is not competent to make this choice? What if illness, youth, old age, or other circumstances have rendered him unable to decide for himself? What if he is legally incompetent — that is, mentally incapable of making an informed, rational choice about his condition? These are the really tough — often heart-rending — cases, which can involve a great deal of emotional agony and soul-searching on the part of the patient's loved ones, as well as considerable uncertainty on the part of the courts and the medical profession.

Let's take an actual case. Joseph Saikewicz was a sixty-seven-year-old man who had spent most of his life in state institutions; he was mentally retarded, with an IQ of ten and a mental age of about two years and eight months. He had never learned to talk, and could communicate only by means of gestures and grunts.

Saikewicz was terminally ill with leukemia. The question for the doctors was whether he should be given chemotherapy to try to make the disease go into remission, which is not a cure but a temporary halt in its progress. Remission occurs in only 30 to 50 percent of the cases in which chemotherapy is tried, and typically lasts for only two to thirteen months. Moreover, whether it works or not, chemotherapy has serious side effects, including pain, severe nausea, and loss of hair.

So what were the doctors to do? If Saikewicz had been competent, he could have made the decision himself, but he was totally incapable of understanding his situation and the available options. There was no family with whom the hospital authorities could confer, so they went to the Massachusetts courts to resolve the question.

That state's highest court reasoned that Saikewicz had the same right as a competent person to decide whether to forgo treatment. It then employed what it called substituted judgment to decide the issue: The court asked itself what the incompetent person would have chosen had he been able to understand the situation. To do this, the judge imagined himself as the incompetent patient and weighed all the factors of the case from Saikewicz's standpoint to determine what he would have wanted done. Looked at from that angle, the factors in favor of chemotherapy were that most patients who choose for themselves elect to have it, and that it offers the chance of a longer life. Weighing against treatment were Saikewicz's advanced age, which could have prevented remission from taking place; the suffering that the treatment would cause; and the fact that he would be unable to cooperate with the treatment and wouldn't comprehend the reason for the severe disruption of his life that it would cause. On balance, putting itself in Saikewicz's place, the court decided that he would have refused chemotherapy.

Does this "substituted judgment" approach make any sense to you? How can a judge, who may well never have seen the patient, much less come to know him, decide what he would have chosen? Is the decision whether the patient lives or dies one that we want a court to make? Or is it more properly a decision that should be left to the medical profession or to the patient's loved ones? Before answering these questions, let's look at how well — or badly — involving the court works in a situation in which the incompetent patient has a family that wants to have a say in the decision.

Consider the case of Earle Spring. Here was a man who had lived a robust, healthy life until, at the age of seventy-six, he developed a foot infection, then pneumonia, and then suffered kidney failure. His condition was diagnosed as "end-stage kidney disease," which is total and irreversible loss of kidney function, and required that he be subjected to dialysis treatment. Dialysis is not a cure; it is simply a substitute for the absent kidney function. Without dialysis, Spring would have died within a month. His physical deterioration was accompanied by a deterioration of his mental capacities; he became belligerent, destructive, unable to care for himself, and in time was unable to recognize his wife or son, who were looking after him. Eventually he had to be institutionalized.

Spring's condition placed a severe strain upon his family, particularly his wife, who suffered a stroke as a result. The family decided that, considering all the circumstances, it was best to discontinue the dialysis treatment and have Spring die a natural death. But under the rationale of the *Saikewicz* case, which was the controlling precedent since Spring lived in Massachusetts, the decision was up to the court. When the family asked the court for an order to stop the treatment, the judge appointed an independent guardian to represent the patient's interests. This started a series of highly publicized legal proceedings that went on for more than a year. By the time the court finally ruled that yes, the treatment could be discontinued, Spring had died of other causes.

The *Spring* case illustrates several of the problems with asking courts to decide these issues. A court case can drag out for months or even years; yet a situation like Spring's cries out for a quick resolution. Moreover, it seems a cruel procedure to force the patient's loved ones into the position of seeking to end his life, while an "objective" guardian — someone who probably doesn't even know the patient — argues against them. Yet it's hard to avoid this sort of adversarial procedure, since our courts basically are set up to resolve disputes through the presentation of competing arguments and not through consultation.

If you have doubts about courts settling this kind of question, who do you think should resolve it? What do you think of leaving it to the patient's family and attending physician to decide?

That's the general approach that the New Jersey Supreme Court used in the well-known Karen Ann Quinlan case. The patient was a twenty-two-year-old girl who, for reasons never fully discovered, had gone into a coma a year earlier and remained in a totally vegetative state in which her mind had ceased to function on a conscious level, and from which there was no reasonable possibility of her ever emerging. She was on a respirator, and the question was whether it should be disconnected so that she could die a natural death.

The court noted that Karen Ann's constitutional right of privacy entitled her to have the respirator disconnected. But it took a different approach to the problem than the Massachusetts court would take a year later in *Saikewicz*. It said that the decision to discontinue treatment should not be made by a court, but rather by the patient's family in consultation with the attending physicians, and then only with the approval of a hospital "ethics committee." Significantly, this decision would be made without court review or approval. The court added, however, that if the procedures it laid down were followed, then the physician and hospital would not be subject to criminal or civil liability for the decision to disconnect the respirator.

Although this case involved a comatose patient, its approach could be extended to terminal patients who are being maintained artificially by life-support systems. (Indeed, unless these two conditions are seen as substantially the same, the court in *Quinlan* could be accused of making a qualitative judgment about the value of Karen Ann's life.) In either event, the decision to discontinue the treatment would be made for the patient by his family and doctors, with the court pretty much staying out of the process.

Do you think this is the best way to handle the situation? At least it would avoid the delays that kept Earle Spring's family in turmoil while the court proceedings dragged out. Also, this approach allows the decision to be made by those who know and love the patient, instead of by a judge who in all probability has never laid eyes on him.

But wait a minute. Doesn't the *Quinlan* approach place too great a burden on the family? Remember that the patient's loved ones are under immense pressure already. There's the anguish of seeing the patient in pain or comatose, their own suffering (such as Spring's wife's having a stroke), and the possible financial drain caused by the expense of continued treatment. Is it fair to subject them to the further pressure of determining whether to terminate the life? Isn't there the risk that they'll be too emotional to judge what's best for the patient? If they choose to have him die, how might they feel later on? Would they wonder whether they did the right thing? At least the *Saikewicz* approach relieves the family of the burden of assuming final responsibility for discontinuing treatment.

The *Quinlan* procedure also creates another problem: Just how much should the courts rely on the medical profession to make these choices? Will the doctors treat all patients equally, or will they be influenced by factors that arguably should not be considered, such as the shortage of life-sustaining equipment and the quality of life of those already using it, or the desire to divert the already strained resources of the hospital to those who can be cured? The law may hesitate to question the integrity of another profession in this way, but it has no choice but to consider these possibilities. Moreover, although judges know less about the situation than doctors (and must rely heavily on their expertise and judgment even under the *Saikewicz* approach), they may be in a better position to make a dispassionate decision, precisely because they are removed from the day-to-day pressures that confront the doctors who handle these cases.

Still, on balance, unless court proceedings on these cases can be significantly speeded up, the *Quinlan* approach seems to be preferable. At present judicial intervention is just too slow and cumbersome to deal effectively with a problem of this nature. Of course, there may be special reasons for court review, such as a dispute among the relatives on what to do, or among the doctors on whether the patient really is incompetent — after all, it's not always easy to determine whether a person is in control of his faculties, particularly if he's ill. There's also the possibility that the family will not act in the patient's best interests, that other motivations, such as hatred, a desire to inherit, or the wish to end a burdensome situation, will influence their decision. In these circumstances, the law should intervene to resolve any disputes and to protect the incompetent. But it must do so on an expedited basis. Otherwise, the decision to terminate treatment probably is best made within what the *Quinlan* court called the patient-doctor-family relationship.

Under either approach, the law must provide the medical profession with clear standards under which to act. Although the *Quinlan* court made an attempt to do this, its efforts were not wholly successful. It is not clear, for example, how active a role the attending physicians are to play in the decision to discontinue treatment. Nor is it clear exactly what the function of the ethics committee is to be. A literal reading of the case indicates that the committee doesn't do any more than confirm that the patient has no reasonable chance of recovery. Yet the term *ethics committee* suggests a group imbued with more than technical medical knowledge. Indeed, the New Jersey court indicated that in addition to doctors it could consist of social workers, lawyers, and theologians. But assuming that the committee is to employ ethical, religious, or legal principles, and not merely make a medical judgment on the patient's condition, the court offered little in the way of guidance on how this disparate group was to apply these principles to the question of when an incompetent patient should be allowed to die.

This lack of guidance was to affect the resolution of the Quinlan matter. Even with the court's approval, the hospital refused to take Karen Ann permanently off the respirator. (It was found she could breathe without it, but apparently the hospital determined to put her back on it if she developed trouble breathing.) Karen Ann's parents were forced to move her to a publicly operated nursing facility to get her completely weaned from the respirator. (Ironically, terminating the treatment did not lead to her death, and she is alive today, although still comatose.)

If you think the hospital authorities were too timid, look at the situation from their standpoint. They're subject to lawsuits for malpractice and to possible criminal prosecution if they deviate from the legal standards of proper medical care. The state, for example, might press criminal charges for homicide, or perhaps a relative — one not consulted in the decision — would bring charges. So if the law is confused or unclear, then they can't be sure that their participation in terminating the patient's life-support system won't get them into legal trouble. The court in *Quinlan* said that if they followed its directions, they would be relieved of liability. But the hospital authorities apparently weren't convinced. And given the general uncertainty of the law in this area, perhaps they were justified in their reluctance to assume the responsibility that the court tried to delegate to them.

* * *

One solution to the problem of preserving your right to die should you become incompetent is to make your wishes known while you are still in control of your faculties. A number of states have passed, and others are considering, statutes that allow a person to express in a written document, called a living will, the desire to die a natural death, rather than have life preserved by artificial means. Typically, the will states this desire, and then absolves the doctors and the hospital of liability for terminating treatment.

Some of these statutes require that the declaration be made after a person learns of the terminal illness; others allow a healthy person to decide what he would want done should illness or accident render it impossible to make the decision. To prevent a rash decision, one statute requires that at least a two-week period pass between the time when the condition is revealed to the patient and when he signs the will; safeguards include the right to revoke the will orally at any time, and a set period after which it lapses.

As is true of any "preventive medicine," however, the living will offers a cure only to the extent that its availability is known and people choose to make use of it. Perhaps the most serious barrier to employing a living will is facing up to the prospect of an incapacitating, terminal illness. It's not a pleasant thought, but consider how much heartache you may save yourself and your loved ones by planning ahead for this eventuality.

* * *

The right to die is really the right to be let alone to meet one's fate privately and with dignity. But like all rights, it's subject to limitations, especially when the death will affect third parties, or can only be brought about by the active intervention of others.

The extent of the right is currently being tested around the country by the cruel paradox that modern medicine can preserve life in situations in which it cannot offer any hope of a cure. Thus far, the law has been feeling its way and has not reacted effectively — or consistently — to this dilemma. Perhaps as legal guidelines become clearer, families such as Earle Spring's no longer will have to spend their loved one's last months enmeshed in emotionally charged public court battles. Eventually, the law, reflecting the society it serves, will broaden its support of the right of every person — competent or not — to allow life to end quietly and naturally.

POINT OF LAW:
The Right to Live

Kerri Ann McNulty was born with multiple birth defects, including cataracts on both eyes, deafness, probable mental retardation, and a congenital heart condition. These were the result of her mother's having had German measles during pregnancy.

The infant would die of her heart condition unless she had an operation, and it was estimated that there was only a fifty-fifty chance the surgery would be successful. After consultation with their minister and with the attending physicians, Kerri Ann's parents decided that it was better not to proceed with the operation; in effect, they preferred that she die.

Since the situation arose in Massachusetts, where *Saikewicz* was the governing law on the question of the right to die, the hospital authorities thought that a court would have to determine whether to withhold the operation. The judge decided they should go ahead and operate, stating, "I am persuaded that the proposed cardiac surgery is not merely a life-prolonging measure, but indeed is for the purpose of saving the life of this child, regardless of the quality of that life." The operation was a success, and Kerri Ann lived.

Note that the court had no choice in its decision. This was not a case in which the judge could apply substituted judgment, à la *Saikewicz* and *Spring,* to determine what the incompetent would have chosen under all the circumstances. Substituted judgment applies only when the incompetent patient is *terminal,* and only permits life-sustaining treatment to be discontinued; it does not allow *life-saving* treatment to be withheld. Kerri Ann was not terminal; although her life was in jeopardy, she had an even chance of surviving the operation and of living for many years — she was terminal only if she didn't receive the operation. Thus her situation was entirely different from that of Joseph Saikewicz, who would die relatively soon even with chemotherapy, or Karen Ann Quinlan, who could never return from a vegetative existence. The question for Kerri Ann was whether she would be given the chance to survive; what was at stake was not her right to die, but rather her right to live.

You might be wondering how the question came up. After all, wasn't it obvious to the hospital authorities that this was not a case in which treatment could be withheld? The answer may lie not only in confusion on the part of the medical profession about the exact meaning of the *Saikewicz* case but also in a conscious or unconscious determination by the doctors, along with the parents, that Kerri Ann's life would be of such poor quality that the most merciful thing to do was to "allow" her to die.

But merciful for whom? For Kerri Ann? Just for perspective, try the substituted-judgment approach. Put yourself in Kerri Ann's place and ask if you would desire death. Wouldn't the answer probably be no? Kerri Ann may not have the prospects of a full life by most people's standards, but how can we say that from her own viewpoint life is unacceptable? Remember, she knows no other existence than her present condition, and cannot regret the loss of what she has never experienced. Does she enjoy her life? We may never really know. What we do know is that, with only the very rarest of exceptions, all living organisms cling to their existence. So how can we say that a retarded human being, even one who is blind and deaf, does not value the life she has been granted?

What of the parents? Should we consider their suffering? They face the prospect of raising a child who will never be normal in the traditional sense, and who cannot help but be a great psychological and perhaps financial burden to them. Possibly their own anguish leads them to believe that the child suffers as they do, and so does not wish to live. Under the circumstances, it isn't all that difficult to understand their view that the child's life should not continue. But should their opinion be weighted heavily, let alone be determinative?

Unfortunately, their reluctance to have her live is itself a factor that casts doubt on her future. The parents, after all, are the ones who will care for Kerri Ann, not merely during childhood but through her entire life. Even if they place her in a home for the mentally retarded, the extent to which they are willing, or able, to bear the expense involved and their readiness to bear the heartache and the emotional distress of visiting her will largely determine the quality of care that she receives and life she leads. There is, of course, always the possibility of placing her in a public facility, but state institutions are understaffed and overcrowded; and it's hard to be optimistic about her chances of getting the attention she needs in one of them.

But isn't the parents' attitude just another "qualitative" factor? There are perfectly normal children whose parents don't want them, yet no one would seriously suggest they shouldn't live because of that. The right to live is not a right to happiness, or to an easy passage; it's the right to have the experience of being alive, with all the risks and difficulties life entails. Thus it seems that Kerri Ann is entitled to her own destiny, whether or not the rest of us think it worth her while.

As discussed in this chapter, qualitative distinctions on which lives are "worthwhile" and which aren't tend to subvert the principle that each life is of unique value and should be allowed its natural span. Seen from that perspective, we might consider children like Kerri Ann McNulty as exemplars of this principle, and conclude that their lives are of extra special value.

13

ABORTION:

Who Really Owns Your Body?

MENTION ABORTION to your next-door neighbor and you're bound to get a reaction. Take a position on it and you may get some heated response. And watch out! If you and your neighbor feel differently about abortion, you might very well get embroiled in angry debate. The bottom line probably is that your opposing views are completely irreconcilable. There will be no winner — only verbal stalemate.

The abortion issue is like an intersection where none of the lights work. It's a virtual traffic jam of competing rights. Collisions between these differing interests are inevitable. Eventually, only a policeman can avoid chaos.

In the political arena, abortion is a hot potato. It already has burned a few politicians, targeted by antiabortion organizations for their pro-abortion stands. It spawned a presidential candidate, Ellen McCormack, who ran in 1976 on an antiabortion platform. It even made it into a plank in the 1980 Republican platform, which urged the appointment of federal judges who have a proper concern for the sanctity of human life. Indeed, the nomination of Sandra Day O'Connor, the first woman to sit on the United States Supreme Court, was attacked by right-to-life groups because of her voting record on abortion when she was a legislator.

Well, the legal debate over abortion isn't too much different. On one side of the arena are those most concerned with protecting the "rights" of the mother. On the other side are those worried about the "rights" of the fetus. Throw into the fray the interests of others also affected by the abortion decision — the parents of a pregnant teenager, the father of the unborn child, the government that is funding (or refusing to fund) abortions for women who are poor. When all those interests and rights come together, what you have is all-out philosophical and emotional combat. It seems impossible to reconcile them so that everyone's interest is sufficiently protected. But the law can't settle for a stalemate. It has to make choices about whose rights are most important.

In 1973, the Supreme Court seemed to make that choice when it recognized that a woman has a constitutional right to an abortion without being treated as a criminal for exercising it. But it qualified that right. And it has been qualifying and refining the rules relating to abortion ever since in hopes of finding some middle ground. Every question the Court has answered seems to create another question. As a result, its docket always seems to have cases on it about just what that right means. It's a tough task for the nine justices, and it has all the earmarks of a no-win situation. A few critics say that the Court should have stayed entirely out of the war; some enthusiastically applaud its 1973 decision; while others charge it with "overruling" the Almighty.

This chapter will explore the right to an abortion as well as the rights of others affected by the abortion decision. And we'll see how the Supreme Court has been struggling to strike a balance. We'll go back through history, then forward through different people's lives. Hold on to your hat. It's going to be a wild and crazy ride.

* * *

The ethical and moral debate over abortion is centuries old. It hasn't always had the same content, however; reasons for opposing or favoring abortion have differed over time. Nor has the debate always been as intense as it is today. Abortion in the past was too infrequent and clandestine to become a significant topic of public discussion; as we shall see, a woman who submitted to abortion took her life in her hands. Finally, the opposition to abortion hasn't always expressed itself through the law. Until the nineteenth century, antiabortion laws were either nonexistent or little used.

Of course, some laws are so old that no one is really sure how often or for what purpose they were used. A few thousand years ago, there were laws that punished assaults on pregnant women. Since for many centuries physical beating was considered the best way to cause an abortion, the laws could have been intended to outlaw abortion as well. Not surprisingly, the penalties varied widely over time and from society to society. For example, under the Babylonian king Hammurabi in 1728 B.C., someone who caused a miscarriage by striking a woman had to pay a fine of silver. Three centuries later, the Assyrians had upped the ante to flogging, hard labor, and sometimes death.

In ancient Greece and Rome, however, abortion was not only tolerated but approved. Both Plato and Aristotle thought of it as a population control device. The ancient gynecologist Soranus of Ephesus, who

himself prescribed abortion only rarely, saw it as one way to maintain
feminine beauty; it also was helpful if the woman wanted to conceal the
consequences of adultery, he noted. Some propertied families reportedly practiced it in order to keep down the number of children among
whom they would have to divide their estates. If abortion was prosecuted at all, it was under a theory that the father's rights had been
violated in that his consent had not been given. His claim to the
unborn child, not the fetus itself, deserved protection.

The Pythagoreans, however, who were followers of the Greek phi-
losopher and mathematician Pythagoras, opposed abortion. It is said
that they were primarily responsible for what is now known as the
Hippocratic oath. The oath, a touchstone in medical history, forbade
giving a woman a "pessary to produce abortion" or any other "abor-
tive remedy." Hippocrates, the Greek physician after whom the oath
was named, was not above giving advice to pregnant women about how
to miscarry, however. On one occasion, he reportedly instructed a
pregnant woman to jump in the air and strike her heels against her
buttocks. On the seventh leap, she miscarried.

Nevertheless, with the rise of Christianity, the Hippocratic oath took
hold and the Pythagorean position on abortion became that of the
Catholic Church. Abortion was a double-barreled sin. First, it was
associated with lechery and adultery. Second, aborting the fetus was
a sin against God, in whose image a child was made. According to
Christian theologians, abortion was a crime.

Christian opposition to abortion did not crystallize into an absolute
legal ban, however. Instead, early English common law was a bit more
discriminating. Abortion was illegal only after the fetus became "viable." A fetus became viable at "quickening," when it began to move
in the womb.

The common law, of course, is judge-made law; until it was embodied in a statute (which wasn't for many centuries) there was considerable disagreement among judges about just how serious a crime abortion after quickening was. In the thirteenth century, ecclesiastic and
judge Henry de Bracton ranked it as a homicide. In the seventeenth
and eighteenth centuries, English legal scholars Sir Edward Coke and
Sir William Blackstone called it a misdemeanor, not murder. Just how
to punish abortion was largely academic, however. Abortions were
rare, so prosecutions were few and far between. Until 1800, for example, the number of reported abortion cases in English legal history
could be counted on one's fingers.

No wonder. Abortion techniques were extremely primitive; few
women would dare submit to them, much less make it to court if they

were caught at it. Deadly potions were regarded for centuries as the most effective way to induce a miscarriage. They ranged from stewed bananas, herbs, and raw eggs to goat dung and snake venom. If they didn't work, the woman was told to drink arsenic, cedar, or oil of savin — with usually fatal results. Physical blows to the abdomen and strenuous exercise generally accompanied the ingestion of the bizarre mixtures. The painful procedure may have aborted the fetus, but it often killed the woman. Even the stigma of having an illegitimate child seemed preferable.

It wasn't until the nineteenth century that legislatures in England and America attempted to give shape to the amorphous common-law prohibitions against abortion by passing statutes clearly delineating the crime and punishment. In England, Lord Ellenborough's Act in 1803 made abortion after quickening a capital offense, punishable by the death penalty. In 1821, Connecticut became the first American state to enact antiabortion legislation (although the death penalty was not imposed). By midcentury, twenty of the then thirty states had followed suit. An American Medical Association committee in 1859 called upon the remaining states to revise their laws to protect against "unwarranted destruction of human life." In 1871, a second AMA report called the clergy's attention to what it called the "perverted views of morality entertained by a large class of females — aye, and men also — on this important question."

Why the sudden blossoming of antiabortion statutes? Certainly, some of the opposition to abortion had Victorian overtones to it; banning abortion was designed to discourage illicit sex — an example of the law's moralism discussed in Chapter 10, Living Together. But more important, certain technological developments had occurred. First, doctors discovered anesthetics and adopted techniques for abortion that presaged the medically safe procedures used today. As a result, abortions (though still dangerous) became feasible enough to draw public attention to the practice. Second, scientists made advances in embryology that provided support for the theory that a new being came into existence with the fertilization of the ovum. More members of the public — and legislators — became concerned that abortion amounted to taking a life.

By the twentieth century, changing attitudes about women's role in society and concern for overpopulation and unwanted or defective children created pressure to reform laws making abortion a crime. At the same time, doctors were able to photograph fetal development and keep prematurely born babies alive, making it more difficult to dismiss the fetus as a mere conglomeration of cells. The rights of the pregnant

woman seemed to stand in clear conflict with those of the unborn
child. Everyone started choosing sides. The Catholic Church issued
edicts against abortion, and religious groups proclaimed a right to life.
Feminists argued that abortion was a personal matter and claimed
freedom of choice. The conflict inevitably reached the courts. How was
the law to resolve the clash? How would you?

*　　*　　*

Assume you're a state legislator. You're a member of a subcommittee
assigned the task of coming up with an abortion statute. First, you'll
have to figure out what you think about abortion. Then, you must
decide how best to carry out your beliefs in the law.

To help you think it through, let's take the case of Jennifer, a sixteen-
year-old senior in high school. She's an excellent student and hopes
to go to college next year on scholarship. Jennifer always has minded
her p's and q's, spending most Saturday nights at the library or with
the family and attending church every Sunday. A few months ago she
fell in love. One thing led to another, and now, only a few weeks after
a traumatic breakup with her boy friend, she finds out she is pregnant.
Jennifer decides to get an abortion. It seems the only way out.

Suppose you are against abortion under any circumstances because
you believe that it violates the fetus's right to life. But what about
Jennifer's life, which she fears would be ruined by the stigma of unwed
motherhood and burdened with the task of raising a child she doesn't
want? At the very least, she would lose her opportunity to go to
college. That doesn't matter, you say; the fetus's rights must be given
priority over hers. In order to preserve its life, the law should force
Jennifer to make sacrifices affecting her own future.

All right, let's test that out. Your belief in the fetus's right to life
means that you think the law should make Jennifer give up the free use
of her own body so it may live to term. After all, physical discomfort
and even pain are a small price to pay for another life.

Would you also be in favor of a law that required Jennifer to donate
a kidney to a dying relative? Suppose the doctors said that she would
undergo no more physical pain than she would in childbirth, and her
sacrifice to save another's life certainly would be the morally right
thing to do. Or what about a law requiring people to be Good Samari-
tans? The statute would provide that if you didn't try to rescue someone from a burning building or from drowning when you had the
opportunity, you'd go to prison. Of course, there's a risk you'd be
burned in the rescue attempt, or might drown along with the person
seeking help. In effect the law is saying that the risk to you is worth it

to save someone else's life. Certainly, there are many things we think people should do for others, even when it means making sacrifices themselves. But do we want those moral obligations to have the force of law, with penalties attached for nonperformance?

Wait a minute, you say. Abortion is different. Jennifer got herself into her predicament; the life inside her came into existence because of something she knowingly did. But what if she had been raped or had taken precautions against getting pregnant, and, by a fluke, the contraceptives didn't work? Can she really be blamed for her present condition? In one instance she is a victim of a heinous crime and in the other she did her best to make sure that pregnancy didn't occur.

Even if Jennifer hadn't taken precautions, maybe she didn't know enough to realize she could get pregnant so easily if she didn't use contraceptives. She was a pretty strait-laced sixteen-year-old before her boy friend convinced her to have sexual intercourse. If she had been more a woman of the world, a little less morally upright, she would have known about contraception and wouldn't be in this fix. Should we penalize her for naiveté? You might respond that she never would have gotten pregnant if she simply had said no, and since she didn't, she should face the consequences of her act. But then aren't we in effect denying Jennifer an abortion in order to punish her for her "sin"? Should a baby that Jennifer doesn't want become the tool by which we teach her a lesson? Is childbirth a penalty, motherhood the equivalent of a prison term? Besides, Jennifer's boy friend doesn't have to face the physical discomfort and consequences of raising a child. Why should she?

Of course, Jennifer's life need not go to rack and ruin if she does have the baby. Maybe Jennifer's ex–boy friend, particularly if he knew of the pregnancy, would kiss and make up and marry her so they could live happily ever after. But what if he told her to get lost? A shotgun wedding isn't a good way to begin a happy home life, and a man forced into marriage is not an ideal father.

If marriage is out of the question, Jennifer could put the baby up for adoption, you say. But her parents certainly would find out, even if she went to a home for unwed mothers, which could lead to a rift in family relations. And the psychological trauma of having a baby only to give it up could leave permanent scars. Abortion may not be the only way out for Jennifer, but it may be the most painless and least harmful way from her standpoint. Should she be allowed to make that decision?

Let's turn your thinking around. Suppose that, in light of the consequences of having an unwanted child, you're among those in favor of recognizing a right to an abortion. You think that Jennifer should be free to choose whether to terminate or continue her pregnancy. After all, it is her body, her life.

But are you fully prepared to disregard the fetus completely? It's not yet a fully productive human being like Jennifer, but if it were allowed to be born — who knows? — it could become another Einstein. Also, the mere fact that the fetus is nonproductive would not necessarily justify taking its life. Otherwise, a lot of handicapped and elderly people would qualify for death. It's true that the fetus doesn't have the thoughts and emotions of a child and that it cannot live outside the womb; in the first few months, it cannot even move. But does that make its life any less important? A comatose patient does not move, at least not consciously; a retarded person has only the most basic of thoughts. And what happens when medical science becomes able to maintain a fetus outside the womb from shortly after conception so that the distinction between born and unborn that we understand today becomes meaningless?

Having explored some of the pros and cons of abortion, let's get down to writing that law. You've consulted your conscience and your constituents. What should an abortion statute look like?

If you're against abortion, you may favor a flat prohibition. To put teeth into the law, you attach a criminal penalty. But who should be punished — the doctor who performs the abortion, the woman who seeks it, or both? And will the penalty actually prevent abortions? Wealthy women may be able to buy off a doctor willing to risk his medical license for a price. The law may stop poor women — or it may instead drive those who are sufficiently desperate into the hands of an abortionist who doesn't have a medical license to lose. That thought gives you pause, since that kind of an abortionist may be more a butcher than a doctor, and his "clinic" may not be a hospital but some dirty room off a back alley. Abortion under those circumstances may mean death. Finally, a flat prohibition may be too harsh in some cases. Jennifer may be pregnant because she was raped, or she may be the victim of incest. Her doctor may have told her that she would die if she had the baby or give birth to a child without arms or legs. Maybe some exceptions to our draft antiabortion law are in order.

We could make an exception that would allow an abortion when the mother's life is in danger. But that exception is far from clear or easy to apply. First, how much of a danger must exist before an abortion is justified? Suppose Jennifer's doctor says she has a 75 percent chance of surviving childbirth. Should the law brand her a criminal because she doesn't want to take even a small risk of death? Second, it may be difficult for the doctor to calculate the chances of death from childbirth until late in the pregnancy. The longer the mother waits, the more risky an abortion becomes and the more the fetus resembles a child.

Let's take another possible exception to our law: A woman may get an abortion if she is the victim of a rape or incest. If you don't want it to be a loophole for those who weren't actually victims of these acts, but simply claim they were, there will have to be a requirement tacked on that the rape or incestuous act must be reported to the proper authorities within a certain time of its occurrence. Of course, many victims of rape or incest are too fearful or embarrassed to report the incident. What do we do about them?

We could put a third exception in our law and allow abortions when the fetus is defective. But what types of defects justify an abortion? Suppose Jennifer's baby will be physically normal but mentally retarded. Or it will have only four fingers on each hand. Perhaps the baby will be a girl and Jennifer wants a boy, so that in her eyes the fetus is defective. Certainly that wouldn't qualify as a defect. But what would?

These exceptions are getting out of hand. They're either too broad, and therefore provide loopholes, or too narrow, excluding those who should qualify for an abortion. What if we lump all these exceptions into one big one, and allow abortion only when "medically necessary"? That would place the decision about whether an abortion is proper with the doctor, who is in the best position to deal with contingencies that we legislators cannot foresee. Of course, we could be accused of abdicating our responsibility as lawmakers by letting the doctor be the sole judge of when an abortion is proper. And, in the end, we may not prevent many abortions. Doctors differ as to what is medically necessary. By hunting for the right doctor, a woman may be able to get an abortion on the thinnest medical excuse.

If you are a middle-of-the-roader who can't quite make up your mind on the subject, the law is especially difficult to write. You're torn between the woman's right to decide what to do with her own body and the belief that abortion on demand is just a little too close to homicide for your taste. What about allowing abortion only after the woman gives her written consent following a "waiting" period? That would assure that she had thought about what she was doing. Moreover, so that the woman may be fully informed about what an abortion means, the doctor could be required to explain to her how the fetus develops — when it grows arms and legs, at what stage its facial features emerge, and so on. Maybe the doctor might even show her pictures to impress on her the fact that what will be aborted is not just a shapeless conglomeration of cells. But does this procedure really do anything more than render the woman a psychological wreck? Chances are she's already done battle with her own conscience before coming to the doctor. Why open the wounds?

All the possible laws that we have discussed in fact have been considered and adopted by various state legislatures. Prior to 1973, most states took a pretty hard line on abortion. The doctor who performed one was subject to criminal prosecution regardless of whether the fetus was "viable" or not. Even the toughest antiabortion laws often made exceptions, however. Abortion generally was permissible if the mother's life was in danger or if she had been the victim of rape or incest. But in 1973 everything changed. That's when the Supreme Court handed down its controversial decision in *Roe* v. *Wade*, which, as we shall see, made your life as a state legislator easier in one sense and harder in another.

* * *

The case began in Dallas, Texas. Jane Roe — a fictitious name (for various understandable reasons, a litigant may not want to use his or her real name and the law generally respects that desire) — was an unmarried pregnant woman who wanted an abortion, but Texas's antiabortion law stood in her way. So Roe brought suit in federal court challenging the law's constitutionality. She claimed that the statute interfered with her personal right to control her own body, and that she had a constitutional right to make up her own mind. When the case eventually reached the United States Supreme Court, seven of the nine justices concluded that a woman has a "fundamental right" to an abortion. Thus, in the absence of any "compelling" state interest in stopping her, abortion no longer could be made a crime.

Where, you might ask, does this "fundamental right" to an abortion come from? Justice Harry A. Blackmun, writing for the majority, found it in at least five places in the Constitution. He said it was part of a general "right of privacy" implicit in the First, Fourth, Fifth, Ninth, and Fourteenth Amendments.

Of course, none of these amendments specifically says that there is a right of privacy, much less a right to an abortion. But it was not the first time the Court had gone beyond particular rights expressly guaranteed by the Constitution to find other rights lurking in the penumbras, or shadows, of those freedoms specifically protected. Especially in matters pertaining to family, marriage, and children, the Court has been unwilling to let state legislators regulate too much. For example, the Court previously had struck down a law allowing the state to sterilize certain criminals because that interfered with the personal right to have children. It also had held that laws prohibiting the dispensation of birth-control pills interfered with an individual's right *not* to have children. In addition, the Court has said that the Constitution does not allow government to limit people in their choices of whom to marry or where to send their children to school. Given these precedents, the Court reasoned, the Constitution surely extends protection to the abortion decision as well.

Nevertheless, the Supreme Court admitted that the right to an abortion was not unqualified. Since competing interests were at stake, the state could step in and protect them. This obliged the Court to identify the reasons that could motivate a state legislature to forbid abortion. First, the state might want to discourage sex outside marriage. But the existing antiabortion laws went much further than that, since they prohibited abortion for married women as well. Also, the Court said, there was something decidedly wrong in trying to discourage illicit sex in this manner. Even the Texas attorney general, in defending the state's antiabortion law, did not claim the statute was meant to promote a certain moral code. Two other reasons for state legislation against abortion were thought legitimate, however. The state had an interest in protecting a woman's health, which could be jeopardized by an abortion. It also had an interest in protecting the unborn child.

Now comes the tricky part. Justice Blackmun had found a constitutional right to an abortion, but at the same time, he recognized that the state had legitimate reasons for preventing one. He was caught between the proverbial rock and a hard place. Remember how much trouble you had as a legislator in drawing up a law that successfully resolved the interests of everyone affected by the abortion decision. Justice Blackmun is not a legislator; courts simply decide the particular cases put in front of them. But he faced the similar problem of balancing competing rights. At what point in the pregnancy did the state's two interests become "compelling" enough to justify curtailment of the "fundamental" abortion right?

To find the answer, Justice Blackmun turned to medical journals and historical tracts. That itself is somewhat unusual. You would expect a judge to concentrate his research in the law books. But the law didn't provide any answers to Justice Blackmun's dilemma, while medicine and history did.

The justice found that in the initial stages of pregnancy, abortion was medically safe, so the woman's health was not in danger. Moreover, the fetus was not yet "viable," which was important because, at least historically, it had not been accorded the protection of the law at that point. Remember that at common law abortion was illegal only after the fetus was viable. Later in the pregnancy, however, abortion became more dangerous and the fetus more like a child. Certainly, abortion in the ninth month of pregnancy was not only risky but close to infanticide.

To strike a balance between the state's interests and the woman's rights, Justice Blackmun hit on a scheme that divided the months of pregnancy into three three-month periods. In the first "trimester," he said, the state should stay completely out and leave the abortion decision to the woman and her doctor. In the second trimester, the state could regulate abortion as long as the regulation was "reasonably related" to protecting the woman's health. In the third trimester, abortion could be completely banned, if the state chose to do so. At this stage, the fetus was viable and the state could act to protect its life.

What do you think about Justice Blackmun's solution? He seems to have fared better than we did in coming up with an abortion law. But wait a minute. We were acting as state legislators. The Supreme Court is not supposed to "make" law; as we discussed in Chapter 1 in connection with school prayer, its business is interpreting the Constitution. Isn't it best for politically accountable officials, not unelected judges, to strike the balance between competing interests, particularly in an area in which emotions run high? The Court's approach prompted Justice William H. Rehnquist, who dissented, to charge a few years later in another abortion decision that the Court purported to be "not only the country's continuous constitutional convention but also its ex officio medical board."

But let's be realistic; it was the problem of constitutional interpretation that got Justice Blackmun into his dilemma in the first place. If he had stopped writing once he decided that there was a right not to be criminally punished for an abortion but that the state had a legitimate interest in preventing one under certain circumstances, he would have raised more questions than he had answered. The states would have been left completely in the dark as to just what they could and couldn't do.

Of course, the Supreme Court might have avoided the problem altogether simply by recognizing that the *fetus* had a constitutional right to life. In that case, state antiabortion laws would be upheld as proper prohibitions against killing. To find that constitutional right, however, the Court would have had to interpret the word *person* in the Constitution to apply to embryos as well. To many that sounds a bit far-fetched. But if the Court can interpret the Constitution in a way that allows a right to an abortion to be discovered, it seems that the Court could expand the meaning of *person* to find a fetal right to life.

(Powerful forces in the United States Congress are pushing for a federal statute that would define life as beginning with conception. Whether this statute would give the fetus a constitutional right to life is unclear.)

But let's see where that leads us. If the fetus is a person from the moment of conception, would that mean that birth-control methods such as "morning-after" pills and certain intrauterine devices would have to be banned? After all, they essentially work by causing an already fertilized egg to be expelled from the womb. Would there have to be laws against pregnant women smoking or drinking alcohol or doing anything that could injure the fetal "person," possibly infringing its constitutional right to life? What would happen if a pregnant woman was injured in an auto accident and sued for damages? Could she collect on behalf of the embryo? At present, most state laws only allow for injuries to the fetus if it is "viable." But if the embryo was a "person," that distinction could not be drawn.

Also, antiabortion laws before *Roe* v. *Wade* didn't go far enough if they were designed to protect the fetus's right to life. First, most states allowed abortion in certain extraordinary circumstances (such as incest or rape). But if abortion amounted to killing, it seems that no exceptions could be made. Second, the laws punished only the doctor who performed the abortion. Wouldn't the woman have to be considered an accomplice to the fact and punished as well?

No, recognizing a constitutionally based fetal right to life was not the simple way out. But as the Supreme Court was soon to discover, neither was *Roe* v. *Wade*. The decision opened up a Pandora's box. Let's take a look at some of the problems that remained.

* * *

Thus far, we've been talking about the rights of those immediately affected by an abortion: the fetus and the mother. But what about those who, because of their relationship with the mother, may want a say in whether she has a baby? A woman may have a constitutional right to an abortion. What about the rights of her parents or her husband?

Consider Marjorie, a thirty-year-old physicist with a brilliant career ahead of her. She has neither the time nor the desire for a child, but then she finds out she is pregnant. She wants an abortion but her husband, Bob, objects. Marjorie had promised him a family when they got married. Now he is approaching forty without a child and feels that he will soon be too old to enjoy one. Besides, Bob has deep religious convictions against abortion. He'll do anything to stop Marjorie. Should the law help him out?

The law would if it conditioned a woman's right to an abortion on the consent of her husband. It wouldn't be the first time the law required both spouses to agree before one of them acted. For example, if they jointly own their home in some states both must consent before it is sold. If one parent puts a child up for adoption, the other must agree. If one seeks sterilization, the other's consent may be required. Because of the marital relationship, what one spouse does may have a profound impact on the other. So it makes sense for the law to require agreement when a particular action affects them both.

Abortion certainly affects Bob. It deprives him of a child — something he had come to expect under their marriage contract. Abortion also could affect Marjorie's reproductive capacity if there were any complications. Like adoption and sterilization, it's a decision that has an enormous impact on the family structure. Surely, Bob should have a say.

Yet, it is Marjorie, not Bob, who will have to carry the child for nine months with the accompanying physical discomfort and undergo the pain of childbirth. The law doesn't require Bob's consent if Marjorie needs an appendectomy. It's Marjorie's body. So are you really so sure that the abortion decision shouldn't be hers alone? The marriage contract doesn't seem to justify the kind of claim Bob is making. He doesn't own Marjorie. A woman can't be compelled to function as the human equivalent of a broodmare. Certainly the law could not force a man to impregnate a woman, forcing him into service as a "stud."

Moreover, there are certain practical problems with a law requiring a husband's consent. What if Bob and Marjorie were separated and Bob could not be found? What if he was available, but out of spite refused to give his consent simply to punish his wife? The law, designed to ensure marital harmony, may do just the opposite. If Marjorie and Bob couldn't patch up their differences, the law could even precipitate a divorce.

After considering all these pros and cons, the Supreme Court, in 1976, found a law requiring a husband's consent to be unconstitutional. The Court said that such a statute gives the husband an absolute veto power over the abortion that the state itself, under *Roe* v. *Wade*, cannot exercise in the early stages of pregnancy. Although the Court recognized that the father may have an interest in the unborn child, the Court noted that "it is the woman who physically bears the child and who is more directly and immediately affected by pregnancy." When the father's and mother's interests collide, the balance must be struck in her favor, the Court said. Three justices dissented. They argued that the mother's interest in avoiding the burdens of child rearing should not automatically snuff out the father's interest in keeping the child.

Let's change our hypothetical case and say that Marjorie is not a mature career woman but a sixteen-year-old high-school junior. She wants an abortion, but she knows her parents would just die if they found out she was pregnant. Do you think she should be able to get an abortion on her own? Or should the law require her to secure her parents' consent first?

Suppose Marjorie were your daughter. Would you want her making this decision on her own? Perhaps more than any time in her life, you might think, she needs your help in deciding what would be best for her to do. Chances are her friends can't really help her in this predicament. And the emotional strain of pregnancy — with its accompanying feelings of guilt and shame — may mean she is not capable of calmly assessing her alternatives. Without you to advise her she may be all alone. Shouldn't the law require Marjorie to turn to you for her own good? Besides, don't you have a right to know? A woman may have a constitutional right to an abortion, but a sixteen-year-old is a mere youngster. And as her parents, you have rights and responsibilities too.

Given society's special concern for children, it should come as no surprise that laws restricting the freedom of minors or requiring their parents' consent before they act are rather common. Teen-agers under a certain age cannot drink, drive, purchase firearms, or work in factories. In many states, they cannot marry, make an enforceable contract, or have surgery without their parents' consent. They can't even see certain movies without parental supervision. Surely abortion is more important a decision than whether to allow a child into a theater to see an R-rated film. If you, as Marjorie's parents, would have to consent before she had a tonsillectomy, your consent should certainly be required for her to abort a pregnancy.

Let's look at it the other way — more from Marjorie's perspective. What if her parents refused to let her have an abortion? If the law gave them an absolute power to veto it, doesn't that undermine the constitutional right recognized in *Roe* v. *Wade*? Should she lose it just because she is not an adult in the eyes of the law? Ideally, Marjorie's right to make up her own mind about an abortion should depend not on her age but on her maturity. At sixteen, she may be as mature as a woman of twenty-two. And yet under an abortion law requiring parental consent, she doesn't have a twenty-two-year-old's rights.

Also, we have to recognize that not all parents will provide love and support — or even sound advice — when they find out their daughter is pregnant. Requiring consent may do nothing for the girl at all. Marjorie's parents may beat her on learning about her pregnancy. They could be alcoholics. They could even be mentally ill. Marjorie may not be an adult, but she may be a better judge of what is best for her than they are. A law requiring parental consent — designed to protect the family — may have the effect of promoting disharmony instead. The truth is that the legal system cannot compel trust and confidence between child and parent — that must come of its own.

All right. Like rational people we've looked at both sides. Now let's see how the law resolves the conflict. The Supreme Court has dealt more than once with the constitutionality of requiring parental consent to a minor's abortion. In 1976, it held that a law giving parents an absolute veto power over their minor daughter's abortion was unconstitutional. The court saw it as just as bad as a law giving the husband the same power over his wife's decision; both types of law impermissibly interfere with a woman's constitutional right.

Many states reacted to the decision by fashioning a judicial alternative to parental consent. Unwilling to give a young girl an unqualified right to make up her mind alone, the laws required her to get approval for an abortion from a judge, if not from her parents. And they provided that she at least try to get her parents' consent before going to court.

However, when the inevitable challenge to these statutes reached the Supreme Court in 1979, the Massachusetts version of this law was struck down. The Court said that consultation with parents should not be required in all cases. Also, the law was defective in that it allowed a judge to veto an abortion regardless of the girl's maturity. The Court said approval could not be withheld if the girl is mature enough to make up her own mind, despite what the judge thinks her best interests are.

So where does that leave us? A minor can get an abortion without her parents' consent. But, in some states at least, she may have to go to court and convince a judge that either an abortion is in her best interests or that she is mature enough to decide for herself. The judge, acting as surrogate parent, may decide that her parents should be consulted, but not necessarily. As a result, the minor may be able to keep her parents from ever knowing about her pregnancy.

Evaluating this procedure is an exercise in totaling up pluses and minuses. On one side, it strikes a balance between the girl's right to an abortion and the state's interest in making sure the decision is supervised by an adult. Also, it avoids those situations in which consultation with parents would do more harm than good. Moreover, a judge may be more objective than parents, and thus better able to decide what is best for the minor.

On the other side, this procedure encourages secrecy and deception. It lets a teen-ager lie to her parents and possibly lock them out of the abortion decision completely. Also, who says that a judge is in a better position than parents to decide a girl's best interests? Most likely, a pregnant teen-ager won't even feel comfortable in talking to a judge. Suppose your daughter was pregnant. Would you want a judge — a total stranger — taking over what is rightfully your responsibility? He doesn't know your daughter. How can he even begin to decide what is best for her?

The problem of secrecy and deception may have been solved by the latest round of litigation in the Supreme Court concerning parents and teen-ager abortions. In 1981, it upheld a Utah statute that requires a physician to notify the parents of a minor upon whom an abortion is to be performed. The Court concluded that a mere notice requirement was constitutional as applied to minors who were dependent upon their parents and who hadn't made any showing as to their maturity. One might ask, however, if requiring that parents of a dependent minor have notice of the abortion is really any different from giving them power of consent.

As you can see, the Supreme Court decisions on state consent requirements strengthen a woman's constitutional right to an abortion. Her interests prevail not only over the fetus in the early stages of pregnancy, but also over the interests of her husband, if she is married, and of her parents, if she is a minor. In the years following *Roe* v. *Wade,* the Supreme Court seemed committed to striking down state-erected obstacles to abortion. There remained only one major hurdle to effectuating the right — poverty. What if a woman was too poor to pay for an abortion? Must the state pick up the tab?

*   *   *

Nora Mae is a twenty-two-year-old unemployed waitress. She is married but her husband has abandoned her. Two of her three children are in foster homes because she couldn't afford to care for them. The third is up for adoption. Nora Mae is now living with her parents and her eight brothers and sisters in a small apartment. There are too many mouths to feed as it is. Then Nora Mae finds out she is pregnant. She isn't sure who the father is. She decides to have an abortion, but neither she nor her parents have more than a few dollars to spare.

Nora Mae has a constitutional right to have an abortion, but what good is it without the wherewithal to use it? Nothing but a lot of fancy words out of some lawbook — a right reserved for the rich, she thinks. Telling Nora Mae that nothing is stopping her from having an abortion is a little like Marie Antoinette's comment, "Let them eat cake." If the state cannot constitutionally erect obstacles to an abortion by insisting upon consent, why shouldn't it be constitutionally required to remove the obstacle of poverty?

Hold on. The state didn't create Nora Mae's poverty. Her being poor is a hard fact of life she has to face on her own every day. There's a difference between the state directly interfering with the abortion decision by putting up procedural roadblocks or making it a crime, and simply failing to alleviate a condition not of its own making that blocks access to the right. It might be nice to help Nora Mae out, but a constitutional right to an abortion does not imply a constitutional entitlement to government funding.

Besides, there are a lot of rights that cost money to enjoy that are not financed by the government. You have a right to send your child to private school, but the government doesn't have to pay the tuition. You have a right to learn a foreign language; but in structuring the curriculum of a public school paid for with tax dollars, the state need not include that language. You have a right to publish a newspaper, but the government doesn't have to pay for a printing press. You can worship as you please, but the government doesn't have to build you a church. If the government had to pay for the enjoyment of every constitutional right, it would go broke or we would be taxed to death.

But there's a special consideration here: The government has decided to provide free medical services for the poor by enacting the Medicaid program. It wasn't required to, but having decided to assume the responsibility, can it make an exception for abortion, which is unquestionably a medical expense? Can the government pay all of Nora Mae's medical costs, *including the cost of having the baby,* but then single out abortion — a constitutionally protected right — and decide not to pay for that?

There is no good economic reason for the government's refusing to fund abortions. Sure, money that otherwise would go to pay for an abortion can now be used to give extra benefits in other areas. But there is no real net saving of tax dollars. Childbirth alone costs more than abortion. And Nora Mae's unborn child may well go on state welfare rolls as soon as it comes into the world, just as her other children have.

Maybe there's a moral reason for not funding abortion. The people who write statutes simply don't think it's right and have the political muscle to impose their view on others. *Roe* v. *Wade* may prevent the state from prohibiting abortion, but the decision didn't say the state couldn't make it less attractive. Therefore, in order to encourage the alternative of childbirth, the government withholds Medicaid funds for abortion, while at the same time offering to pay for the expense of having the child.

That's what the federal and some state governments have done. At the local level, several states began withholding their portion of Medicaid money for abortions not deemed therapeutically required. A poor woman no longer could get an abortion just because a child would be inconvenient or expensive. Congress went a step further. In 1976, it passed the Hyde amendment, which prohibited the use of federal Medicaid funds for abortion except when pregnancy endangers the mother's life or is the result of rape or incest. Even an abortion to protect the mother's health or to prevent the birth of a seriously defective fetus could be excluded from Medicaid coverage. Those opposed to abortion finally had gotten through to their legislators. Their tax money no longer would be used to pay for what they regarded as legalized murder.

But wait a minute. Are these funding decisions by Congress and the state legislatures just a clever way of circumventing *Roe* v. *Wade*? Instead of using the "stick" of criminal sanctions to prevent abortion, the government is using the "carrot" of funding to encourage childbirth. It seems to be doing indirectly what it cannot do directly. A poor woman faced with a choice between a fully paid childbirth and an unpaid abortion may not have a choice at all. In effect, the government has made a poor woman like Nora Mae an offer she can't refuse.

Moreover, the impact of the legislation falls only on the poor. Forcing a woman like Nora Mae to have a child may have a significant financial impact on her, possibly cutting off all chances of her escaping the cycle of poverty and controlling her own life. If she does decide to get an abortion, her lack of money may drive her to a "discount" abortionist whose techniques may be medically crude. The discrimination against the poor is justified as a concern for the unborn child. But its right to life may be nothing more than a right to a "bare existence in utter misery," as Justice Thurgood Marshall once said.

Armed with these arguments, critics of the funding decisions went to court, fought all the way to the Supreme Court, and lost. In 1977, in two separate decisions, the Court upheld state regulations withholding funding for medically unnecessary abortions. (It is interesting to note that in 1981 the Supreme Judicial Court of Massachusetts held that although a state funding cutoff did not violate the federal Constitution it did transgress the Massachusetts Constitution.) Three years later, in a case called *Harris* v. *McRae,* the Supreme Court said that the federal Hyde amendment was constitutional. Five of the nine justices said that the constitutional right to an abortion did not require the federal government to pay for its exercise. Neither did the Constitution prevent the state from making a value judgment in favor of childbirth, then implementing that judgment in the way it allocates funds, the Court said. A poor woman can still secure an abortion by paying for it, of course. That prompted the dissent in one of the state funding cases to quote Anatole France: "The law, in its majestic equality, forbids the rich as well as the poor to sleep under bridges, to beg on the streets, and to steal bread."

Those of you unhappy with *Roe* v. *Wade* may applaud *Harris* v. *McRae.* It would be quite natural for you to think that, for once, the Supreme Court has decided an abortion case right. But let's see how happy you are when we apply the Court's reasoning in *Harris* to a hypothetical case. Consider the following.

The state of Iddylia is plagued by problems that primarily are due to its burgeoning population. In an effort to curb population growth, Iddylia's government decides to fund only abortion, not childbirth. Religious groups are up in arms. The government is denying women their right to have children, they complain.

Now let's apply the Supreme Court's analysis. First, the government is not abridging any right in this situation, it's merely failing to pay for its enjoyment. The poor woman still can have children; she just has to pay the associated medical costs herself. Second, the government decision to withhold funding for childbirth is a value judgment designed to encourage the alternative of abortion in order to keep the population under control. The goal is a legitimate one. No matter that the decision primarily affects the poor. Iddylia's proposal appears at first glance to be constitutional. Does *Harris* v. *McRae* cut both ways?

* * *

Of course, there's no state of Iddylia, and with antiabortion sentiment running high nowadays, it's doubtful there will be one during our lifetimes. But those of you who oppose abortion should ask yourselves whether the government's refusal to fund it for poor women is a fair way to cut down on abortion itself. Should the enjoyment of a right depend on whether you are rich or poor? You may say that the Supreme Court should never have found a right to an abortion in the first place, given the fact that many people believe it is wrong. But should constitutional rights exist only if the majority recognizes them? Should your own views about abortion be imposed, through the law, on someone else?

Those of you in favor of abortion also should be asking yourselves some questions. The Supreme Court found a right to one without pointing to any specific words in the text of the Constitution. Do we want nine unelected justices to infer rights that the framers of the Constitution never meant to be there? You might agree *this* time with the Court's conclusion about what is constitutionally protected, but what about the *next* time? The Supreme Court may infer a "right" that you don't think should be a right at all. You may be helpless to change the Court's decision by complaining to your elected legislator. Is that democracy? Is that what we mean when we say that this is a country of laws, not men?

POINT OF LAW:

The Story of Chad Green

On August 30, 1977, twenty-month-old Chad Green awoke in his Nebraska home with a fever of 106 degrees. The subsequent diagnosis was acute lymphocytic leukemia, a blood cancer most common in young children. Under the indicated treatment, he had no better than a fifty-fifty chance of survival. In September, that treatment — chemotherapy — began. It consisted of ingestion and injection (sometimes directly into the spinal fluid) of a variety of drugs over a period of three years.

Chad's disease quickly went into remission, but his parents were far from happy with the treatment's side effects. Particularly fearful of the prospect of cranial irradiation, which the Nebraska doctors wanted to include in the therapy, the family moved to Massachusetts, where radiation was not considered essential by doctors at Boston's Massachusetts General Hospital. The side effects from the drug treatment, however, continued.

Over the ensuing months, Chad experienced cramping, diarrhea, vomiting, and constipation. He found the chemotherapy terrifying; according to his mother, the ordeals would leave him "completely drenched from head to toe, soaking wet from the fight." He had difficulty sleeping and would cry out "Don't hurt me" at night. In November the Greens stopped administering drugs to Chad at home, though they continued the monthly hospital visits for injections. A few months later, the leukemia reappeared. When the Greens admitted that they had stopped giving Chad the drugs, the doctors went to court. A legal maelstrom ensued.

Over the next year, the Greens fought two legal battles in the state

courts. They lost both. The first time, the Greens argued that they had
a right to refuse to give the drugs to their son. The courts disagreed
and ordered that the treatment be resumed. The Greens then began
to supplement the chemotherapy with a regime of vitamins, enzyme
enemas, and Laetrile, a natural substance derived from apricot pits.
The courts, finding the supplemental treatment to be ineffective and
potentially harmful, ordered it discontinued. At no time were the
Greens' motives impugned. The courts admitted that they only wanted
what was best for Chad. But each time the parents' view as to *how* Chad
best could be helped was rejected.

If Chad had been an adult, the court decisions would have been
different. Part of the constitutional right of privacy is the right to make
decisions about one's own body. As discussed in Chapter 12, The
Right to Die, an individual can refuse medical treatment, even when
the decision could result in certain death. Thus, courts have upheld an
elderly woman's right not to have a gangrenous foot amputated, and
agreed that a patient could refuse use of an artificial respirator. In fact,
a doctor who does not get the informed consent of the patient before
treatment risks being sued. The medical decision lies with the patient,
not the doctor, no matter how unwise or irrational that decision is.

A key condition is imposed on the individual's right to choose,
however. He or she must be competent. In the eyes of the law, a child
is incapable in most situations of making decisions for himself. As a
rule, it is up to his parents to make decisions for him. But that power
does not clothe them with absolute power or life or death authority.
Their right to raise their child as they choose implies a corresponding
duty to care for and protect him. Thus, a parent who could refuse to
have a life-saving blood transfusion for himself cannot refuse to let his
child have one; nor could a parent refuse to allow a heart operation
needed to save the life of an infant with nonterminal birth defects. (See
Point of Law: The Right to Live.) The state can step in and substitute
its judgment for the parents' if the best interests of the child are not
being served.

In reaching the two decisions in the Greens' case, the courts had to
decide between the competing claims of Chad's parents on one side,
and the state, represented by Chad's doctors, on the other. The focal
point of the judicial inquiry was Chad himself: What was best for him?
The courts found that chemotherapy offered Chad an opportunity for
a longer life and a substantial chance of cure. To forgo the treatment
would mean almost certain death. As to the supplemental treatment
of vitamins and Laetrile, the courts found that it could interfere with
the chemotherapy and prove harmful to Chad. (At the time, Chad was

suffering from a low-grade cyanide poisoning, apparently from the Laetrile.) Despite expert testimony offered by the Greens that Laetrile helped cure cancer and could ease the side effects of the chemotherapy, the courts noted that most of the medical and scientific community regarded it as totally ineffective. Laetrile had been banned from distribution in the United States by the Federal Drug Administration — a ban upheld by the Supreme Court.

The Greens did not stay in Massachusetts to hear the state's highest court spell out the reasons for their defeat. On January 24, 1979, they fled to Tijuana, Mexico, where Laetrile clinics flourish. That August, the Greens announced that Chad was "cured." But on October 12, 1979, the three-year-old boy died.

The Green case raises difficult questions about just how far the state can and should intrude on the family unit and second-guess parental decisions in the name of helping the child. First, in ordering Chad to undergo the chemotherapy, the courts in effect were deciding that a longer life, even though full of pain, was what was best for the boy. Chad's mother, Diana, said that she would prefer that her child have a short, full life free of fear and the interminable rounds of hospital visits, needles, and pain. Who can say that the quality of life is any less important than its length? Second, this was not a case in which the parents medically neglected their child. The Greens at no time refused *all* medical treatment, and they acted only because they couldn't bear Chad's suffering. Laetrile may be unorthodox and have uncertain results, but neither could the courts predict with any certainty that the chemotherapy would be successful. Was it clear that the Greens were wrong in what they did?

The case has one other dimension. The Greens' flight to Mexico illustrates how difficult it is for a state to enforce its decision even though we may agree that it is right for its courts to have acted. As it was, the courts forced the Greens' hand. Willing to continue the chemotherapy as long as they could supplement it with Laetrile, the Greens gave up chemotherapy entirely when they took refuge in the Tijuana clinics. It is possible that Chad would be alive today if the courts had been a little more tolerant of the Greens' "home remedies." The state's court "victory," as it turned out, is thought by many to have been a hollow one indeed.

14

GENETIC ENGINEERING:

How Should the Law Deal with Our Burgeoning Power over Life Itself?

REMEMBER THOSE SCIENCE-FICTION FILMS in which the mad scientist, usually played by someone like Vincent Price, created a monster — a massive fly, a gigantic gopher, or a huge, malevolent hedgehog? One day Vincent would forget to lock up the lab and the monster would get loose and run amuck. Finally, after it had knocked over half the city and trampled or devoured the greater part of the population, the army would close in and blow it up or dump it in a volcano or send it off to monster obedience school. With order restored, the film would end with Vincent Price making a pontifical and somewhat ominous statement about science and the future that amounted to: "Well, back to the drawing board."

Just a crazy fantasy, right? Perhaps not. Today science is investigating the very core of the life process, raising awesome possibilities — and problems. Scientists are now working on ways to alter and to duplicate the gene structures that determine the make-up of all living things. Known variously as recombinant DNA research (after deoxyribonucleic acid, which has been called the "master molecule of life"), gene splicing, and genetic engineering, it involves the transplanting of genes, which control the transmission of hereditary characteristics, from one living organism to another. These techniques have made it theoretically possible to create variations, or mutants, of living creatures, and even to duplicate them exactly, a process called cloning.

Of course, so far no one has made a monster or cloned Cheryl Tiegs or Paul Newman. Indeed, the present practical uses of genetic engineering are quite benign. For example, by altering the gene structure of certain bacteria, scientists can create an organism that produces interferon, a protein substance that may aid in the battle against cancer. Another bacterium created through gene splicing "eats" crude oil, or reacts with it to break it down into its more basic components, and thus may be helpful in cleaning up oil spills. It's also expected that as scientists are able to engage in more sophisticated experiments, countless other useful products will be developed through genetic engineering. Predicted future "inventions" include vaccines against hepatitis and malaria, self-fertilizing plants, and fuels manufactured from what are now viewed as waste products.

Unfortunately, there may be a dark side to genetic engineering. Some people already have called attention to the potential dangers created by the experiments that are now being carried on. For example, there is the possibility that they could result in a new or hybrid bacterium immune to all present antibiotics. If one of these microorganisms were to escape from the lab, it could lead to a plague to which mankind would have no defense. Even our oil-eating bug raises dangers; it has been suggested that it might get out of control, invade the Persian Gulf, and end up consuming most of the world's oil supply.

Beyond the threats presented by the present levels of recombinant DNA research, there are troubling moral and philosophical problems raised by our growing power over life itself. Arguably, the day is not so far off when we may be in a position to create or alter life forms on a much higher level than mere microbes; indeed, we even may be able to conduct experiments rivaling those carried out by Vincent Price. When that time comes, we will have to face the question of whether we really want to play God, or to risk upsetting the delicate balance of nature with experiments that could backfire with catastrophic results. As with nuclear energy, we can say in reference to genetic engineering that the genie is out of the bottle. But we may wish he had never escaped should he prove to be an evil genie.

*   *   *

Imagine yourself as living in a small, peaceful town. Everything is very rustic and quiet, just the way you like it. Then one day a new company opens a plant up the street from your house. It's called the American Mutant Company, and according to its prospectus (it's a hot issue on the New York Stock Exchange), it specializes in creating "exciting new life forms, tailored to your every need." This makes you a bit nervous. You get even more nervous when you notice certain strange phenomena — for example, all the grass in the plant compound has turned purple, your neighbor's dog has just given birth to puppies that look more like pelicans, and at night there's a strange howling sound on the wind. You're beginning to get the feeling you're living in Transylvania.

What to do? Well, let's say you feel there's a simple solution to the problem — you want to outlaw genetic engineering. That way the American Mutant Company will be closed down and everything will return to normal.

But wait a minute. Are you sure you want to do that? Keep in mind that one of our traditions is to allow free play to scientific inquiry. To a large extent, our advanced technological society is a fruit of that policy. Now you want to crack down on scientific research, to cut back on the exploration for knowledge about the life process itself. Is that position consistent with our claim of being a free society? With our commitment to free expression? Your response is that despite our tradition of free inquiry, we have to draw the line someplace in our meddling with the forces of nature.

There's certainly a great deal of precedent for your attitude. No doubt there were cavemen who thought the best thing to do with the newfangled invention called fire was to put it out. The wheel probably had its detractors. Later on, the Inquisition was established in Europe to make certain there wasn't too much independent thought. Indeed, the Inquisition versus Galileo is a perfect example of an attempt to prevent the spread of "dangerous" knowledge. The secular and religious authorities believed that the stability of Catholic Europe was threatened by Galileo's support of the Copernican theory that the earth and the other planets revolve around the sun. After all, the Church had supported the Ptolemaic belief that the earth was the center of the universe, and its authority would be undermined if it were proved wrong (a particularly grave matter at a time when Catholic Europe was engaged in an ideological struggle with the Protestant states). Seen from that perspective, it's not altogether surprising that Galileo was tried, found guilty, and forced to recant his heretical views on astronomy.

The Galileo case suggests two reasons for not outlawing recombinant DNA research. First, it reminds us of the unsavory nature of "thought control"; most of us have little sympathy for the Inquisition and all it stood for, and would not want to pursue a course that resembled its operations in even the slightest respect.

Second, it suggests the futility of trying to prevent the spread of knowledge, for despite the Inquisition's best efforts, the Copernican theory of planetary movement triumphed. As they sometimes say in whodunits, the truth will out. Outlawing genetic engineering in this country wouldn't necessarily stamp it out (as, for example, laws against educating blacks didn't prevent them from learning in secret); nor could we prevent its being pursued in other places. Thus the direst predictions — worldwide plague or a total ecological collapse — could still come true. Moreover, by banning it, we would lose the opportunity to regulate its development and keep it headed in the safest possible direction.

Finally, are you sure we can afford to forgo the benefits promised by the supporters of genetic engineering? The rewards may be greater than the risks — cures for disease, a nearly endless supply of fuels, a new "green revolution" in agriculture, and who knows what else. Rather than being an evil genie, it may be simply a powerful one, with the decision of how that power is to be applied left to us.

All in all, an outright ban on genetic engineering doesn't seem like such a good idea. So why not have Congress pass laws that would allow research to continue but control how it develops so that no "accidents" happen? Congress already regulates many aspects of applied science, from the labeling of drugs to the production of nuclear energy. Regulation would not unduly interfere with freedom of inquiry, and would enable us to gain whatever benefits the research has to offer.

The quest for regulation probably would start with a congressional investigation into genetic engineering. For example, hearings would be held at which scientists and other experts would testify on the dangers raised by the new technology and the best ways to prevent their occurrence. Theoretically, once the information had been collected, Congress would be in a position to enact legislation that would ensure that all recombinant DNA research was carried on in the safest possible manner. Since scientific research is a complex, ongoing process, a flexible scheme of regulation probably would be best. Thus Congress could empower an agency — either one created for the purpose or an existing one — to monitor genetic engineering as it develops and adopt rules and procedures as they are needed.

It sounds great, but there's a hitch. So far there has been no significant progress toward the adoption of a comprehensive scheme of regulation. So what's the problem? After all, here we have a potentially dangerous technology, and our elected representatives, whose job is to pass laws to protect the public interest, aren't doing anything.

The problem is very basic: It often takes the law a long time to react to new circumstances. This especially is true in the case of broad social developments or technological innovations. We saw in Chapter 9, Products Liability, how long it took the law to adjust to the mass production of consumer products, and in Chapter 11, Landlord and

Tenant, how the law still hasn't fully emerged from the Middle Ages.

There are a number of reasons for the law's inertia. For one, it is a conservative discipline, populated by conservative practitioners who by and large would prefer that human affairs be self-regulating, at least to the extent that is possible. Closely allied with a reluctance to impose on the activities of people is the knowledge that in acting too quickly or in trying to accomplish too much, the law can end up doing more harm than good (as, for example, in the case of Prohibition).

Inertia is characteristic not only of the dynamic — or lack thereof — of the law itself, but also of Congress, which often moves at somewhat less than a snail's pace. With regard to regulating genetic engineering, the situation is exacerbated by the complex, technical nature of the subject. It's all very well to say that Congress is going to hold hearings and get the facts, but what if the facts aren't available or the experts give conflicting testimony on what dangers are posed and what precautions should be taken? (Remember when hearings were held to determine if the ozone layer was about to be destroyed by aerosol spray cans or the Concorde? The experts disagreed so much that no clear conclusions could be reached.) Few, if any, of our legislators, many of whom are lawyers, have any detailed, in-depth knowledge of science, and thus are in no position to resolve conflicts in testimony or to make independent judgments on what should be done.

A further limitation on Congress's ability to act effectively is that genetic engineering is in its relative infancy. Thus even the experts may not know what problems are liable to develop and what form of regulation is needed. Although a number of possible disasters have been prophesied regarding recombinant DNA research, none has yet come to pass. Contrast this to the regulation of nuclear energy; the bombing of Hiroshima and Nagasaki allowed no doubt about the menace posed by splitting the atom.

This brings us to another barrier to congressional action: The tendency of our legislators not to deal with a problem until it has become too serious to ignore. They do so not simply out of a spirit of procrastination, but also because Congress is inundated with a myriad of matters demanding immediate solutions. Asking them to focus on a yet unrealized danger is a little like asking a juggler to add another ball to an already overloaded act.

So it's possible that Congress won't get around to regulating genetic engineering until there's an accident or even a catastrophe. By then, of course, it may be too late.

How about the courts — can't they step in and do something? The answer is that they can't do anything until a genuine controversy is presented to them. As things stand, there's no law against making a monster, let alone experimenting with genes and bugs in the laboratory. However, if the monster breaks out and proceeds to misbehave in standard monster fashion, then its maker presumably would be subject to lawsuits and criminal prosecution for maintaining a public nuisance. It's a little like the scene in Western movies in which the bad guys have ridden into town and are holed up in the saloon. "Why don't you go arrest them varmints?" someone asks the marshal, who replies, "Because they ain't done nothing yet." Similarly, the courts will have to wait until the genetic engineers do something that breaks the law or endangers the populace. Again, it's possible that by then it will be too late.

Keep in mind that even if a case does come up, a court decision is not likely to offer anything like a complete solution to the problems we've been discussing. Courts tend to deal only with the facts of a particular dispute and try to decide lawsuits on the narrowest possible grounds (indeed, anything a court says that isn't essential for the decision is called dictum and is of limited precedential value. In a sense, courts tend to deal only with the tip of an iceberg, with the visible part of what sometimes is a deeper and more far-ranging source of danger. So, at the very least, regulation of genetic engineering through the courts could prove to be a long-drawn-out process (as demonstrated by the slow evolution of the law of products liability). It's also possible that their efforts to steer clear of trouble could prove ineffective — after all, look what happened to the *Titanic*.

An illustration of how court review usually focuses on narrow issues is the one case in which the Supreme Court has dealt with genetic engineering. In *Diamond* v. *Chakrabarty,* the question was raised whether a manmade organism — a form of bacteria useful in dissolving oil spills (our "oil-eating" bug) — could be patented. The bacterium had been created through gene splicing by scientists at the General Electric Corporation, and the company sought a patent to help it profit from its "invention." The Patent Office denied the application on the ground that patent protection does not extend to living creatures, such as bacteria.

The Supreme Court, however, took the position that the bacterium could be patented, since it was not found in nature but rather was the product of human ingenuity. Thus, like any other invention, it fell within the ambit of the patent laws. Four justices dissented. They argued that Congress had never intended that living creatures be treated as inventions for these purposes. They thought the better policy was to refuse the patent, and let Congress decide whether it wanted to allow the products of genetic engineering to be patentable.

Note the difference in approach. The dissent says in effect, "Don't give them a patent on these things until Congress specifically acts to allow it." The majority says, "Let them have it until Congress steps in to stop it." If the dissent's view had prevailed, the natural inertia of the legislative process might have acted as a brake on the development of genetic engineering, at least to the extent that the prospect of patent protection would not have been available to act as a spur. But the majority passed the buck to Congress, and so far Congress hasn't done much with it.

The significance of the *Chakrabarty* case isn't as great as some people — particularly in the media — have suggested. Even before it was decided, a number of companies were working on developing the commercial uses of genetic engineering. But the case probably will provide an incentive for private industry to get involved in research and development, and has focused the attention of investors on the new field, so much so that shares in one genetic engineering company that went public proved a "hot item" on the stock market.

Note that the failure of Congress and the courts to step in and get a measure of control over genetic engineering means that private industry is operating in a regulatory vacuum — one in which it's only too free to do as it pleases. These companies are not subject to even the limited government regulation that now exists in this area. Several years ago, the National Institutes of Health drew up guidelines applicable to academic institutions — principally Harvard, the Massachusetts Institute of Technology, and Stanford — that were doing recombinant DNA research under federal grants. Violation of these standards, which generally were directed to the dangers of contamination, could result in termination of government funding. Private industry, however, can fund itself, and so isn't subject to the guidelines. Given the reluctance of both lawmakers and judges to interfere with the private sector, it seems unlikely that much will be done, at least in the near future, to rectify this "imbalance."

Moreover, attempts by the scientific community to regulate itself are less apt to succeed in the private sector than they are within university confines. A number of universities have developed their own safety procedures to protect against accidents, and some have even imposed a moratorium on further experimentation. But companies seeking a profit will be under considerable pressure to develop their products before their competitors do, and may be inclined to forge ahead rather than to proceed with caution.

*   *   *

So it doesn't look like you're going to get much help from either the Congress or the courts. But don't give up. There's always the possibility of a local ordinance banning genetic engineering. After all, local government is one of our most cherished traditions, and since the research is going on right here in the community, what could be more appropriate. So here's a chance for the townspeople to stand up to the dastardly imprecations of murderous microbes and greedy technocrats.

But hold on. Do you really want to be a mini-Inquisition, banning the pursuit of knowledge in your little corner of the world? Suppose you successfully close down the plant or zone it out of the town limits, and in the process cut off the possibility of discovering a cure for cancer? Of course, it doesn't seem likely that our imaginary American Mutant Company will find a cure for anything, but in the real world, companies involved in genetic engineering promise great benefits to mankind. Does a single community like your town have the right to close off even the possibility of these promises being fulfilled?

You respond by saying, "Let them discover a cure for cancer somewhere else, like in the next town." But if the people there take your attitude, they'll ban it too. If everyone follows suit, genetic engineering soon will be barred from every community in the United States. In effect, we'll end up with a national ban imposed through local legislation. And we saw earlier that a complete ban on research isn't a good idea; aside from not being all that effective, it eliminates whatever possibility exists of controlling how the technology develops.

Instead of banning it, why not regulate it through local ordinance? Indeed, a number of communities including Boston and Cambridge (extensive recombinant DNA research goes on at Harvard and MIT) have passed local legislation of this nature. One problem with this approach is that the town authorities may lack the scientific expertise to develop a coherent regulatory pattern or to enforce it. The task, unfortunately, is a bit more complex than seeing that restaurant kitchens are kept clean, a typical matter for local regulation. The Boston and Cambridge city councils finessed this problem to a certain extent by relying on the National Institutes of Health guidelines; but by now they may be out of date, given the rapidly developing pace of genetic research, and it remains to be seen how effectively the guidelines can be implemented by local health officials.

In general, it seems that genetic engineering is too complex a field to control through town ordinances. Regulation necessarily will tend to be uneven and to lag behind the state of the art — or science. Only Congress, with its capacity to collect information and to enact comprehensive national legislation, enforced by experts, is in a position to deal with the problem. Trying to make do with a multitude of local ordinances is a patchwork solution at best, one that simply may en-

courage research companies to move into communities that do not
have regulation.

* * *

What shall we conclude, then? That it's all out of control? Certainly
we'd have to say that thus far it hasn't been brought under meaningful
regulation. It may take a disaster, something comparable to Three Mile
Island, to get Congress to enact legislation regulating genetic engineering.

It's possible that the dangers presented by this new technology have
been grossly exaggerated. So far nothing untoward has happened, and
there are those in the scientific community who assure us that safeguards are in place and no one should be unduly concerned. Perhaps
they're right. But the problem is that we have no firm basis for knowing
one way or the other, since no authority is monitoring these experiments. Who knows? We may wake up one day and find ourselves
trapped in a manmade version of the black plague. So we're proceeding on either ignorance or trust. The future may tell us, in no uncertain
terms, just which one it is.

However things come out, the issues raised by genetic engineering
illustrate a significant fact about the law: It's unrealistic to expect it to
provide a quick fix for complicated problems. We sometimes think of
the law as something that emerges full-blown, ready in a moment to
latch onto any troublesome phenomenon and bring it immediately to
heel. The truth is the law tends to proceed at a slow, halting pace,
much like the famed tortoise who won his race with the hare on the
basis of sureness rather than speed.

It may be that the law is *too* slow, that it proceeds at too leisurely a
pace to deal with the accelerated rate at which modern science raises
problems as it searches for panaceas. Delays in establishing legal controls that were tolerable in the horse-and-buggy days conceivably
could prove disastrous in our high-speed technological age. Yet it's
hard to see how the law can be speeded up, since, like the tortoise, it's
just not built to go fast. Perhaps all we can do is hope that it doesn't
fall so far behind in the race that science's deleterious side effects,
whether manmade monsters or something else, end up winning.

POINT OF LAW:
Sterilization

Seventy-five years ago the law showed less reluctance to enter the
world of genetic engineering when Indiana enacted the nation's first

compulsory sexual sterilization law, covering inmates of state institutions who were confirmed criminals, idiots, imbeciles, and rapists. By the beginning of World War II, Indiana's example had been followed by thirty-one other states, some of which extended their sterilization laws to the "feeble-minded," epileptics, or "moral degenerates and sexual perverts."

These laws represented an enthusiastic, although somewhat premature, response to the eugenic theories of Sir Francis Galton for improving the human race by controlling hereditary factors and to Gregor Mendel's laws of heredity. The basic idea wasn't new: Plato recommended in the *Republic,* and the Spartans even engaged in, selective breeding or pruning of the genetic stock in the hope of "improving" the human race.

And who could say nay to science? Certainly not the law in this instance — not even the United States Supreme Court. In 1926 a case reached the high court challenging an order under a Virginia statute that Carrie Buck, who had been committed to the State Colony for Epileptics and Feeble Minded, be subjected to a salpingectomy to sterilize her. Apparently Carrie was "feeble-minded," had a "feeble-minded" mother, and had given birth to a "feeble-minded" illegitimate child.

The challenge fell on deaf ears. Without so much as a passing reference to, let alone an inquiry into, the legitimacy of the scientific basis for eugenic sterilization, Justice Oliver Wendell Holmes, certainly one of our legal giants, upheld the sterilization order with these observations: "We have seen more than once that the public welfare may call upon the best citizens for their lives. It would be strange if it could not call upon those who already sap the strength of the State for these lesser sacrifices . . . , in order to prevent our being swamped with incompetence. It is better for all the world, if instead of waiting to execute degenerate offspring for crime, or to let them starve for their imbecility, society can prevent those who are manifestly unfit from continuing their kind. . . Three generations of imbeciles are enough."

Enthusiasm for sterilization has been on the wane since the 1940s. Many people justifiably have come to doubt that some of the traits mentioned in various state statutes are inherited or that applying these laws will have a significant effect on society. And there is no doubt that the dark cloud of Nazism and its eugenic practices tipped the balance against these procedures.

Even though activity under sterilization laws has been on the decline, it has not ended. Has the time come to outlaw it altogether? After all, doesn't the absence of incontrovertible scientific proof of the value of eugenic sterilization coupled with today's sensitivity to personal rights, particularly the right to control one's own body, justify banning it? Or do you believe that if the practice offers some prospect of being socially useful we should continue to subject "criminals" and the "fee-ble-minded" to a relatively "harmless" medical procedure? And, hav-ing learned earlier in our discussion about legal analysis and the im-portance of honoring precedent, you might feel that the law must respect the Supreme Court's recognition in Carrie Buck's case that the states have power to pursue sterilization programs.

Of course, you've also learned that the law has enough flexibility to avoid being irrevocably painted into a conceptual corner. So you won't be surprised to hear that there have been a number of successful attacks on state sterilization laws in the past forty years. A high point was reached when the Supreme Court concluded that Oklahoma's Habitual Criminal Sterilization Act, which applied to those convicted of two felonies involving moral turpitude, violated the equal-protec-tion clause of the Constitution. The Court gave lip service to the Buck precedent and struck down the Oklahoma statute on narrow grounds: It treated virtually identical criminal acts — theft and embezzlement — differently for purposes of sterilization without any showing that the propensity to do one was more likely to be biologically inheritable than the other. Nonetheless, it was a start, a foot in the door, and the Court, now speaking through Justice William O. Douglas, did go out of its way to characterize procreation as "one of the basic civil rights" and ex-press concern about the power to sterilize falling into "evil or reckless hands."

A number of state courts have reached the same result using a variety of legal theories, including cruel and unusual punishment, due process, and vagueness. But there have been just as many cases upholding the state's power to sterilize.

Thus, the law continues to vacillate between shaky genetic evidence suggesting sterilization may help the long-term battle against crime and sensitivity toward human rights and values. It simply can't make up its mind. You be the judge: Would it have been better for Indiana and the states that followed it to have waited for better scientific proof? In any event, aren't three generations of legal indecision enough?

EPILOGUE:

The Court of Last Resort

NOW THAT WE'VE COMPLETED our journey, let's look back at the highlights of the trip. Perhaps the single dominant theme that emerges is that the law constantly is engaged in weighing competing interests and values in its efforts at resolving disputes. For example, in Self-Defense, we saw how the law attempts to reconcile the individual's right to defend himself and his property with society's interest in maintaining the peace; in Landlord and Tenant and in Products Liability, we saw it try to balance the competing economic and social interests of various groups; and in Free Expression, we talked about the law's efforts to balance the political right of free speech with moral objections to obscenity. Indeed, in every chapter we had a lively dialogue over one or more attempts at this difficult and often exasperating task.

Because the law seeks to draw a measure of harmony out of considerable discord in our society, its basic approach to any significant problem generally involves a compromise. The judicial model therefore may be closer to that of Solomon than to the Roman emperor at the Colosseum deciding the fate of a fallen gladiator by signaling thumbs up or thumbs down. Perhaps it is this constant element of compromise that many people find so annoying about the law; for, looking at it from almost any set standpoint, the law always seems either to go too far or not far enough. (Hardly anyone, for example, is wholly satisfied with the present Supreme Court stand on abortion.) The law is a little like the cop on the beat called on to referee a domestic dispute, or to get an especially vexing traffic jam unsnarled — no matter what he does, there are going to be complaints, and, inevitably, some of them are going to be justified.

Only a Utopian would believe that the legal system could function to everyone's satisfaction. In addition to the limitations imposed by the sheer complexity of human affairs, there are practical and philosophic restraints on the law's capacity to solve our problems. As we saw in Job Contracts, the law doesn't like to bite off more than it can chew, and this self-imposed sense of what it can accomplish and what it can't is a pervading, if usually unstated, influence on its work product. There's a further sense of limitation that operates on a philosophic level. We belive that as much as possible human affairs should be self-regulating; we leave it to totalitarian states to attempt to control, by fiat or other methods, every aspect of human life.

But let's not get carried away in the law's defense. Not all its failures can be blamed on the complexity of human affairs, or on a practical or philosophic urge not to overextend itself. As Landlord and Tenant and Living Together indicated, the law often simply is slow to adjust or is downright resistant to changed circumstances; and, as illustrated in Genetic Engineering and Sports Violence, it may decline to act at all in new situations until an emergency develops. To some extent, this lethargy is part of the law's conservative demeanor and that of its practitioners, but it also can reflect a certain amount of complacency and lack of adventuresomeness.

In fairness, however, it should be noted that this approach has a saving grace, since it protects us from being inundated with hastily drafted and ill-conceived laws that might make matters worse. American society does have a tendency to stumble when it tries to run before it can walk or when it overreacts or panics in the face of some perceived crisis. We've been doing that periodically since the Alien and Sedition Act of 1790. Although not inevitably true, deliberateness often helps to guarantee sureness. As noted in Genetic Engineering, the tortoise did beat the hare in one of the most famous races ever run.

Nor have we seen any rebuttal of the charges that there are crooked lawyers and lazy judges (as well as incompetents in both categories), that the courts move at a snail's pace in resolving disputes, and that the whole process is too expensive and thus favors the rich over the poor. Perhaps the best response is to plead *nolo contendere*, which, loosely speaking, is legalese for, "I give up. You've got me there."

But put things in perspective. The law is a labor-intensive institution, one that is under the direction and operation of human beings; thus, its administration is bound to suffer from all the weaknesses of human nature. Of course, it would function better if all lawyers and judges were diligent and professional, and certainly there is a great deal of room for improvement, but it's never going to work perfectly. Although not a terribly comforting proposition, the truth probably is that the law functions no better or worse than most of the other professions in our society. And forget any notion that it was better in the good old days. Shakespeare, through Hamlet, rued the "law's delay" and Dickens's *Bleak House* is a condemnation of the English legal system of a century and a half ago as told through the anatomy of one of the longest cases in history — *Jarndyce* v. *Jarndyce.*

Moreover, our legal system is influenced by the strains and tensions in the world around it. If American litigiousness produces a multitude of disputes at the same time that there is a shortage of public funds, then there won't be enough judges and support staff to handle the workload, and the inevitable result will be what we have today — overcrowded dockets and painfully slow justice. Also, the complexity of our society in such areas as technology and the economy contributes to delay and makes it difficult to predict the exact consequences of legal decisions.

Perhaps the most difficult task for the nonlawyer is to differentiate between those failures and foul-ups that result from corruption or poor administration or inadequate financing, and those that derive from the inherent limitations of the legal system itself. As to the former, we can justly complain and seek reform. Indeed, as informed citizens, it's our duty to do so, given the law's pervasive influence on our lives. But to eliminate the inherent limitations on the legal system, we would have to do away with the existing structure itself and try to find some other way of governing our affairs. And as to that, we must beware, for the pathway of history is strewn with the wreckage caused by failed social experiments and doomed attempts at Utopian reform.

Index

INDEX